MORE
PREACHING VALUES
in the
EPISTLES OF PAUL

Halford E. Luccock

MORE
PREACHING VALUES
in the
EPISTLES OF PAUL

Volume II

SECOND CORINTHIANS
GALATIANS
PHILIPPIANS
COLOSSIANS

HARPER & BROTHERS PUBLISHERS
New York

Grateful acknowledgment is made to the following for permission to quote from the works indicated:

Harper & Brothers, New York: "Do As I Tell You" from *Not Mine to Finish* by Genevieve Taggard, copyright 1934 by Harper & Brothers; *The Bible, A New Translation* by James Moffatt, copyright 1954 by James A. R. Moffatt.

Holt, Rinehart & Winston, Inc., New York: *A Child Is Born* by Stephen Vincent Benét, from *United We Stand and Other Radio Scripts,* copyright 1942 by Stephen Vincent Benét.

The Macmillan Company, New York: *Letters to Young Churches* by J. B. Phillips, copyright 1947, 1957 by The Macmillan Company.

The National Council of Churches, New York: the *Revised Standard Version of the Bible,* copyright 1946 and 1952 by the Division of Christian Education, National Council of Churches.

Library of Congress catalog card number: 61-12828

CONTENTS

6   CONTENTS

The Epistle of Paul to the Galatians

The Epistle of Paul to the Philippians

The Epistle of Paul to the Colossians

PREFACE

Halford Luccock finished writing this manuscript in late September of 1960, six weeks before he died. The final fifty pages came from the typist after the brain tumor which was so swiftly to take his life had made further work impossible. In the final days of his capacity a sense of urgency was upon him. It is revelation not only of those days but of a lifetime that the last typewritten page upon which he worked ended with the line "my Father worketh hitherto and I work." It fell to other hands to complete the correction of the typed manuscript (from the last handwriting that sometimes could scarcely be deciphered). A number of repetitions were found in the book. Some were omitted, others allowed to stand, as it seemed the author might have revised his own work.

My father was not able to complete the work on the notes to this book. In many cases the written manuscript gives no clue to the source of his quotations. Quite a number were found by subsequent search, and these are listed on pages 249-255, but many remain which could not be located.

A number of people worked with patient and painstaking care to trace every reference to its source. Much credit and appreciation is due Miriam Wooding and Marietta Edmonds of New Haven for their persistence in these labors. Librarians at the Yale and New Haven Public libraries were cooperative and helpful. I apologize to any authors, editors or compilers whose work may appear here without credit. My mother gave much loving care to the "finishing" of Hal's book, checking the accuracy of the transcription and final proofreading. These all made it possible to publish the work faithfully and completely.

Scriptural texts, unless otherwise indicated, are quoted from the *Revised Standard Version of the Bible*.

ROBERT E. LUCCOCK

HALFORD E. LUCCOCK: An Appreciation*

by Ralph W. Sockman

Near the close of the fourth century a boy was born in Syria. He entered a monastery near Antioch, where he spent some ten years in extreme seclusion. About the year 423 he left the confinement of his narrow monastery cell and built a pillar on the top of which, only a yard in diameter, he took up his position. From this pillar he moved to several others in succession, each higher than its predecessor, till at last he came to dwell on one some sixty feet in height. There he spent thirty-seven years. The fame of his sanctity brought crowds of pilgrims from distant countries to see him. His name was Simeon Stylites or St. Simeon.

It would be hard to picture two personalities more widely different in spirit and method than Simeon Stylites of the fifth century and Halford Luccock of *The Christian Century*. St. Simeon withdrew from the world; Hal Luccock entered into it with zest. Simeon was austere; Hal was contagiously genial. Simeon was a cold saint living on what must often have been a cold pillar; Hal was a glowing mental fire before which men warmed their spirits. Yet both had a magnetism which drew spiritual pilgrims. And it was a mark of Halford Luccock's original and stimulating mind that he should choose Simeon Stylites for his pen name in writing his incomparable column which revealed what man does with his solitariness, to use Whitehead's words, and what man does or should do with his society. Hal knew St. John of Patmos as well as St. John's-by-the-Gas-Station.

I never was enrolled under Halford Luccock. But I have studied under him ever since I began to prepare for the ministry. When I entered Union Theological Seminary, Dr. Henry Sloane Coffin told us in class of a promising young alumnus who was writing some of the most arresting sermons of which he knew. He commended them to us for study. Another teacher, Dr. Harry Emerson Fosdick, trying to help us in finding illustrations, which is a baffling task for young ministers, cited Halford Luccock as the best man in the art of illustrating. Thus, guided by two great preachers, I began following in the footsteps of Hal Luccock, and seeing

* Delivered at the Memorial Service for Halford E. Luccock at Marquand Chapel, Yale Divinity School, New Haven, on April 5, 1961.

that I was compassed about with such a distinguished company of witnesses, I laid aside every weight of conscience and ran with perseverance the race that was set before me, looking unto Luccock, a pioneer and perfecter of the homiletic art.

But Hal was more than a luminous leader and a superb illustrator. He was a preacher's pastor. We characterize some pulpiteers as preachers' preachers because their colleagues come to study their methods and profit by their material. But Halford Luccock drew ministers with affection as well as admiration. Time does not permit me to quote all the heartfelt comments made to me by ministers since his death.

But in all my ministry, and weighing my words, I have never heard so many expressions of genuine grief over the passing of a colleague as in the case of Halford Luccock. I share the sorrow. I did not see him often. But the world to me seemed a brighter place as long as I knew he was letting his light shine in it. The world which could produce a Halford Luccock is no mean place. The God who could develop such a gay and gracious spirit is truly a Christlike Heavenly Father. Just by being what he was Hal gave sanction to our Christian gospel.

When Henry van Dyke unveiled a bust at the Hall of Fame for Great Americans he gave a definition which I venture to use on this occasion. He said, "Fame is durable good renown, earned by service, approved by the wise, applauded by the common voice." Halford Luccock fulfilled all of those conditions.

His renown is as wide as Christendom. It is as durable as Christianity. He took the materials of his messages from the simple essentials of everyday living which are as timeless as Bethlehem and Calvary. He illustrated them with insights as fresh as the morning paper. He did not try to make the headlines with extreme utterances or flashy references to the latest sensations. Thus, he avoided notoriety, which, according to van Dyke, differs from true fame as a loud noise differs from a noble symphony. He dealt bravely with controversial questions but he did not capitalize controversies to attract attention to himself.

In his religious outlook he was truly progressive because he was sufficiently conservative to view the seen and temporal against the background of the invisible and eternal. He recognized the weakness of the old-fashioned evangelism which regarded mere commitment of the will as a satisfactory "coming to Jesus"; but he was alert to the fallacy of a mere educational program which left out the element of decision, as witness his statement that we "cannot ooze our way into the Kingdom of Heaven."

He proclaimed the social gospel with every effort of his pen but he did not prescribe enlistment in reform as a substitute for personal repentance and redemption. He was concerned to save souls but he was aware that we must change social systems and avert international perils if we are long to have souls to save.

Because of his penetrating insights and pungent words, his blending of the personal and the social, the timely and the timeless, I predict that future historians will study his writings in appraising this twentieth century. Personally I have long thought that Hal Luccock was to the young ministers of America something like that which Socrates was to the young men of Athens.

Let us go on to van Dyke's second element of fame: "won by service."

Coleridge and Wordsworth had an agreement that the former would treat the supernatural to make it credible and the latter would present the commonplace to make it wondrous. While Hal Luccock rendered both services, it was in the latter, I think, that he excelled.

He brought God down to earth. Yet not in the sense of the popular "down-to-earth preaching" which he so frequently decried. How often he thrust his rapier of ridicule into the preaching of God as our servant to help us win friends and influence people! He abhorred the pulpit efforts to make the cross into a success story.

Hal proclaimed God as a sovereign. But he did bring God near enough to feel a presence which disturbs us with the joy of elevated thoughts. Read the opening paragraph in his first book, *Fares please,* written in 1916 and I think the first published, at least in book form, of anything he said. These are the lines:

> *The smile on the face of the conductor of the 7:29 to the city every morning is a real event in the daily life of scores of commuters. His genial "good morning" goes to make up for the lack of sunshine on cloudy days. Yet all the passengers know that behind the warmth of the smile and the unfeigned cordiality of the greeting is the stern insistence of "Fares, please, gentlemen!" For the 7:29 every day is not a charity outing; it is a pay-as-you-go enterprise.*

There in the beginning of this first book is to be seen the combination of divine grace and human effort needed to correct, on the one hand, the softening type of preaching which stresses relaxation and, on the other hand, the stern hortatory preaching which steadily flogs the will without feeding the mind.

In his *Minister's Workshop* he did not provide ready-made patterns for preaching. He made his students more ready to create their own patterns. He was too inimitable to copy. Foolish would be the preacher who tried to plagiarize verbatim one of Hal's sermons. But dull would be the preacher who could study his sermons without feeling his creative impulses quickened.

I have often wondered how Hal got his flashing insights and forceful expressions. I recall that at a church dinner in my own parish some thirty years ago he told my people that he thought I got my texts by the "hunt and peck" method as an amateur fingers the keys of a typewriter. He surmised that I got my ideas and then hunted for a text to fit them—and he was too near the truth for my comfort. His volumes on Preaching Values in the Old Testament, the New Testament, and the Epistles of Paul reveal that he was steeped in scripture. But his intriguing and arresting titles made me think that he started his sermons and meditations at the sidewalk level with the problems people were facing and then led them back into the Biblical uplands to the springs of renewal and strength. Listen to such themes as these: "Doorkeepers"; "What's the News?"; "The Sunny Side of Ten"; "Dutch Courage"; "Everything Upside Down." Every human situation seemed to be grist for his mental mill, and from his mind came the bread of life. Yes, like Wordsworth, he made the commonplace wondrous.

He held the mirror up to life. He let us see our weaknesses. He made us laugh at our foibles. As one former student said, he had wit without barb or malice. But he knew the perils of too prolonged introspection. He once wrote that the trouble with the Versailles Treaty at the close of World War I was that it was signed in a hall of mirrors rather than in a room of windows. Hal was aware that we need windows more than mirrors, showing that he who would really see himself, must look away from himself.

Hal Luccock's productive years spanned four decades, during which America ran the cycle through the psychological searching of the early 1920's, the jazz era of the late 1920's, the depression days of the 1930's, the war years of the 1940's, and the return to psychology in the 1950's. Only God can measure the value of his service as, through all the fluctuations of social mood and the flux of fads, he kept his eye clear, his pen sharp, and his heart courageous. Take Halford Luccock out of these last forty years and contemplate the void.

We pass to the third feature in Henry van Dyke's definition of fame: "approved by the wise."

There are tricks in all trades and the clerical calling is no exception. Clever preachers can draw crowds by catering to popular desires. Hal Luccock preached to the needs of men, not to their wishes. True, he did phrase his themes to arouse popular interest, but he did not prostitute his gospel to please light-minded listeners. To my knowledge no man equaled him in deflating pretense and sham. He was so dedicated to the truth that any false note irked him.

Henry Pitney Van Dusen declares that there are two human needs which have given rise to religious cultivation. These are: the longing for light on the mystery of things and the longing for power for the mastery of things. Since World War II we have had a spate of "how to" books offering quick recipes for getting power and peace of mind through faith, prayer, and the Holy Spirit. Hal kept a balanced perspective on life as a quest and a conquest. He was concerned for the "know how," but he saw beyond to the need of the "know why."

Hence he was able to command the confidence of the man on the campus as well as attract the attention of the man on the street. If anyone had called him a theologian, he would no doubt have denied it with some quick quip. But he was respected by the theologians. He was not a specialist in social ethics but his moral insights were regarded as sound by the scholars in that field. He stood where the specialties meet and helped men to see life steadily and see it whole.

In this age of specialization a person may be approved by those who are wise in his own department and yet not be appreciated by the general public. In fact, the public is usually so far behind the advance of truth that it ridicules its pioneers and stones its prophets. But give the people time and they usually arrive at true estimates of greatness.

Henry van Dyke climaxes his criteria of fame by adding a fourth test: "applauded by the common voice." Hal Luccock never sought the klieg lights of public acclaim. I do not know that his name will ever be a household word throughout the land. But I would predict that Halford Luccock's reputation will grow with the passing decades and fifty years hence will outshine the names of those who at the moment may be more in the public eye. And I make that prediction because his work was founded on fundamentals and fashioned by universals. To him "the church's one foundation is Jesus Christ her Lord." He built on the ultimate values, beauty, truth, and goodness. He dealt with the basic needs of human nature. He transcended denominational lines and aided the ecumenical movement. He was a fighter for racial brotherhood and international peace. His sympathies were as wide as the world and as deep as human suffering. He lived with lasting things. He died with faith, hope, and love abiding and abounding in his heart. His influence was still growing when he went to his grave. We believe he lives now with his Lord and will continue to live in an ever-widening circle of those who love and bless him.

It was Hal Luccock who first called my attention to some lines which appeared anonymously in the London *Times* during World War I. I think you will see the fitness of quoting them here:

> *Jesus, whose lot with us was cast,*
> *Who saw it out from first to last,*
> *Patient and fearless, tender, true,*
> *Vagabond, carpenter, felon, Jew,*
> *Whose humorous eye took in each phase*
> *Of full rich life this world displays.*
> *But evermore kept fast in view*
> *The far-off goal it leads us to.*

*The Second Epistle of Paul
to the Corinthians*

1. THE COMFORT OF GOD

The God of all comfort. 2 COR. 1:3

One of the most beautiful and beloved names for God—"The God of all comfort." A good name for the God of a world-wide family in desperate need of fortification of mind and heart.

The very word "comfort" as it appears in the beginning of the great prophecy in Isaiah 40 is almost a new watershed in spiritual world history. It leads into a larger experience of a God of love, with its culmination in the revelation of the comfort of God in Christ. "I will not leave you comfortless: I will come to you" (John 14:18, AV).

There is no deep and adequate comfort for man facing a mysterious and frightening universe except in God. Men have tried to find it elsewhere. They have tried it in nature. There have been in nature both beauty and restoration of spirit. But if man is to face "the heavy and weary weight of all this unintelligible world," the love of nature is not enough. Here is an experiment made by one whom John M. Mecklin calls "a great teacher who confesses himself a complete non-believer in the Christian God." He writes,

Nature is to me the great healer of the sickness born of man's social stupidities, his moral nightmares, and religious superstitions. Nature that long ago gave birth to man, her last and most dubious offspring, often seems to me like a mother stilling her restless child. She is there to soothe his ills, too often self-created. She never lets him slip from her all-encircling arms.

This glowing description makes one think of the phrase, "The still small voice that whispers, 'Fiddlesticks.'" Could more pure sentimentalism be packed into one short paragraph? Real empowerment must be made of sterner stuff, "the God of all comfort."

Yet in our time that word "comfort" has sadly degenerated in many quarters. In religion many have made a cult of comfort. In the very much shorter catechism of many moderns the chief end of man is to get comfortable and enjoy himself forever. And a religion has been shaped to meet the tastes and clamors of a genera-

19

tion to which comfort is the highest good. We sing,

> *Must I be carried to the skies*
> *On flowery beds of ease,*

and forget that a large part of our inventive genius and manufacturing skill has been devoted to designing flowering beds of ease. Perhaps not always flowers, but at least ease.

An indication of the way in which the word has slipped from its high New Testament meaning is found in a book of a few years ago, *The Art of Comfort*. It sounds as though it were a book of counseling and effective sympathetic action. But no; it is a collection of "hundreds of ways to achieve comfort" in more comfortable houses.

The comfort which God gives is not a mental aspirin tablet or a tranquilizing pill. Many who follow the cult of comfort, in the words of one onlooker, "drag the deity around like a dancing bear."

The comfort of God includes "fortification" in our life. That is the root meaning of the word. To give comfort is to fortify. In this very passage the idea goes from comfort into affliction. It moves and has its being in a real world. It does not portray a romantic, sentimental world, rather one where pain and suffering and toil are real things, but for which the God of all comfort gives fortifying strength for all demands. True Christianity is not a self-centered search for ease. It does not put itself in the center of the universe, as in the parody of the childhood verse,

> *Twinkle, twinkle, little star*
> *How you wonder what I are.*

Before the august God the worshiper is "lost in wonder, love and praise."

2. TERMINALS AND TRANSMITTERS

God . . . who comforts us in all our affliction, so that we may be able to comfort those who are in any affliction.   2 COR 1:4
So that we in turn may be able to give the same sort of strong sympathy.
(Phillips)

This verse is a picture of what is designed to be an endless chain. God's comfort is given, not that it may come to a dead end, but be transmitted to others. The realm of electricity pictures the meaning here. There are terminal wires where the electric impulse ends.

There are transmitter wires which send the impulse on, whether across the room or across a world. An inevitable question confronts us—are we terminals or transmitters? The strengthening, the fortification, the re-creation which come to us from God are to be sent on to others, as through a channel. There is a purpose through it all—"He gives us comfort, so that we in turn may be able to give."

The high significance of a life is not the personal dazzle it may emit, drawing attention to itself. Some people can make a great show fizzing like a Roman candle. But there is nothing left but a burnt-out stump. In electrical terms they have a short circuit to their powers. Nothing is passed on. We get a picture of the same lives in the remark of a gardener to the effect that there is nothing more exasperating than a hose which just isn't long enough. No water transmitted to a thirsty garden.

One great stress of this whole passage is on the truth that comfort and strength which one has found in any affliction is a tremendous equipment for service. There is nothing to match it. Phillips renders this affirmation clearly, "We know how to encourage you to endure patiently the same sort of troubles that we have ourselves endured." The supreme curriculum for encouragement is not eloquence. It is the power of one gleaming sentence, "He has been through it."

A demonstration of that was given in dramatic form by Sir Cyril Arthur Pearson, the publisher, in England, during and following World War I. He was afflicted with failing eyesight and finally became blind. He founded St. Dunstan's Home for Soldiers blinded in World War I. His very presence, serving them in his own affliction, proved a power. So it was with the unfailing dramatic word "we" as pronounced for the first time by Father Damien, speaking to the lepers in the colony on Molokai Island. To their great astonishment he began his talk to them one Sunday, "We lepers. . . ." They knew that he had served them so long that he had become a leper himself. That was a new tremendous bond of brotherhood. His own affliction gave him a new power of encouragement.

The supreme example, of course, is Jesus. If Jesus had had a happy and serene and carefree life, if his acquaintance with grief had been a very distant one, he would have had nothing to say to people in the toils of suffering or to a world in distress. He would have been a sort of Hebrew Seneca. He knew how to encourage, because for the joy that was set before them he endured the cross. If we have had affliction and have known the comfort of God, it will save us from the empty commonplaces and maddening clichés, which, as mere talkers, we are likely to indulge in. Moffatt uses an expressive word, that our affliction and comfort will *"nerve* others to endure affliction." What could be greater than *nerving* another person in distress, paralyzed except for strength transmitted by us.

Pain and trouble are wonderful entrance tickets to other lives. We "know how to encourage," not by exhortation but by demonstration.

How many marvelous transmitters of God's comfort there have been! Parents, teachers, housemaids! A church can be a terminal or a transmitter. A church can become like a railroad terminal, the Grand Central in New York City, for instance. Everything stops there; nothing goes through. Or a church may be a transmitter, like the little churches which met in the homes of some of the early disciples.

3. A NEW TESTAMENT LIBERAL

For if I have a liberal share of Christ's sufferings, through Christ I have a liberal share of comfort, too.   2 COR. 1:5   (Goodspeed)

Here is a picture of what might be called "a New Testament liberal." He is defined differently from the usual party label of "liberalism"; he is one who has a liberal share both of Christ's sufferings and of his comfort.

This passage gives a fresh view of a "liberal." It is a word that has been thrown back and forth, a convenient stick to beat a dog with. For a long stretch of years, and particularly in recent years among theologians, the word has been too much of a party cry— the things which Paul protested against so vehemently and frequently. It has become a divisive word, with something of complacency and self-satisfaction among those who have looked askance at old-fashioned liberals.

> *Shall we whose minds are lighted*
> *With wisdom from on high*
> *Withhold from the poor "liberal"*
> *Our truth for his dark sky?*

Among the newer lights of theology there has grown up quite an imposing bit of historical fiction, that pillars of liberalism such as Rauschenbusch and Gladden were just softhearted optimists who were incurable romantics. Some of them sound as though they had

never heard of Rauschenbusch's *A Theology for the Social Gospel.*
In certain quarters in recent years, the liberal, never sharply defined,
has been given the treatment described in the classic story of the
woman who visited a silver fox farm. She asked the owner, "How
often do you skin them?" He gave her a gentle answer, "We used
to do it twice a year, but that made them nervous, so we skin them
only once a year." But the "liberal" has been "skinned" every week
at least by *avant-garde* theologians.

But this picture of "a New Testament liberal" lifts the word out
of party conflicts and divisive labels. And what a glorious liberalism
it is—"a liberal share of Christ's sufferings," a generous, wide share
of this, "As the Son of man came . . . to give his life as a ransom
for many" (Matt. 20:28). "I am crucified with Christ" (Gal. 2:20,
AV). That is more than a slogan. It is a redeeming life.

4. THE END OF OUR TETHER

We had this experience of coming to the end of our tether.   2 COR. 1:8
(Phillips)
We were so utterly, unbearably crushed.

This is a spot which most of us know—the end of our tether. We
have been there. And how well some people know it, every inch of
the rugged ground! And what a short rope our tether seems to be!
We often make the lamentation, "If this tether that holds us back
from opportunities were just a little bit longer!" We don't ask for
a square mile to roam at will in. All we ask is a little bit more
tether!

In our present world, short tether is the lot of most of us. Some
cynic tells us, "If you don't worry, you will go to the poor house;
if you do worry, you will go to the lunatic asylum." Evidently, you
can't win. One of the sharp insights in George Bernard Shaw's murky
play has to do with what "The Ancients," who lived to the age of
Methuselah, finally die of. He says there are two causes of death,
accidents and *discouragement.* Not so far from our own world with
its standard span of life running to threescore and ten. Every year
we are appalled at the increasing number of accidents on the road
and in mine and shop. And how many diseases, all the way from
a stomach ulcer to heart disease, stem from discouragement. Ask any
psychosomatic specialist. Men and women at the very end of their
tether are so deeply discouraged in many ways that people are ready

to ask the question which Juliet, in a moment of discouragement, asks in *Romeo and Juliet*:

> *Is there no pity sitting in the clouds*
> *That sees into the bottom of my grief?*

That is all familiar country and a living place we all know. Our passage here from Paul points out the tragic confusion and misunderstanding that is so commonly made. Hosts of people tend to think that because they have come to the end of their tether that God has come to the end of *His* rope. Too many people confuse themselves with God. They take their fears, their discouragements, their weaknesses and frustrations, and transfer them to God. That was the procedure of a man who lived most of his life as a romantic optimist, and ended in a state of deep-dyed pessimism hardly matched in our time: H. G. Wells. In his last despairing day he wrote a book entitled *Mind at the End of Its Tether*. A gloomy farewell to a doomed world. There was no God in the picture—all black! Part of the explanation is that Mr. Wells never had a truly realistic view of the world. He had a romantic idea of science, and a trust in a new breed of human aristocrats who would soon take over the world and set it to rights. In essence, most of the works of this great worshiper of science were as the Alger books. When world disasters showed that this Wellsian optimism had no real foundation, he swung clear over to the extreme of despair. This is a swing of position made so often that it can be put into a kind of equation. When a person begins by believing that man can do *everything*, he ends up by believing that man can do *nothing*. Both extremes are wrong. The missing factor is God. A real faith in God keeps the believer out of both pitfalls, romantic optimism and dogmatic pessimism.

Many people hold to a deep pessimism because it is the most fashionable style of thinking. There is a widely accepted delusion that unless you are a pessimist you cannot be a deep thinker. So there are thriving schools of pessimism, the hydrogen bomb pessimists, who know the world will be blown to bits, and that right soon. There are the population pessimists who know that there will be so many people in the world in forty-seven years, six months, and nine days. There are the exhausted resources pessimists, who see a world where oil, coal, and food have given out. Their invitation is constant: "Come sit down in a comfortable seat by the wailing wall, and wail hard. You will be in good company."

Of course, every one of these matters is occasion for deepest concern and demands vigorous action to prevent disaster. But they do not mean the end of God's rope.

Notice in this passage—2 cor. 1:8-11—Paul hardly finishes declaring that he was unbearably crushed and felt as though he had been condemned to death, than he makes clear that he was not unbearably crushed. But he has set his hope on the God who has delivered and will deliver again. At the end of every tether we have an appointment with God.

5. WHERE YOU COME IN

Here you can join in and help by praying for us.   2 COR. 1:11 (Phillips)

These words, "here you can join in," echo a question that runs through many lives like a continued beat of a drum: "Where do I come in?" Often when any kind of project is proposed, the question springs out of hiding to the foreground, "What is there in it for me?"

It was heard in the very beginning of Jesus' teaching of his disciples. We read, "Then Peter said in reply, 'Lo, we have left everything and followed you. What then shall we have?" (Matt. 19:27). The persistent question gets a start in the history of the gospel and the church, "Where do I come in?" So down to the present have we heard in one form or another, often unspoken, "What do we get out of it?" The request resembles that of desiring to be first-class passengers on a cruise. These people feel that special attention is due them.

Paul uses here almost the same words, but in a vastly different sense. He tells the Christians at Philippi, This is where you come in. He does not mean the distribution of gifts and advantages. He lifts the question to a higher level, to the highest level, that of prayer and communion with God. He asks the converts that he may have their co-operation in prayer. The place where they come in is in a fellowship of intercession. There are many places and undertakings where they come in, but this is one of them, partnership in communion with God in prayer. Paul asks their prayers for him, that blessings to him may be carried to others.

The emphasis falls on unselfish prayer, the prayer for others. So often prayer is dragged down to a form of self-seeking. Thus the highest employment of human powers, prayer, becomes a practice of seeking a reward for the question, "Where do I come in?" A rather perfect picture of degenerate prayer is given in a story from the Department of Agriculture in Washington. A fussy woman was parading up and down the offices of the Department, demanding to see the Secretary of Agriculture. She was permitted to see one of the staff, but that was declined wrathfully. She said that she must see the Secretary. She was told that this was impossible and that she had better give her request to another official. She finally agreed, and told the official, "Well, I have a geranium at home that isn't doing very well."

We might say that there is a great deal of "geranium religion," that is, an attempt to use God as a means of getting some selfish gain for oneself. C. S. Lewis, in his autobiography, records a somewhat similar restricted idea of prayer. He recalls that in his childhood he prayed to the magician God whom he wished to heal his dying mother and then go away. That childish idea is all too often carried into an adult life, adult in years but childish in motive, to get something from God and then dismiss Him from life. There is no better question for the lips and the heart than this: "Where do I come into God's plan for the world?"

This plea for a fellowship in prayer comes down through the centuries to our day and to us. We need urging to *practice* prayer. We are in an analytical age. We are busily engaged in destroying the flower to see what it is made of. Many of us are far more ready to explain prayer than to pray. Yet no one can reduce intercessory prayer to a diagram or a syllogism. We cannot have it and tie it up with a neat Q.E.D., either negative or positive. But we can practice prayer for others. We know that God touches the world through human lives. God makes a larger entrance into human lives through lives that are open to his coming and influence. So the world is "bound by gold chains about the feet of God."

That is our first service. Some years ago E. S. Waterhouse pointed out that when Jesus said the harvest was too big for the available help, he did not say, "Work harder," or "Get more helpers," but he said, "Pray to the Lord of the harvest." First things first.

We should never forget that prayer is an active affair. It has been said of Rodin's statue of "The Thinker" that the man thought with his whole body. The person who makes an effective prayer prays with his whole life.

6. PROUD OF US

You can be proud of us. 2 COR. 1:14

This seems like a terribly complacent thing to say. It savors strongly of self-praise, self-satisfaction, and conceit. This does not sound like the language of the Letter to the Ephesians, "I am the very least of all the saints" (Eph. 3:8), and the words the author of First Timothy puts into the mouth of Paul, "I am the foremost of sinners." (1:15). Few of us, certainly, would be so calloused as to tell people that they "can be proud of us."

Yet it is a goal to put before one's eyes, and, in that sense, Paul used it and also reached that goal. With Paul, when he tells the church at Corinth that they "can be proud of us," it is not complacency that speaks but realism. Paul was making his defense against the slanders that had been cast on his conduct by some of the Christians at Corinth. He tells them frankly and firmly that they can be proud of all he has done. This can be appreciated and applauded by a generation of Christians who have been taught to put self-acceptance far above self-depreciation as an equipment for spiritual service. Robert Louis Stevenson found a good word for undue playing down of one's worth. He called it "crushed wormery." There is no virtue in calling oneself, or thinking of oneself, as a crushed worm. A true Christian attitude calls for the recognition of one's integrity and sincerity. Such a recognition of one's genuine achievements, with God's help, is a feeling which Paul has urged on others. Thus, "I bid every one among you not to think of himself more highly than he ought to think, but to think with sober judgment, each according to the measure of faith which God has assigned him" (Rom. 12:3). In other words, think realistically, barring conceit and also refusing to wallow in an orgy of self-depreciation.

Of course, a genuine conceit is not only wicked, but often is screamingly funny. Thus we look at the words of Gertrude Stein, "I know that I am the most important writer writing today," and "I am the only person who has ever known what poetry is." Exit Dante and Aeschylus, followed by such small fry as Shakespeare and Milton. Such exhibitions of conceit are not to be disregarded. For they give a hearty laugh which is good medicine for soul and body.

When we think of pride, we may well be warned by the trivial things over which people have prided themselves. Benjamin Haydon, the English painter, related a well-known story of a man in Stratford who was always telling the town that they could be proud of him, for he was ninety years old and had never had a toothache or lost a tooth. Another man prided himself inordinately on having never missed a train in his life. What, if anything, happened because of catching these trains never came into the picture!

But there is a place for solemn pride. Paul told his friends and enemies that in his life and work there had been holiness and godly sincerity, not worldly cunning but the grace of God. They could be proud of him for that. We are all of us miserable sinners. But fidelity to God in a crisis, and integrity in one's whole life, are cause for pride. Remember the words of Hebrews: "Therefore God is not ashamed to be called their God." Such people could say truthfully to the whole company of archangels, "You can be proud of us." That is the highest decoration man can wear, God's distinguished service medal.

7. A GREAT DAY COMING

On the day when Christ reveals all secrets.   2 COR. 1:14 (Phillips)

This verse suggests a picture to stir the imagination. It recalls the spiritual, "There's a Great Day A'-Coming!" For one thing, on the day when Christ reveals all secrets, we will want to be there. We are interested in other people, and we will be excited to learn their secrets; especially are we curious to see skeletons in the opened closets.

This little bit of imaginary anticipation has two bad flaws. For when we stop to think—an upsetting habit, stopping to think— we have to revise our thinking about the great day of secrets. First of all, the spotlight swings from other people to *ourselves*. It is *our* secrets with their carefully arranged camouflage and their clever disguise which will be revealed. The inner self which we have tried so hard at times to conceal shall appear in the daylight. That is something to think about, deeply and painfully and penitently.

The second common mistake about the Great Day of secrets revealed is that too exclusive an emphasis has been placed on evil secrets. All secrets are not bad. A great multitude of the secrets of many lives are among the most beautiful and lovely things of earth. The familiar words of the Collect, "O God . . . from whom no secrets are hid," very often have only a forbidding sound and an upsetting quality. Thank God there are other secrets. They are not great scandals. They are such golden secrets as a great sacrifice, done quietly and kept hidden, with no fanfare. There is the secret of endurance of those who have carried heavy loads, too heavy for them, from a great loyalty and a great love. There are the secrets of the handicapped, stumbling through life as best they can, but with no sourness, no complaint. There are those who have met disappointed hopes, yet played bravely a role they never expected to occupy. God sees those secrets. They are written down in the Lamb's Book of Life.

If we could only see people as God sees them! They may look like rather ordinary folk to our shortsighted gaze, but they carry a precious secret known only to themselves and God. They may have nothing of genius, but they have a great self-forgetfulness which God rates much higher than genius.

The familiar words should bring not fear but reassurance: "From whom no secrets are hid."

8. YES AND NO

We have never given you a message meaning "yes" and "no." 2 COR. 1:18 (Phillips)

Paul did not say "yes" or "no." He did not talk out of both sides of his mouth. That is where many in our day have made a big improvement on St. Paul. We have made a fine art out of double talk. Indeed, the skillful use of "yes" and "no" in the same breath —the kind of talk that is double talk de luxe—has been made into a profession. Many who have mastered the art have climbed to the seats of the mighty. We read, on good authority, "If therefore thine eye be single, thy whole body shall be full of light" (Matt. 6:22, AV). It is also true that if thy speech be single, and not double, thy whole talk shall be full of light. But if thy speech be "yes and no," thy speech is a chaos of darkness.

The hazards of "yes and no" speech are increased greatly by two popular features of our time.

The first feature favoring "yes and no" talk is the great prestige of the open mind. The open mind, of course, in the true sense is a fine quality in any person or situation. But, as practiced, the open mind is often made an excuse for never reaching a decision, of being always a retreating neutral, and of making one's life motto, "There's much to be said on both sides." And it is said that people with perpetually open minds frequently become disciples of the saving religion of "on-the-other-hand-ism." The equation which accurately represents the "yes and no" fraternity is $X=0$. The whole impact of their speech adds up to an eloquent zero. G. K. Chesterton dealt with this common masquerade of the open mind by saying that the purpose of an open mind is to close it on something. Selah!

Another force against which our minds must fight their way to the prize of positive convictions is the cult of adjustment. The chief end of man, in this philosophy, is to get adjusted. In pursuit of this ideal end, parents have sacrificed the individual qualities of children's minds on the altar of conformity. The goal seems to be to agree with everything, till the whole population becomes as exciting as a picket fence. The last state of that man is the tragic one of being robbed of the power to say "No!" clearly and decisively, or to say "Yes!" with a thundering accent which leaves no doubt.

"Yes and no" talk is found in what is often an adjusted religion. That is, one adjusted to the ruling ideas of the environment in which it wilts instead of thrives. Such a company may well feel that the harsh saying, "No man can serve two masters," is a rather extreme position. What they do is to demonstrate the truth of what Jesus said.

To cure this fatal speech defect, Jesus highly recommended two words to be used separately, "yes" *or* "no."

9.   THE DIVINE "YES"

All the promises of God find their Yes in him.   2 COR. 1:20
He is the divine "Yes."   (Phillips)
The divine "yes" has at last sounded in him.   (Moffatt)

A tremendous word—the divine "Yes"—for a world of so many negations. It is a positive affirmation sounding like a roll of thunder amid and above the many denials of human speech, its fears, its frustrations, its betrayals. Our world is full of road blocks. It stretches out like the streets of Paris during its many turbulent revolutions. There are barricades erected across so many roads which say sternly "No!" Multitudes ask of our dark world, "Watchman, what of the night?" The answer is often ready before the question is finished. They leave out the first part of the classic answer in Isaiah, "The morning cometh," and hurry on to the negative, "The night cometh." Hope for the world hangs by the slenderest of threads; hope is often regarded as really an illusion clung to by naïve minds. To the question of the good of life, the answer made by many is a "No!" as emphatic as the slamming of a door.

Yet the ancient thunder still sounds, the divine Yes to all the hopes and aspirations of humanity. "All the promises of God," writes Paul, "find their Yes in him." The hopes and dreams of man find their yes in him. The lines of Phillips Brooks seem like a translation of these words of Paul:

> The hopes and fears of all the years
> Are met in him tonight.

There can be no mathematical proof of this thunder of affirmation in Christ. There are no logarithms by which salvation for the world through Christ can be proved. But a caution must be expressed against taking vociferous negations of hope in God too seriously. Dean Inge said that he had no ear for music, that he could not tell the difference between the songs "Pop Goes the King" and "God Save the Weasel." But that is not a fact about music. It is just a somewhat pathological fact about Dean Inge. So when a person says that there is no dependable "yes" to man's hopes and yearnings, that is not a fact about the universe. It is just a fact about the orator of the day who is sounding off.

When someone says that there is no spiritual world beyond the five senses, that ultimatum does not abolish it. It merely describes the limitations of a man's perception.

The divine affirmation, the divine "Yes" in Christ, brings a multitude of men of every race, color, and nation to respond by their whole being. Occasionally there are volunteers ready to improve Jesus. Margaret Fuller wrote condescendingly,

> With regard to Christ, I am grateful here, as everywhere, when spirit bears fruit in fullness. The very greatness of this manifestation demands a greater. We want a life more complete and various than that of Christ.

More complete and various! Miss Fuller would doubtless have been pleased had Christ shown a fuller grasp of New England Transcendentalism! Had Christ been "made over" to fit her specifications, he would have been only a footnote to history, in small print.

In the story of "Ali Baba and the Forty Thieves," one of the tales of the *Arabian Nights,* is a passage suggesting a truth about Christ:

The forty thieves lived in a vast cave, the door of which opened and shut at the words, "Open, Sesame!" and "Shut, Sesame!" Ali Baba tried saying, "Open, wheat!" and "Open, barley!" but there was no movement of the door. Then one day he accidentally discovered the magic word, "Open, Sesame!"

The door swung wide. The magic word which opens life's treasure is Christ. "The divine 'yes' has at last sounded in him." H. M. Tomlinson has a postwar picture which culminates in what is a good name for Christ in our badly dented world. In his *Wreckage at Sunset* he muses on a passing gun wheel in a military parade, and writes,

Just for an instant we surmise that those wheels cannot be endlessly turning; a calm morning will come, with no ships blowing up, and no houses on fire. Only the silent ruins will be there, waiting for the recreative Word.

The Word made flesh is for our broken world the Re-creative Word.

Christ was born into a world sunk in negative pessimism. Like our world it had its longings as well as its depressions. Gilbert Murray wrote of it, "How earnestly the world was looking for peace at this time appears by inscriptions set up in Asia Minor and elsewhere in honor of Emperor Augustus. The nations had received the *Pax Romana,* but as a philosopher was to say before the century was out, that while Caesar may give peace on land and from piracy at sea, he cannot grant peace from sorrow and envy." A greater than Caesar was here! All the promises of God, and all the deep hopes of men, find their yes in him. With him it is always Yes.

10.   SATAN'S TRICKS

To keep Satan from gaining the advantage over us; for we are not ignorant of his designs.   2 COR. 2:11
I know his manoeuvres!   (Moffatt)
We know what he is after.   (Goodspeed)

Here is pictured a salvation which everyone desperately needs, salvation from gullibility. It often seems that as much, or more harm is done by gullibility, the capacity of being easily deceived

One of Satan's most reliable tricks is found in his rule, "Never call a thing by its right name." The forces of evil do not like the words "whatever things are *true*." Ugly realities are covered up by fair names. The embezzling cashier in the bank is not really stealing. Horrors, no! He is *borrowing*. A good place to study this process is in the parable of the Prodigal Son. When he left home and was wasting his substance, he was "seeing the world." When he was bankrupt through riotous living, he called it being "a little wild." Dissipation was given a much softer term, "independence." Only in the barnyard did he find the right name, "I have *sinned*."

A trick which has been a reliance of Satan is getting men to avoid responsibility. "This isn't my fault" is a constant whimper which is music to Satan's ears. A common instance of this is the man who makes his living in the city but makes his voting residence in the suburbs. Very often this enables him to evade responsibility at both ends of his commuter's trip. He feels no responsibility for making the city a decent place to live in, or to take his share of the responsibility of the suburban town. So his inertia enables the racketeers, gangsters, and all immorality in politics to go on.

A simple trick, but a mystifying one, is to lead people (perhaps we had better say, "to lead *us*," for we all swallow it) into thinking we have *done* something about an evil when we have merely *talked* about it. Not quite the same thing. After a vigorous talk, we are tempted to dust off our hands and say, in self-congratulation, "Well, I guess that's telling them off!" That's the trouble. It is *telling* them, not really *fighting*. It was rather easy, in the North, to denounce Little Rock, Arkansas, for its enormities, easier than it was to make a visible contribution to racial justice.

The tragic gullibility of a host of people is never better demonstrated than the acceptance of the holy faith that we must not interfere with business. For the forces of evil, this is gullibility de luxe. The most heartbreaking example of this is found in the years of the industrial revolution in England, when the machine age stole in without any protection for labor, without any protection even for children. Parliament voted in the 1860's £30,000 for education of England's children, and £70,000 for the royal stables and kennels. "How much is a man better than a sheep?" It took twenty-five years of legislation to restrict a child of nine years to a sixty-nine-hour week, and that only in the cotton mills. All over England women and children descended into the dank dark-

or cheated, than by deliberate evil-doing. A great many people
much attention to part of Paul's list of things to give your min
(Phil. 4:8), such as whatever is "honorable, just, pure,
lovely." But they do not look with X-ray eyes to what is named
in that list, "whatever is *true*." The search for the truth sh
be one of life's first explorations. Give your mind, Paul say
finding whatever is *true*. Let loveliness and good report fo
along. Be saved from gullibility!

A knowledge of Satan's designs is a necessary equipmen
avoiding his deceptions. Paul wrote, "We know what he is a
We had better *all* know what he is after, better be familiar
all his tricks, so that when one is brought out we can say witl
dain, "That's an old one. Get going." Then, also, there are d
tions of evil that we must be aware of. Here are a few star
"designs":

1. A common deception in these psychological days is the
pretation of all sin and evil as just subjective mechanisms wh
doctor will be able to control. Denis De Rougemont calls t
dangerous Utopia. It is a great quelling of mind and consc
to consider sin as an out-of-date idea, replaced by a form of m
disturbance.

Again, Denis De Rougemont points out a masterpiece of d
"We have lost," he declares, "the cosmic sense, the immediate
sciousness of our bonds with the whole of the universe, its k
laws and its mysteries," and the moral sense, "the immediate
sciousness of the absolute, which, independent of ourselves, v
be the universal measure of good and evil."

More familiar to us, and hence more devastating, is Satan
surance that "there is no hurry about it." That saves us the tr
of doing anything about any evil *now*. No hurry, whispers S
Many tragedies have been brought about by accepting this c
narcotic. No hurry. Remember Thomas McKean. Who wa
and why should he be remembered? He was the last man to
the Declaration of Independence. He signed in 1781, four
after it was adopted. If the other signers had been as slow
was, there would have been no American Revolution. The n
ing song of this noble company of "no hurry" saints might
be:

> *Sleeping in the morning, sleeping through the crises,*
> *Sleeping in the noon-tide and the dewey eve;*
> *Waiting for the harvest and the time of reaping,*
> *We shall come remorseful, bringing up the rear.*

ness of the coal pits to work as much as thirteen hours a day. Many of the bishops in the House of Lords voted against every effort to lighten the slavery of the children and their mothers. It was one of the great masterpieces of evil in all history.

One of the most destructive of the deceits of evil is furthering the illusion that this affair or time is not important, or that "this little slip" makes no difference. This develops a neglect of moments that do not seem to be vastly important major matters. Life does not announce the great important hours through a megaphone. There is no loud blare: "Oyez! Oyez! A great class event is now going to take place. Watch it carefully, folks. Right over there. Don't miss it!"

Life does not have that kind of public address system. There is no shrill fire alarm to warn of its great moments. It never screams, "Here is the crucial decision."

May we be able to say with truth, "We know Satan's methods."

11. TRIUMPHANT TRAIN

He makes my life a constant pageant of triumph in Christ. 2 COR. 2:14 (Moffatt)
Thanks be to God, who in Christ always leads us in triumph.

Poetry? Of course. But was there ever a more monumental triumph than Paul's: beginning with being beaten with thirty-nine lashes, and with rods and stones, and, as incidental features of the triumph, "hunger and thirst, often without food, in cold and exposure" (2 Cor. 11:24-28)?

Yet beyond the poetry there is truth. Paul's was a triumphant life, far beyond any gaudy triumph of the Roman Forum. Paul, in this passage, is comparing his life in Christ with the triumphs of the Roman emperors or victorious generals. Rome really gave the populace memorable "circuses" as well as bread. Imperial Rome had a genius for showmanship which far surpassed the greatest achievement of Barnum and Bailey. For in the Roman triumphs there were wild animal acts as well as military glory.

As a spectacle, compare the parades, any one of the many triumphs which wound their progress along the Appian Way, and Paul's parade along the same highway. Here it is recorded, and the record will help the imagination to make the contrast:

And so we came to Rome, and the brethren there, when they heard of us, came as far as the Forum of Appius and the three taverns to meet us. [Acts 28:15]

A pitiful little spectacle, according to Roman standards, three or four men walking along the highway, one of them a prisoner! Yet Paul's triumph far surpassed any triumph ever staged at Rome or along the road to Rome. Just for one slight measure of the triumph, step over to the public library, and drop in on the court of the card index. Look up the name of the Roman emperor under whom Paul was executed. That is, if you can remember it. Oh, yes, Nero. Look up Nero in the catalog. One or two entries, largely a case of retarded mental development, arsonist and third-rate violinist (perhaps "third-rate" places him too high!). Try any Roman emperor in Paul's century. You will not find much but a name and a date. Paul will occupy a whole tray of cards, giving some idea of the way he has been plowed into the world's mind and life and history, and is still one of the towering figures in the world's thought. Paul's triumph was that of mind over matter, of spirit over material. No matter how many lashes, it was the ultimate triumph of the presence and companionship of God, of being a co-worker with Him. "It is no longer I who live, but Christ who lives in me" (Gal. 2:20).

And what a big parade of those who have followed in Paul's train and finished the course in the same triumph! The well-known knights of the spiritual realm come first to mind: St. Francis, John Bunyan, and George Fox. Bunyan and Fox, at least, could match Paul's record of "perils," "danger in the city, danger in the wilderness, danger at sea, danger from false brethren" (2 Cor. 11:26).

Who follows in their train?

> *A noble army, men and boys*
> *The matron and the maid.*

A triumphant processional winds its way through country lanes and city streets all over the earth with Christ at its head. We are all familiar with the inscription on the tomb of the Unknown Soldier, "known but to God." There are uncounted hosts in this triumphal train "known but to God." They are unknown to fame, unknown to *Who's Who*, often unknown to their near neighbors. There is the Unknown Homemaker, wife and mother, who marches in the triumph of a sacrificial life, who, like Another, gave her life, piece by piece, a ransom for many. There is the

Unknown Farmer, the Unknown School teacher, the Unknown Factory Worker. Of many of these we speak in scriptural terms, "the world was not worthy."

The endless procession moves not through the aisles of a cathedral, but through the long aisles of time and space.

12. PEDDLERS OF GOD'S WORD

We are not . . . peddlers of God's word. 2 COR. 2:17
I am . . . not adulterating the word of God. (Moffatt)

Evidently, the peddler in the Mediterranean world had a reputation for cheating. For here the opposite to peddler is sincerity. The peddler in this passage sounds like a man concerned for his own profit, in selling things, often adulterated goods. His concern was with tricks that make a profit. The peddler has, in part, a noble tradition in America, for the peddler was often a man who performed a great public service, particularly to people in remote locations. He was often a man of integrity, such as that notable Yankee Peddler, Bronson Alcott.

The true opposite of being a peddler of God's word is being a *commissioned* servant of the word. Against the person who makes profits from small gadgets is the man of great dedication. This applies both to the public proclaimer of the word and to its private demonstration. For the peddler is concerned with something he can use for his advantage. The commissioned messenger is the servant of a gospel which uses him.

Carlyle's description of Thomas De Quincey fits the peddler of God's word—"full of wire-drawn ingenuities, and bankrupt of enthusiasms." The peddler is caught in a terrible bankruptcy. Enthusiasm has oozed out of him. He is not carried on by any surge of come-what-may commitment. He is a peddler. "Here is a cute little item, folks." George Bernard Shaw called Henley "an Elizabethan, . . . a man with extraordinary and imposing power of saying things, and nothing whatever to say." Diminutive excitements aplenty in the peddler's pack, but no burning commission, no resounding echo of great words, "Go," "Tell," "Do."

The peddler takes his message casually. One question: How can I adulterate it a bit to appeal to an unconcerned audience, so that they will buy it, and I will make a profit? Sometimes the man who peddles God's truth is like the horrible thing imagined by the young Walter Pater. Pater took up the cult of shocking people. "What fun it would be," he once said, "to be ordained and not believe a single word of what you are saying." But many peddlers of the word seem to have reached that high estate of felicity.

Against the peddler, set that great sequence, "I believed, and so I spoke"; we too believe and so we speak (2 Cor. 4:13). Speech was not the chatter of a huckster. It was the explosion of a great belief.

13.   A LETTER FROM CHRIST

You show that you are a letter from Christ delivered by us.   2 COR. 3:3

A rather constant feature in the literary life of the nineteenth century was a set of *Life and Letters of John Jones* or whoever. It sailed the library seas like a three-decker. Here we have something different, not life and letters, but a life as a letter. And more than that, a letter from Christ. Could imagination go farther than this tribute to a life: he carried so distinctively the qualities of Christ, that receiving him was like receiving a letter from Christ?

Some people seem to be little more than *advertising circulars.* They recommend their own virtues heartily and continuously. They seem to be printed in large 42-point type, with a dependable supply of exclamation points. They recommend themselves with all the frantic earnestness of a television announcer.

Other people seem to resemble a bill. Their appearance on the scene is welcomed with the joy with which we welcome the bill that drops in on the first of the month. Their very features at times seem to say, "You owe me so and so. Please pay now."

But there are some, by the grace of God, who are letters, people in whom we can read in clear letters a message of Christ. If we look carefully enough, we can make out the words of Christ. In their outgoing sympathy we catch the echo of his words, "Come unto me, all ye that . . . are heavy laden" (Matt. 11:28 AV). In the persuasiveness of their action and character, we hear one saying, "Follow me." In their invitations to an abundant life the prayer is granted,

> And wing my words that they may reach
> The hidden depths of many a heart.

In their vision of a world's need and their response to it, we hear old words, "Go ye into all the world."

It is one of the great achievements and privileges of life to represent something beyond oneself. Matthew Arnold writes,

> The night wind
> Brings up stream
> Murmurs and scents of the infinite sea.

There are people whose lives bring up stream murmurs and scents of the infinite sea of God. These are people who are described with some truth as "letters from Christ." Their very life is persuasive. Michelangelo said of Donatello that he made a St. Mark so strong and simple and sincere that "it would have been impossible to reject the gospel preached by such a straight forward man as this." The ultimate tribute!

Questions as direct as an arrow shot from a bow come to us from these words. Do our lives point to anything beyond us or above us? Does our life have any emphatic reference? If we aspire to fill that highest role in life, or "letter from Christ," can people read it in us? It was said of a contemporary artist that "she began as a primitive, and is now an abstractionist." There are people whose progress in being legible letters from Christ has been downward. They were once "primitive," clear and sharply defined. No one could miss their meaning. Then they became blurred abstractions.

Lord, is it I?

14. CHANGED BY BEHOLDING

And we all, with unveiled face, beholding the glory of the Lord, are being changed into his likeness from one degree of glory to another.
2 COR. 3:18
We are being transformed into the same likeness as himself.   (Moffatt)

This verse brings a rewarding study of New Testament grammar. That sounds dull. To many pople grammar is one of the most painful memories of youth. But this exercise in grammar is thrilling. It illustrates the fundamental point of the New Testament, that the Christian life and experience begin in the *passive* voice. "We are being transformed." It does not begin in our acting, but in being acted upon. This is a hard lesson to learn, and many have not mastered it; they like to jump into the active voice, with no great experience of the passive voice, that of being transformed by the spirit of God. God takes the initiative. We are acted upon. We do not change ourselves.

But there is a large active part. We are not carried to the skies. Our response to God's invitation is made by beholding, that is, bringing our whole powers to beholding the glory of God. That is the part that is often missed. We lead busy lives in a busy world. Who has time to "waste" in a contemplative life? We do, of course, spend much time in looking. But what we do so often is stare at the changing wonders of our mechanical world, rather than beholding the glory of God. So it happens that if there is no continued beholding of God, there is no "behold!" exclamation point in our lives. A life is in dismal poverty which has no beholds in it. Even in the Christian life, the favorite text of many is not "Be still and know that I am God," but "Let us then be up and doing."

It is true in many realms in addition to religion that true beholding is the beginning of wisdom and power. We can see this in art more clearly than in many other spheres. Here is a picture of the artist Whistler's power of actually seeing what he was looking at:

Leaning on the embankment wall, he [Whistler] would look long and steadily at a scene that appealed to his fancy, taking in all the details until the picture was stamped in his mind. If he had a companion, he would turn his back to the river and test his memory, saying in a spurt, "The sky is lighter than the water, the houses darkest. There are eight houses, the second is the lowest, the fifth the highest, the tone of all is the same . . . the first has two lighted windows, one above the other . . . the second has four . . ." and so on. If his companion said he was at fault at some point, he would turn around, look again, correct his mistake, turn again and once more recite from memory. That might happen a dozen times. . . .

The same power of beholding is true in science. The details of the legend of Galileo beholding the swinging chandelier in the Cathedral of Milan no doubt are untrue, but we do know that the beginning of wisdom with Galileo lay in beholding the skies with unveiled face. Rodin's statue "The Thinker" represents this power of man beholding, and that makes the statue a symbol of science far more accurately than the figure of a man running a machine.

In the life of the spirit transformation begins with beholding God in His glory and grace, a look that has in it awe, wonder, and adoration. And we may add, a look that has the consciousness of evil in it. That beholding is nothing "once and for all." It is a continuing activity of the whole being. We are "being transformed," progressive tense. That does not mean a casual glance at God. Beholding the glory of God involves reading, meditation, and prayer.

Some people build a ceiling over themselves, and prevent any possibility of being transformed or changed progressively into the image of Christ. Such men and women are rarely stirred by any vision that lets them see and realize their true potential. But true beholding brings into life a transforming process. Here is the very essence of Christian experience, which many people do not grasp. The Christian gospel is not "Try hard." There would be no saving power in that advice. It is a secret of "beholding" the glory of God, so intense and continual that we are transformed by its power.

There is a task that requires divine power. Goethe once said, rather playfully, that it was regrettable that nature made only one of him, since he had material for both a rogue and a gentleman. But that is a profound truth, and in no playful mood. There is in each of us material for a sinner and a saint. The rogue, the sinner, can be transformed into a son of God. "Now are we the sons of God."

15. DO NOT LOSE HEART

We do not lose heart. 2 COR. 4:1
Nothing can daunt us. (Phillips)

This affirmation was evidently very important to Paul. He repeats again a few paragraphs on, verse 16.

That is one of life's great risks—losing heart. It is a disaster that easily besets us. When we hear a man urging us not to "lose heart," we feel like giving him a challenge as a sentry and cry, "Halt, who goes there?" We have a right to know that the speaker has a right to give such an exhortation. Paul has won that right. Surely no one ever met greater temptations to lose heart. He fulfilled the commission, given in Proverbs, "Keep they heart with all diligence; for out of it are the issues of life" (4:23, AV).

Losing heart is so often a fatal risk—fatal to any more accomplishment and to life's deep joy. It is a peculiar hazard today. We keep our *minds.* Our generation has made greater strides in the mastery of nature than any preceding generation. But we "lose heart." The odds are against us. That is often true of an individual.

It is true of an institution, a nation, a generation. Before people have lost battles in personal life, they have lost heart. It is tremendously important not to lose heart. What a record in that respect many of the Christians of the first three centuries made. We love to sing about them:

> They met the tyrant's brandished steel
> The lion's gory mane.
> They bowed their necks the death to feel.
> Who follows in their train?

But these are two lines in the hymnal in which we cannot in all honesty join:

> And blest would be their children's fate,
> If they, like them, should die for thee.

It is staggering to be reminded of the obstacles and agonies before which and under which many did not lose heart.

In our world today there are so many ways to lose heart, some of them more overbearing than anything before our century. In many ways our times seem to have developed an equation or relative measurement: the more mind, the less heart. In the midst of the most dazzling intellectual achievement of science, we have terrified hearts. Multitudes have already lost heart over the future of our world.

We have varieties of pessimism, dark blacks and deep blues. There is a popular brand that has been called "cosmic pessimism," in part taken up as a fad, a pose of those who accept homage as the intellectual elite. Much of it is tragically sincere, the feeling that man is under a sentence of death, predestined to doom with a universe with evil purpose or with none at all. The difference at times is small. Thomas Hardy was a cosmic pessimist. He lost heart over the whole of the world. In the *Dynasts* he pictured an unconscious deity blindly knitting.

There is also "local pessimism," a feeling about humanity which ranges all the way from Swift's bitter invective on man to a less venomous portrait of man. But still a view of man taken by those who have lost heart. Jonathan Swift wrote that the fault in the world was in man, "the most pernicious race of opious little vermin that nature ever suffered to crawl on the face of the earth."

Not many can join that hymn of hate to the human race. But an uncounted multitude do lose heart. There are so many fears to steal away their confidence and hope. More than fifty years ago,

William James set down a few of the fears, many of them ridiculous but deadly, which rob life of a high heart. He wrote,

There is a long line of particular fears and trouble-bearing expectations, such, for example, as ideas associated with certain articles of food, the dread of the east wind, the terrors of hot weather, the fear of catching cold if one sits in a draught, the coming of hay fever upon the 14th of August. . . . Yet this is not all. This vast array is swelled by innumerable volunteers from daily life—the fear of accident, the possibility of calamity, the loss of property, the chance of robbery, of fire, or the outbreak of war. And it is not deemed sufficient to fear for ourselves. When a friend is taken ill, we must forthwith fear the worst and apprehend death. There is "an ocean of morbidity."

But no pessimisms, cosmic or local, no specific difficulty, ought to cause us to lose heart. For a gift of God in Christ is the gift of heart. It was that gift of heart which enabled Paul to face the appalling difficulty and the appearance of disaster in the church in Corinth. One might easily have said, "Well, if this is what the Christian church amounts to, it will soon come to an end." But he did not lose heart.

How does one "keep heart"? Two preliminary observations may be made.

1. Don't go around piling up disasters so that they form a wailing wall. Centuries ago Jeremy Taylor put this advice picturesquely: "How many people are busy gathering thorns to *sit on*." They multiply the obstacles so that they lose heart before the heart really has a chance to get into the battle.

2. Do not expect to go through the world like a teacher's pet. Some people collapse like a punctured balloon and lose heart entirely when the slightest difficulty in life appears. The world is not arranged for teacher's pets.

There are ways of keeping heart.

1. One is having a *fortified heart*. Paul has this in his mind and heart all the time. It shows through all his letters, as a traveler in mountain country gets long glimpses of high mountains. He asks, "If God be for us, who can be against us?" That fortification sends people to conquer.

If God be for us, our song is a Hallelujah Chorus.

2. All through the centuries of struggle since Christ, men have kept heart by putting their hands to the plow and their backs to the load. To the outward view, the people most likely to lose heart in any warfare against evil would be those in the midst of the

fight. That is not true. It is the people who are immersed in the effort who keep their heart. It is the armchair legion who do nothing but sit and watch who lose heart. It is not the missionaries facing tasks beyond their power who lose heart; it is the indifferent Christians at home. In the hard struggle for human welfare in the slums of New York and Chicago, it was not the front-line fighters, such as Lillian Wald and Jane Addams, who threw in the sponge. It was the people who never touched the task.

3. We keep heart by remembering that our labor is not vain in the Lord. It is the steady continuous stroke that counts.

A picture of action is found in the early records of Chicago, a rather vivid picture:

George M. Pullman began his climb to fortune by securing contracts to raise city buildings from their marshland foundations. One of his first assignments was to raise four feet from the ground an entire block of buildings on Lake Street, which he did by placing 6000 jackscrews under the base and hiring a small army of 600 men who, at each signal, gave the screws one half turn, thus raising the block a fraction of an inch at a time.

A fraction of an inch at a time! Slow work, and pretty hopeless. But "our labor is not vain in the Lord."

16.   TAMPERING

We refuse . . . to tamper with God's word.   2 COR. 4:2
We use no hocus-pocus.   (Phillips)

Tampering with the currency has been a major crime through many centuries. It has frequently been punishable by death. Kings have often done it for their own gain. But no one has ever sent them to the gallows or to jail for it!

In our own time, tampering with medicine has been and is a disastrous crime, severely punished.

Paul, here, is proclaiming himself innocent of another kind of tampering, and a worse crime, tampering "with God's word." Phillips translates his plea of innocence, "We use no hocus-pocus." The gospel has been a saving power. "I am not ashamed of the gospel: it is the power" (Rom. 1:16). But it loses power when it is tampered with. It loses power when it is merely half strength, as pictured in Swinburne's stinging line,

For tender souls, he served up half a Christ.

There are so many ways to tamper with God's word. Not all the "tampering" is done in the pulpit, or classroom, or in books. Whenever, by our speech or by our actions, we give a false impression of the gospel, we tamper with the word.

The worst tampering is to leave out the heart of the message. There can be much decoration of the Christian religion, stressing its entertaining features and deleting any sting from it, that makes very interesting and attractive versions of hocus-pocus. This mangling is pictured in Margaret Webster's comment on Sir Henry Irving:

> His productions at the Lyceum Theater, London, interpreted Irving rather than Shakespeare. Everything was done with lavish care. Nothing was cut except Shakespeare.

So, in the tampered word, all too often nothing is cut except Christ.

One common way of tampering with the word is to create the impression that *"the Christian life is easy."* The invitation is not "Take up your cross and follow me," but "Come on in. It is easy. It won't hurt you at all." Canon Raven in his autobiography, *A Wanderer's Way*, gives an arresting memory of the way in which the word of the gospel was tampered in confirming boys in a boys' school in England. It was explained that being a Christian was something like taking an oath in the days of chivalry. Very simple and, in his memory, very innocuous. Then he writes with deep feeling, "Ah, Christ! How some of us wanted you!" To be a Christian is to enter the joy of the Lord. But it is never easy.

Some tamperers do their work by presenting the gospel *"cleared of Oriental imagery."* It sounds impressive, with an air of superior scholarship, but it can be stated so that it leads to no sharp meaning.

Another very common piece of hocus-pocus and vicious tampering is the distortion of the gospel so that it appears *remote from any dangerous action*. People are told that being a disciple "will not get you into any trouble." And, alas, that often proves true. There is no trouble whatever. Henry D. Thoreau, with an unerring eye, describes the way in which the great words of the gospel which demand action are stripped of all consequence. Here he is in full blast:

> I know of no book that has so few readers. There is none so strange, heretical and unpopular . . . "Seek ye first the kingdom of heaven."

"Lay not for yourselves treasures on earth." "If thou wilt be perfect, go and sell that thou hast, and give to the poor and thou shalt have treasure in heaven." "For what is a man profited, if he shall gain the whole world and lose his own soul?" "Or what shall a man give in exchange for his soul?" Think of this, Yankees. They were never read. They were never heard. Let but one of these sentences be rightly read from any pulpit in the land, and there would not be left one stone of that meeting house upon another.

A popular form of tampering is the announcement that *"sin is an obsolete expression."* It does not often come out this bluntly. But a decreasing emphasis on sin has much the same effect in gentler language. To many who have heard the glad tidings of the retirement of sin, guilt is a bad complex which must be exorcised in the well-adjusted man. That clear word of Jesus, who "came into Galilee saying . . . repent," is shrunk in size and importance.
"I did not tamper."

17. BLINDED MINDS

In their case the god of this world has blinded the minds of the unbelievers. 2 COR. 4:4

A strong picture—blinded minds! Harry Kemp wrote a poem entitled "Blind," which pictures sharply the affliction of physical blindness, and yet makes its case that mental blindness is worse.
Here also Paul affirms that a blinded mind is a worse calamity than blinded eyes. For a mind blinded by the god of this world not only misses the singing green of spring. He suffers a darker blindness. "The light of the gospel of the glory of Christ, who is the likeness of God" (2 Cor. 4:4). For the blinded mind walks in glory and misses it all!
There are many kinds of blindness, some temporary, such as snow blindness and sun blindness. But there are also gold blindness and power blindness, which keep men from seeing the things that are more excellent. There is the lust of the eye which results in blinded eyes. The lust of the eye has a subtle power, the Rue de la Paix, Fifth Avenue, and so-called "miracle miles" in many cities, and the veritable holy of holies, the dress designers and the jewelers. No generation in history has had such terrific temptation to have the mind seduced by the lust of the eye!

There was Paul's friend, Demas. The pageant of Rome was too much for him. "Demas had forsaken me, having loved this present world" (2 Tim. 4:10, AV). He went blind.

Here is the word, in a recent novel, of a man afraid of the blindness of conformity to a rigid pattern for the mind. He cries, "I am a fugitive from the suburbs of all large cities. . . . Preserve me from adulterers . . . from basset hounds, and swimming pools, and frozen canapés, and Bloody Marys, and smugness."

Many have been blinded by gold. The lust for profit has so marked our era and order that one meaning of the wide spread of life today, called loosely "juvenile delinquency," is that our values are catching up to us. The corner store hold-ups are a reflection of a larger mood of an adult generation in a determined seeking for profit.

A common form of blindness was described many years ago by Théophile Gautier, who said, "One can go through one's age without seeing it." That today is one of the world's greatest dangers. Many do not see their age, with its terrifying dangers and great possibilities, because they have no time to think. As Norman Cousins has described this blindness to one's age,

We have more food than we can eat. We have more money per person than anywhere else in the world; with 6 per cent of the population we hold 80 per cent of the wealth. We have bigger homes, bigger television sets, bigger cars, bigger theatres, bigger schools. We have everything we need, in fact, except the most important thing of all—*time to think and the habit of thought.* We lack time for the one thing indispensable for safety of an individual or a nation.

Blindness to the background of human need is a form of blinded mind that affects many. Herblock, the Washington cartoonist, put this in a cartoon that almost literally stabs us. Three people in the foreground are seated at a dinner table that is, literally, a "groaning board." We can almost hear it groan under its burden of roasts and chops and a dozen other things. Sketched in the background are a host of thin, emaciated children, with large, staring eyes. One man is asking a woman, "Shall we say grace?"

A familiar miracle in the gospels, indeed a characteristic miracle, is that of Jesus touching the eyes of people and restoring sight to them. When his spirit touches our spirits, he gives sight to see the invisible and to see people.

18. YOUR SERVANT

Ourselves as your servants for Jesus' sake.   2 COR. 4:5
I am simply a servant of yours.   (Moffatt)

This phrase has covered a wide stretch of territory. It can be, and has been, the expression of the last full measure of devotion of a life in self-giving to others. At the opposite extreme, it has been countless times a traditional rubber-stamp phrase. This was a standard usage for all "polite" correspondence in the eighteenth century, with innumerable letters ending, "Your obedient servant." The result often looks to our later eyes ludicrous in the extreme. A letter to a military commander will read thus: "Surrender at once or I will blow you off the earth. Your obedient servant." And today, the idea of being a servant may, and often is, a conventional expression.

Or the same phrase may indicate genuinely the whole focus of a life, a life committed to the welfare of the whole. It is not sentimental, but fundamental, the solid basis of a life's whole outlook and effort.

History is full of stirring scenes of men and women who had that focus of life on the welfare of all. We see it clearly when the richest man in the American colonies left it all at home and became the commander of an unimpressive rabble of untrained and ill-equipped soldiers, George Washington. But he had said in the depths of his being, "Ourselves your servants." We can almost hear the words, "I am simply a servant of yours," from the laboratory of Louis Pasteur. We can hear the same echo every time we seen an audience lifted to its feet by the opening strains of the "Hallelujah Chorus." Handel was a "servant of yours for Christ's sake." So it was with Ridley and Latimer at the stake.

That phrase gives a whole wider frontage of life, and a deeper content of living. The difference between these words of Paul's and saying, in any form, no matter how well disguised, "My servant," is immeasurable. The difference is partially pictured in two groups of men coming home in the early morning. One group is returning from a hoopla festival. The other is a company of firemen on a fire truck, coming back from the saving of lives. On the second group can be hung the accolade of honor, "Ourselves your servants." For they are part of a saving force. So, when one becomes part of a redeeming force, life reaches its summit. That is the motif of so many of Joseph Conrad's novels, in which the isolated man finds redemption through involvement with and for others.

Henry Thoreau wrote of his experiment to be made at Walden Pond, "It will be a success if I shall have left myself behind." Life is always a success under that condition. It is quite an art, "leaving oneself behind," but life's highest art. But it cannot be achieved by gritting the teeth and crying, "I *will.*" Tremendous motive power is involved. "Ourselves your servants," not by whim or exhibitionism, but by the action of the most powerful motive power in history, "for Jesus' sake."

19. THE GLORY IN A FACE

For it is the God who said, "Let light shine out of darkness," who has shone in our hearts to give the light of the knowledge of the glory of God in the face of Christ. 2 COR. 4:6

This is one of the greatest texts in the Bible. A man could preach on it for a lifetime and never feel confined. It is the doctrine of the incarnation put into a sunburst of poetry. A multitude of people have lived in it for a lifetime. It pictures an illuminated world, and an illuminated heart.

"Glory of God in the face of Christ." That is the wonder of the gospel. Yet, how else could the true and full glory of God be communicated except by a face? "The heavens declare the glory of God; and the firmament sheweth his handiwork" (Ps. 19:1, AV). True. But the glory of the God and Father of our Lord Jesus Christ can be shown only in the word that became flesh and dwelt among us and looked out on all men with the face of Jesus Christ. Edwyn Bevan put this with arresting force: "God looks out on men through the eyes of Jesus Christ." There have been so many fears of the eyes of God looking out on men. Even John Milton's phrase —great Christian that he was—is not altogether comforting: the necessity to live,

As ever in my great Taskmaster's eye.

But God appears as a face; He looks on us, and on the whole human family, through the eyes of Jesus Christ. What eyes they were, lighted with sympathy, forgiveness, and yet demanding eyes.

We meet the glory of God in "that one face." Herbert J. Muller has put the essence of Christianity as it seems to him, and to many:

The Christian God, derived from the pure monotheism of Judaism, represented the divine unity that the greater poets and philosophers of the pagan world had for centuries been aspiring to. At the same time, Jesus was both fully human and fully divine. His gospel of love added warmth to the abstract Greco-Roman ideal of universal community, making it an ideal of true brotherhood. His teaching . . . gave the individual even more dignity and worth than the Greeks had given him.

One of the primary tasks of life is to keep the wonder of the glory of God in the face of Christ. One of the risks of any life is to have that wonder fade into the light of common day. We tend to take the glory for granted. When awe and wonder are allowed to slip out of our lives, the glory is lost in the gray of plodding days. When we take the miracle of life for granted, a withering blight of the soul sets in.

This loss of wonder is beautifully and powerfully expressed in Vachel Lindsay's poem "Niagara." Take this poem with a touch of imagination and apply it to the life of the mind and soul. Forgetting the light of the glory of God in Jesus Christ is missing life's great wonder, no matter what kind of trinkets occupy us.

There is one caution never to be forgotten. The word "poetry" was used a few paragraphs before this. Some say the glory of God is revealed in poetry but not in theology. A noble figure in the life and the pulpit of our time, John Haynes Holmes, has given words to this dangerous confusion. The act of God in Jesus Christ is pushed aside in these words of his:

When I say "God," it is poetry and not theology. Nothing that any theologian ever wrote about God has helped me much, but everything that the poets have written about flowers, and birds, and skies, and seas, and the saviors of the race, and God—whoever he may be—has at one time or another reached my soul! More and more, as I grow older, I live in the lovely thought of these seers and prophets. The theologians gather dust upon the shelves of my library, but the poets are stained with my fingers and blotted with my tears. I never seem so near truth as when I care not what I think or believe, but only with these masters of inner vision would live forever.

If the theologians have "gathered dust," the foundation of our faith is forgotten and what is left looks like a sentimental rhapsody.

The birds, the flowers, and skies are beautiful, but they are not the revelation of the Father of our Lord Jesus Christ.

20. EARTHEN JARS

We have this treasure in earthen vessels. 2 COR. 4:7.
This priceless treasure we hold . . . in a common earthenware jar.
(Phillips)

The English title of one of Harold Begbie's books, *Broken Earthenware,* telling the story of "twice-born men," has an arresting and haunting echo of this metaphor of Paul's. The earthenware of God, in the form of man, was broken and restored.

Humanity, meaning you and me and all the human family, is earthenware. We are earthen jars, so undependable, so easily damaged. Yet this picture gives the balanced view of man in the New Testament. There is no sentimental view of man, no overestimate of his godliness. Paul takes a clear view of man free from delusion. Yet there is no cause for wallowing in despair over man under the guise of realism. He is an earthen jar, but in it he has a priceless treasure.

The gift of God, God with us, is the treasure wrapped in earth. This remembrance will save us from having an inflated soul. "Not to us, O Lord, . . . but to thy name give glory" (Ps. 115:1). "Put on therefore . . . humbleness of mind" (Col. 3:12, AV). One of the constant temptations of the man who strives to do God's will is that of harboring an imaginary godliness. The saint always stands in slippery places.

For ourselves is the saving remembrance that we are of the earth, earthy. Our loftiest utterance is but a "lisping stammering tongue." Our goodness, of ourselves, is not gold or silver. Isaiah had a more accurate term, "All our righteousnesses are as filthy rags" (Isa. 64:6, AV).

But Christian history and experience leave no doubt about the treasure. It is a shining jewel. Just as a high mountain may be reflected in a muddy pool, the treasure of God may be found in a life.

When we wander anywhere in Christian history, we are startled by the sheer wonder of the treasure in earthen jars. Augustine, man of the earth in its earthiest form, passed from wastrel into saint. There is the amazing wonder of John Bunyan, "a tinker out of Bedford," in Kipling's phrase, God's treasure in a very un-promising container. Yet out of that earthen jar, by God's grace, came his interpretation of Christian experience, the brightest light of English literature in his century. There is that very earthen vessel, "the monk that shook the world," Martin Luther.

We are earthen jars. Let us never forget it. But never forget that in earthen jars we may have this treasure.

21. "AFFLICTED, BUT NOT CRUSHED"

We are afflicted in every way, but not crushed; perplexed, but not driven to despair; persecuted, but not forsaken; struck down, but not destroyed. . . . 2 COR. 4:8-9.

In two verses of Paul's second letter to the Corinthians, we have a remarkable study in four pairs of words. The words are sharply defined with a precision like that of a lapidary. They are put into memorable and arresting contrast.

Emerson says that every word must cover a thing. These words do exactly that. They contrast vividly the common experiences of life and the way of victory over calamity. They represent the potentialities of the living of the Christian life. More than that, in these four pairs of contrasts we read Paul's autobiography. They may, by the grace of God, portray the autobiography of the Christian disciple. The words open up a panorama of Christian history over the centuries, and vividly describe many living disciples whom we have known.

Look at the shades of meaning as found in three modern transla-tions of the New Testament (2 Cor. 8-9):

REVISED STANDARD VERSION
> We are afflicted in every way, but not crushed;
> perplexed, but not driven to despair;
> persecuted, but not forsaken;
> struck down, but not destroyed.

J. B. PHILLIPS' TRANSLATION
*We are handicapped on all sides, but we are never frustrated;
we are puzzled, but never in despair.
We are persecuted, but we never have to stand it alone:
we may be knocked down but we are never knocked out!*

JAMES MOFFATT'S TRANSLATION

> *On every side I am harried but not hemmed in,*
> *perplexed, but not despairing,*
> *persecuted but not abandoned,*
> *struck down but not destroyed.*

Just looking steadily at these words, and thinking of the chapters of living they represent, is a quickening exercise of the imagination. The figures begin to move. We see, for instance, people, either in the first century or in the twentieth, people who are "puzzled, but never in despair." *We* are the ones who are perplexed. By God's help, we may never in all our puzzlement be driven to despair. These twelve contrasts show in a variety of ways what Christ does for a person.

Take the first pair as a sample of the fruitful way they can be dropped into the mind, "afflicted, handicapped, harried"; that is a picture of all of us at times, is it not? Yet not "frustrated" or "crushed." People have borne handicaps that seemed like the falling of a ten-ton weight on a fly. Can any of us dimly imagine the afflictions of Helen Keller? Yet she was not "hemmed in," shut out from her human and divine heritage. How many of the greatly afflicted, flat on an invalid's bed, yet neither crushed nor frustrated, have gone into a true kingdom of influence! A shining company of the handicapped brings to mind again and again the words of the Old Testament, "The lame will take the prey" (Isa. 33:23).

Again, we read the "puzzled" and "perplexed." That is what we are, all too often. Men and women have come to the end of their map. How often they and we are like children who had just reached long division, confronted with intricate problems of calculus. Life faces us with many problems of advanced calculus. Yet, as Paul writes of his own life, "We are puzzled, but never in despair." God has a key by which we can meet problems. It was said of Napoleon that he had an unquestioned magic for victory, but he had not technique for defeat. The victor of Austerlitz turns into the despairing horseman of the retreat from Moscow. But in Christian faith there is a technique for defeat, for affliction, for handicap. It is in "the transcendent power of God."

And what new glorious chapters have been enacted under the phrase, "persecuted but not abandoned" in our own time! The heroism of Norwegians, clergy and laymen, of some Germans, Christians and Jews, has left a new glory to the race. And in common life, the persecution and being struck down have given a present-day portrayal of one of the greatest pictures of a redeeming faith:

> *Though the fig tree do not blossom,*
> *nor fruit be on the vines,*
> *the produce of the olive fail*
> *and the fields yield no food,*
> *the flock be cut off from the fold*
> *and there be no herds in the stalls,*
> *yet I will rejoice in the Lord,*
> *I will joy in the God of my salvation.*
>   [Hab. 3:17-18]

These words sum up the possibilites of life in trust: "We may be knocked down but never knocked out."

But these pairs are not a study in words primarily; they are a study in life. If one is never "knocked out," a secondhand or casual faith will not be enough. The need of every life to be victorious in God's power is vividly presented by L. P. Jacks:

I began to see that all this hearsay, second hand stuff about God and Christ, in which I was so prolific, was not religion, but at the best only a reminiscence or ghost of religion; that it would soon exhaust itself and give out—in short that though it might *go* it wouldn't *do*.

22. THE GLORIOUS WORD—"BUT!"

Struck down, but not destroyed. 2 COR. 4:9

It would sound like a strange thing to say that the conjunction "but" is one of the most glorious words in the New Testament. But look at the manner in which the word is used four times in the eighth and ninth verses of this chapter. Each time the word says, in effect, "We may be at the very end of our rope, *but* God." This passage proclaims that God has the last word.

There is an expressive line of Strickland Gilland's verse which really says something pertinent about the Holy Spirit:

> *I think God kept on talking when*
> *His book had gone to press.*

The style is colloquial, but the truth is profound. So, God keeps on talking after the world has said its worst, after it has passed

all its sentences and ordered its executions. Drop into your imagination the supreme example of God's use of the conjunction "but."
In the crucifixion of Jesus, Pilate and Caiaphas, Herod and Judas,
had done their worst. It was all over. Pilate had said, "Make is as
sure as you can." The soldiers made it sure. They rolled up an
immovable" stone against the grave, "*but* on the first day of the
week, at early dawn." It was all over, except that God had another
chapter to add! Surely as that word appears in the resurrection
story (Luke 24:1) it is a glorious word!

There is the divine continuation in every perplexity. We are
cast down. Some even plunge into the despair of H. G. Wells in
his last days. He wrote,

Mankind is not the privileged favorite of Mother Nature and in spite
of all my life long optimism, it now seems to me that the whole universe
is utterly bored by the whole species of mankind. I can see the human
race sweeping along the stream of fate to defeat, degradation and final
extinction.

That really is touching bottom. But then, of course, Mr. Wells
had only a sentimental optimism, not any Christian faith, to renounce as he plunged into despair. Yet, his black mood points to
a widely felt feeling of being cast down, a more familiar mood of
a large host of people in dark days. The mood is caught in the
story of a man about to jump off the Brooklyn Bridge, when he
was held back by a policeman. The man showed the daily newspaper he had been reading. And then they both jumped!

A true test of a man's character and religion is found in his use
of the conjunction "but." All too frequently it is used as a reason
for quitting an endeavor, rather than for taking new courage and
going on. So many times the word is used in this fashion: "Of
course I would like to help in this work, *but* I really do not have
any time." Or, "Of course I am all in favor of the visiting nurse
work. It is wonderful. *But* I simply can't do anything this year.
I have so many calls." (Whether any of these calls have been
answered or not is not stated.)

So, on many lives, the word "but" lies like a devastating blight.
In every moral battle it is a ready way of throwing in the sponge.

But it can be the opening door to a new chapter of life. It
signifies that the battle is not over. The word "but" may be God's
word. Learn to say it in the darkest day, "*But* God."

23. DEATH EVERY DAY

*Every day we experience something of the death of the Lord Jesus,
so that we may also know the power of the life of Jesus in these bodies
of ours.* 2 COR. 4:11 (Phillips)

Of course, as they appear in Paul's second epistle to the Corinthians, these words actually meant the possibility of being put to
death for Jesus' sake. Paul came very close to it several times. The
early Christians did not live in a world of metaphor and imagery.
They lived in a real battle.

> They climbed the steep ascent of heaven
> With peril, toil and pain.

But the words have a close and definite universal application to
all disciples who do not live in an age of martyrdom. It means
that our lives as disciples of Christ must have something of the
self-sacrifice that marked the life and death of Jesus.

Death is a strong word, far too strong to be used lightly. What
many people, many Christians, never experience is anything resembling the death of Christ, that is, the spirit of love and sacrifice that led Jesus to the cross. If we have no great sacrificial
quality in our lives, there is no power in the life of Jesus for us.
It is the great Christian paradox: if there is no death, there is no
life. Karl Barth wrote a gleaming sentence which is an expression
of this truth: "A church which has no great anguish on its heart
will have no great music on its lips." But instead of any disturbing anguish of costly love, quite a host remind one of Ambrose
Bierce's definition of a Christian as "one who follows the teachings
of Christ insofar as they are not inconsistent with a life of sin."
Dean Swift, with all his bitterness and cynicism, did see the power
of "death every day." He wrote, "Nothing can render the clergy
popular, but some degree of persecution."

Paul wrote, "We are always facing death, but this means that
you know more and more of life" (2 Cor. 4:12, Phillips). For
with the presence of a sacrificial quality of love, there is the life-
giving quality of love. But this cannot be done by a life on a
spiritual chaise longue. Too often we take our Christian adventure
in an armchair. We do our roughing it de luxe. Philip Hone, the
mayor of New York, left in his voluminous diary a picture of how

he enjoyed his Western adventures in an early part of the century. He wrote of himself,

I have passed a few hours delightfully in reading Washington Irving's "Tour of the Prairies." It is of the very best kind of light reading, killing buffalos, hunting wild horses, sleeping every night on the ground for a whole month, and depending from day to day for the means of existence, upon the deer, wild turkey, and bears which the rifles of their own party can alone procure, matters of thrilling interest to citizens who read of them in their green slippers seated before a shining grate, the neatly printed page illuminated by a bronze astral lamp.

"Green slippers . . . before a shining grate"—that is not in the religious life "death every day."

24. RENEWAL DAY BY DAY

Though our outer nature is wasting away, our inner nature is being renewed every day. 2 COR. 4:16.
The outward man does indeed suffer wear and tear, but every day the inward man receives fresh strength. (Phillips)

Poets agree that the greatest thing in the world is renewal— springtime. For different reasons, the noble company of farmers, among others, cannot truly express the astounding wonder of the earth's renewal. Many have tried it. Many have sung it, from Chaucer with his joy that breaks through any spelling,

> When that Aprille with his shoures sweet
> The droughte of Marche hath perced to the rote
> And small fowles maken melodye;

to our own time, such as in Masefield,

> I have seen the lady April bringing the daffodils
> Bringing the spring in grass and the soft warm April rain.

The wonder of renewal in nature is partly the wonder of chlorophyll, that miraculous sun trap whose chemistry still eludes us.

There is the greater wonder of inner renewal which Paul mentions here, "renewed every day." For the spirit of man is also a "sun trap," receiving the renewal of God who is a sun and a shield. We read in Isaiah that "we all do fade as a leaf" (4:6, AV).

Not only eventually, but every day there is a fading of color and life unless there is renewal. To change the figure, some historian called the years following the Civil War "the age of rusty souls." Rust of spirit is a danger. We can attain it at eighteen as well as at seventy-eight.

How people try, sometimes madly, to keep the outward man, and perhaps even more the outward woman, from "wasting away," from showing "wear and tear"! How many millions on millions are spent on the elusive quest of the appearance, at least, of eternal youth. The preservation of what is regarded by many as beauty has become one of the country's biggest businesses. The advertising man and the television announcer are the great high priests of the cult and their solemn directions have almost a divine sanction.

But, with all this frantic battle with the inevitable years, how little, comparatively, is done for the renewing of the inner nature. It is that inner spirit by which man is truly measured. Salomon De La Silva puts this vividly in a little poem entitled "Measure." She asks herself whether the water in a pool should be best measured by the earth that holds it, or by the heaven it holds. She asks the same question of a life. Man is measured by the heaven he holds, not by the earth.

There are so many ways leading to the day-by-day renewal of the inner man. The pattern is set for all time and all people: "And in the morning, a great while before day, he rose and went out to a lonely place, and there he prayed" (Mark 1:35). And, in Romans: "Be transformed by the renewal of your mind" (12:2).

One important initial step is withdrawal in spirit from the frenzied race of life so that the soul gets a chance.

In this space age, inward space must and can be found for renewed communion, renewed dedication, and renewed activity of body and mind in service.

One guard against the decay of the inner life is to see to it that our professions do not get "bedridden in the dormitory of our minds," to use Coleridge's phrase. For, he continued, such "bedridden ideas do not bring a state of going somewhere wholeheartedly."

Jesus enjoins the double life; the outward life meets wear and tear, while the inward man receives fresh strength.

25. DECISIVE BATTLE OF THE WORLD

For this slight momentary affliction is preparing for us an eternal weight
of glory beyond all comparison. 2 COR. 4:17
The slight trouble of the passing hour results in a solid glory past all
comparison. (Moffatt)

Sir Edward Creasy wrote more than a hundred years ago what became a well-thumbed volume, *Fifteen Decisive Battles of the*
World. If the list were brought up to date many would be added,
certainly Gettysburg and Stalingrad, and that decisive struggle in
the air called "The Battle of Britain."

But, beyond any recorded battles in history, is this battle referred to here by Paul, the battle of today against tomorrow. It is
the struggle men make from the dawn of time till today, to decide
between the affliction of today against the solid glory of tomorrow.
And hosts of men have soon settled that battle summarily. They
have decided to "take the cash and let the credit go." We see it in
Esau's choice: the solid substance of a savory stew, stopping the
affliction of hunger, instead of the intangible gains of a birthright.
He couldn't eat that! The same battle went on in the man who
has come to be known as "the rich young ruler." He chose the
real estate and herds over the distant tomorrow of being one of
Jesus' disciples.

Here Paul comes down on the side of tomorrow against today.
In that he makes a plea for enlisting on the side of the eternal
weight of glory over the prize to be grasped today.

Paul puts on one side what he calls "the slight trouble of the
passing hour." That looks like an understatement! For here are a
few details of "the slight trouble" as he records them later in this
same letter (2 Cor. 11:26): "in danger from rivers, danger from
robbers, danger from my own people, danger from Gentiles, danger
in the city"—a world of danger. Yet here it is—"slight trouble."
And it was not a pose with Paul. *All* trouble was slight against the
gain of an eternal might of glory. But many settle on the spot for
today. We can still smell the savor of Esau's stew, thousands of
years later!

On a lower level, as well as on the higher spiritual, tomorrow
goes beyond today, "beyond all comparison." Socrates, by a shameful compromise, could have decided for today's comfort and avoided

the "slight trouble" with a cup of hemlock. But he chose the greater glory of an imperishable tomorrow. For today is only fulfilled by tomorrow. John Milton had the by no means slight affliction of having his *Paradise Lost* "lie on the hands of a London bookseller as waste paper." But even that was "a slight trouble" bearing no comparison to the greater weight of glory.

On the highest level, that of which Paul was writing, there was no comparison between the affliction of today and the glory which comes from it in the great tomorrow.

In Paul's own generation a glorious company of martyrs chose the greater weight of glory that came from faithfulness under frightful affliction. They could say, in the Roman arena, "Above this circus shine the stars." Balance any "slight trouble" against the glory of God's tomorrow.

26.   THE SEEN AND THE UNSEEN

For the things that are seen are transient, but the things that are unseen are eternal. 2 COR. 4:18
It is the invisible things that are really permanent. (Phillips)

Most of our whole world is a picture of this truth in one way or another. In the ancient world of the Mediterranean, in which Paul moved, the seen was transient. From the pyramids to the Parthenon, the greatness that was seen has passed into ruins. But the unseen, the ideas of the Greeks, the alphabet of the Phoenicians, the monotheism of the Hebrews—these are permanent.

Consider the most impressive ruin of that world, the Coliseum. Byron wrote,

> While stands the Coliseum, Rome shall stand;
> When falls the Coliseum, Rome shall fall;

The Coliseum fell; Rome fell. The seen is transient. But only a short distance from the massive Coliseum were some of the catacombs, where the religion of Christ went underground. There dwelt the unseen faith. On the walls of one of the catacombs could still be traced nineteen hundred years later the sentence, "His kingdom is an everlasting kingdom." The unseen is eternal.

In the ruins of that world, the very stones cry out this affirmation that "it is the invisible things that are really permanent." Solomon's temple has disappeared. Nothing left but a wailing wall.

But the 23rd Psalm, the 40th chapter of Isaiah, the unseen wonders of the spirit to which they attest—these are eternal. It is much the same in the field of art. The world will little note nor long remember Jones' very realistic painting of the architectural wonder, "The Empire State Building." But it will long remember—centuries long—the representations of the unseen world of the spirit. "The Madonna of the Chair" and "The Angelus." The production of a musical composition echoing with remarkable fidelity the sound of a railroad train is transient. The Ninth Symphony is eternal.

Today there is great danger that we get our timing all wrong. We may count the material the important thing in life. We may lose our sense of the eternal. Thomas Carlyle pictured it about a hundred years ago. His warning is even more pertinent today.

If we look deeper, we shall find that this faith in Mechanism has now struck its roots down into man's most intimate, primary sources of conviction; and is thence sending up, over his whole life and activity, innumerable stems—fruit-bearing and poison-bearing. The truth is men have lost their belief in the Invisible, and believe, and hope, and work only in the Visible. . . . The infinite, absolute character of virtue has passed into a finite, conditional one; it is no longer a worship of the Beautiful and Good; but a calculation of the Profitable.

The reality of the unseen is a sustaining conviction of a life that is aware of its total environment. This conviction is put forcefully in the concluding words of William James' *The Varieties of Religious Experience*, that "the visible world is part of a more spiritual universe from which it draws its chief significance; that union or harmonious relation to that more spiritual universe is one true end; that communion with spirit is a process wherein work is really done and energy flows in and produces effects within the phenomenal world."

This spiritual world is no invention of priestcraft. G. K. Chesterton gave the effective answer to that venerable charge when he wrote that "saying that religion was invented by priestcraft for their own gain is just as sensible as to say that sex was invented by jewelers to promote the sale of wedding rings. In both cases the effect is taken as a cause." The unseen is eternal.

27. TENTING TONIGHT

For we know that if the earthly tent we live in is destroyed, we have a building from God, a house not made with hands, eternal in the heavens. 2 COR. 5:1

> *We're tenting tonight*
> *On the old camp ground.*

That bit of an old Civil War song seems like a crude remembrance to associate in any way with Paul's sublime declaration of the Christian faith.

Yet it is true to some of its meaning. We *are* in a *war,* "for we are not contending against flesh and blood, but against the principalities, against the powers, against the world rulers of this present darkness" (Eph. 6:12). And we *are* in a tent, a temporary habitation. We look forward to moving day, to a permanent home, to a house not made with hands. Moffatt's rendering strongly suggests moving day: "if this earthly tent of mine is taken down, I get a home from God." There is an old gospel song, not part of the twaddle which sounded out with such clamor, but true:

> *I'm but a stranger here*
> *Heaven is my home.*

Often it even seems a flapping tent. But do not despise the tent. That has frequently been done, with dire results. Francis Thompson, the poet, at one time in his life despised the earthly tent. He called it "vile corruption." His life was crippled and shortened by his thoughtless abuse of the tent. Our earthly tent is a gift of God to be held in honor. It is a temple of God.

But it is a tent compared to the house prepared for us. When we think of these words, tent and eternal habitation, we are amazed at the amount of decoration that some people put on the tent. They spend a lifetime amassing decorations and hangings for the earthly tent—it becomes their whole concern—but never a thought to the permanent house not made by hands but by God.

What an idiot's folly, a curious show place for the crowd, it would be if a man had fitted out a little tent on the back part of his estate and hung it with priceless hangings and put million-dollar paintings on the sides, and left a great home empty except for dust and echoes. Yet exactly that is a common sight. The point of it all is in Phillips' translation, "We want our transitory life to be absorbed in the life that is eternal" (2 Cor. 5:4).

We look over death. Elizabeth Barrett Browning tells how, at the death of little Joe Story, the playmate of her boy, Pen, she was so much overcome that she almost fell off the seat of the carriage. She sat beside the bereaved mother and she wrote her, "I can't look on the earthward side of death. I flinch from corpses and graves. When I look deathwards, I look over death upwards." Over death —upwards! Tent and house!

The tent is God's gift. Cherish it. But don't forget Moving Day.

28. ALWAYS OF GOOD COURAGE

So we are always of good courage. 2 COR. 5:6
This makes us confident, whatever happens. (Phillips)
Come what may. (Moffatt)

These words look back to "We do not lose heart" (2 Cor. 4:1, and repeated in 4:16). Paul faced, from the beginning of his ministry to its end on the headsman's block, situations well-designated to make him lose heart. But he declares he was always of good courage.

We all remember the man in Goldsmith's play whose courage was always oozing out of his fingertips. Courage oozes out of fingertips readily. The words of Paul, "whatever happens," cover a lot of territory!

There is a fine word, used in Elizabethan and Puritan times, which, unfortunately, has become obsolete. We find it both in the speeches of Queen Elizabeth and in the writing of William Bradford of the Plymouth Colony of Massachusetts. Both had "answerable" courage, courage to answer fittingly a desperate situation. God grant that while the word is obsolete, the thing itself may still be known to us.

Today we could with truth make up a formidable list of dangers which face those trying to live a Christian life. Different dangers from Paul's, but not negligible. There are dangers from the routine turmoil of life with its attrition of spirit; dangers from the hazards to health; dangers from financial loss. We need courage for efforts for the welfare of the community and courage to work for the Kingdom of God against gigantic difficulties. We need courage to speak the clear word in days when taking cover of conformity seems the safest course. Louis Kronenberger writes truly that "many people today do not want honest answers insofar as honest means unpleasant or disturbing. They want a soft answer that turneth away anxiety. They want the blinds pulled down rather than up on reality." We need a special and demanding courage to plead for those who are not there in the presence of those who are present. That appears in pleas for civil rights for Negroes and for the exploited. The easy conscience to surrender to conformity, to majority opinion of those in front of us, makes life far less troublesome. But Jesus plainly said, "In the world you have tribulation" (John 16:33).

So many people choose the easy way of going through life like a crab, backing away from great issues, duties, and opportunities. The direct frontal head-on approach to any of the major engagements of life is skillfully avoided. They never forget themselves into any sudden madness. Scientists tell us that there are thousands of kinds of invertebrates. We have all met a good many of them in the course of a year's travels. Those who do have a backbone and are not invertebrates deserve the high accolade, "Civilian, first class" and "Christian, first class."

In summoning adequate courage there are two evil women to avoid, Pollyanna and Cassandra. They are very opposite characters, but each is *femme fatale*. Pollyanna chirps that everything is for the best, and Cassandra repeats that everything is going to the dogs. Both sap courage.

But when we hear an affirmation of courage in these verses, look who's talking! One who has a right to speak on courage. For in a few words he has pushed away the disasters he has faced and never flinched or given up. Look with imagination at the passage referred to above, 2 Corinthians 11:23-28: "far greater labors, far more imprisonments, with countless beatings, and often near death." And so on, through forty lashes, beaten with rods, stoned, shipwrecked, the seven dangers recounted, hunger, thirst, etc. Yet, incredibly, he writes, "I have learned the secret of facing plenty and hunger, abundance and want. I can do all things in him who strengthens me" (Phil. 4:12-13).

He had learned the secret of courage. He did not stand alone. As in the beginning, so always. Courage is ready whatever comes "in him who strengthens me."

29. THE LONG WALK UP THE MOUNTAIN

For we walk by faith, not by sight.   2 COR. 5:7
We have to live by trusting him without seeing him. (Phillips)

These words, "we walk by faith," come between two affirmations of courage, "good courage," in the preceding and succeeding verses. Faith is the source of courage for living, and also an effect of it.

The great ventures of life are by faith and not by sight. That is true from the launching of the first boat, back in the dark abyss of time, down to the first memorable flight of the airplane from the sand dunes of Kitty Hawk. The Christian fellowship walked into the Roman Empire; some walked into the arena in Rome to meet the lions by faith, not by sight. Sight could see nothing but lions. Columbus led his three little ships out from the port of Spain by faith. The historic tree in Cambridge, Massachusetts, where George Washington took command of the loose rabble of patriots, marked an act of faith, not of sight.

The reality of the spiritual world which interpenetrates this one has, of course, been denied. The village atheist is a type no longer popular or very often found. But denials of the validity of faith in God go on. Emerson was away off base when he wrote in his essay on "Self-Reliance" that "as men's prayers are a disease of the will, so their creeds are a disease of the intellect." So that is it! The creed, "I believe . . . in Jesus Christ," is a disease of the intellect! At least it has proved a contagious disease!

An affirmation of faith in a moral and spiritual order, and its relation to our threatened world today, is that of Barbara Ward, an editor of the *London Economist*. She writes,

The first foundation of Western freedom is one that has been the support of every great civilization until our day—the belief that underlying the ebb and flow of historical events and human happenings there exists a moral order of right and wrong, of good and evil which transcends every particular interest and which, far from being created by men and events, is the yardstick by which they are judged. . . . The fundamental affirmations of Western society are all matters of faith and it is an historical fact that the faith in which they were grounded and from which they derived their deepest strength, has been the Christian faith.

30. OYEZ! OYEZ!

We must all appear before the judgment seat of Christ.   2 COR. 5:10
Appear without disguise. (Moffatt)
Stand without pretense. (Phillips)

At Judgment Day we must appear. But that, of course, means today. For every day is Judgment Day. How much of the world's
great history and literature is concerned with trial scenes; the trials
of Socrates, of Charles I, of Martin Luther, of Cranmer, have
gripped readers with a strong hold. The world's greatest trial scene,
however, is that depicted dramatically in the 25th chapter of Matthew: "When the Son of man comes in his glory, and all the
angels with him, then he will sit on his glorious throne. Before
him will be gathered all the nations" (Matt. 25:31-32).

But we are judged by attitudes and actions every day. We cannot put off our trial till some distant future. Every day comes the
"Oyez! Oyez! The trial of John Doe is now open! That is one clear
call for me.

Those words of Paul, "without disguise" and "without pretense,"
take away from us the last masquerade. For we all have some pretense. The son of James II of England had an arresting title, "The
Old Pretender." Aren't we all? Not all our pretenses are evil, but
we have grown so used to them, and love them so, that we feel
naked without them. But we shall all appear "without pretense"
before the judgment seat of Christ. And we do appear there every
day.

The trial will not be for crimes that we can readily deny, such
as robbery, murder, and lechery. The trial will be also on unchrist-
like moods, attitudes, and actions, the sins of the disposition, mind,
and heart. The charges of complacency, indifference, laziness, and
irresponsibility will not be easy to refute. We have all come short
of the glory of God as revealed in the mind of Christ. The trial will
not call for defense, but for repentance.

A church is on trial every day before the judgment seat of Christ.
Here is a church leader of other days, under judgment, though he
was too stricken dumb with self-satisfaction to know it. It is a
description of William Warburton, an English bishop of Glou-
cester in the eighteenth century.

He was a frank optimist thoroughly contented with conditions in
church and society. His watchwords were reasonableness and moderation.

The Church of England, he believed, was in a perfectly healthy state as long as she purged herself of foolish aberrations, extremes and enthusiasm. He zealously did battle against the non-jurors, but also against the mystics and Methodists.

A satisfied man or a satisfied church stands under the judgment of Christ the great unsatisfied, to whom a possible ninety-nine sheep saved out of one hundred was not good enough.

A whole generation may be before the judgment seat of Christ. We may merit the description, "this evil generation." What are particular sins of our generation which we cannot fully blame on the preceding generation? Our failure to take the possibility of atomic calamity seriously enough, our failure in long division in dealing with the products of the earth, our forsaking the altar and law of God for the Golden Calf, are some items in the indictment we must face. They are charges against our time, and by so much against us. And may God have mercy on our souls!

31. THE CONTROL ROOM

For the love of Christ controls us. 2 COR. 5:14

The crucial feature of our modern world, with its myriad of mysterious powers, is the control room. We see it in the quiet of a great power plant which controls the light, heat, and power of an immense city. We see it with amazement in the train dispatcher's office where levers and buttons control scores of trains and hundreds of lives.

In a life, too, the crucial spot is the control room. When a life gets out of control, it runs amuck, like an automobile with a drunken driver crashing over an embankment. Power failure in the control room will make a chaos of even the finest set of endowments. As Lord Byron wrote of a man,

> *This should have been a noble creature*
> *With all the energy that should have made*
> *A godly frame of glorious elements,*
> *. . . as it is,*
> *It is an awful choas.*

Something wrong in the control room!

We all remember Tennyson's trilogy, from *In Memoriam:*

> *Self-knowledge, self-reverence, self-control,*
> *These three alone lead life to sovereign power.*

But it is important to remember that more than *self* is needed. For often self cannot handle the levers of the control room. There is a panic in a power plant, or below the control tower of an airport, when the fear spreads, "Something wrong in the control room!"

Control is a supreme necessity of life. Bertrand Russell puts this vividly, writing of Conrad:

> Conrad's point of view is the antithesis of Rousseau's, "Man is born in chains, but he can become free." He becomes free not by letting loose his impulses, not by being casual and uncontrolled, but by subduing wayward impulses to a dominant purpose.

True. But a will all alone needs reinforcement, needs enhanced power. For Paul has told the story of the will alone, even a determined will—"I can will what is right, but I cannot do it" (Rom. 7:18).

In a daze at the daily wonders of the world we easily forget that any endurable future lies not on the launching platform at Cape Canaveral or somewhere in Siberia, but in the control room of the mind of man.

The trouble with man is not in his gigantic arms, nor his ears that can hear the ticking of a tiny satellite on the dark side of the moon, nor his eyes that can see through the far galaxies, but in his mind and heart, in the control room.

Man needs to be centered, to bring every thought into captivity to one master. A woman who quite inaccurately heard William James lecture on pragmatism, went away from the auditorium piously caressing one word: "Ah fragmentism, what a lovely word!" A lovely sound, perhaps, but a word meaning a life split and all out of focus.

The most effective picture of the powerful control room of a life, with the controls in God's hands, is found in the story of the temptation of Jesus. Jesus could say to Satan, "Get out," because he could say to himself, "You must." Life had been brought into the control of a great compulsion, the will of God. That brings the turn of the tide in life's battle: devils leave and the sustaining and re-creating forces come in.

As Phillips translates the verse, "The very spring of our actions is the love of Christ." That is, controlled power.

32. A NEW PERSON

If any one is in Christ, he is a new creation. 2 COR. 5:17
He becomes a new person altogether. (Phillips)

This whole passage is one of the greatest declarations of the New Testament. Its central core is the power of God brought into the center of a life with a transforming effect. It is more than good precepts; more than good advice or earnest exhortation. Something *happens*. When Christ takes over the inner man, it is a news event. As Floyd V. Filson observes, "Paul's emphasis is not on who Christ is but on what he does."

To say that a man in Christ "becomes a new person altogether" means that there has been a change more like a chemical change than a physical one. That inner change is the only change adequate to the making of a changed man, a changed society, or a changed world. Will Durant writes vividly of this inner change as he saw it in Savonarola's ultimate failure:

The grandeur of Savonarola lay in his effort to achieve a moral revolution, to make men honest, good, and just. We know this is the most difficult of all revolutions and we cannot wonder that Savonarola failed where Christ succeeded with so pitiful a minority of men. But we know, too, that such a revolution is the only one that would mark a real advance in human affairs, and that beside it the bloody overturns of history are transient and ineffectual affairs, changing anything but man.

Exhortations fail without an inner transformation taking place in man. The whole message of H. G. Wells is a striking example. He writes that man has become a new animal who can jump a hundred miles, see through brick walls, bombard the atom, and analyze the stars. Yet he goes on acting like the quarrelsome little ape he used to be. But all that Mr. Wells can think of is to shout at man, "Stop being an ape!" A good idea! But shouting does not seem to do the trick. Paul has something better—"If any one is in Christ, he is a new creation." From another century comes the same picture of the failure of man's self-sufficiency. Here is Shellabarger writing of the seventeenth and eighteenth centuries:

Codes are not enough, reason fails, ethics are inadequate to preserve society from the corruption which attends the various forms of self-sufficiency. At this period, from the middle of the 17th to the middle of the 18th century, humanity was more deeply sunk in its mire than usual.

Man has shown in history that he has a capacity to be not only an outer-directed person or an inner-directed person, but a God-directed person. Albert Camus makes an interesting suggestion which carries far more meaning than he seems to realize. He writes, "Man is the only creature who refuses to be what he is." Interesting clue, Watson! Perhaps he is more than he appears to be. He has the potential of new creaturehood.

The phrase "in Christ" goes deep into life. It seems that one's inner being is possessed by Christ. He is the air the person breathes. The injunction "Put ye on the Lord Jesus Christ" means put him on from the inside, not from the outside. It is not a new complexion put on from a bottle, but the health of the whole being.

This is not something done "once for all." Nothing that we do in Christian discipleship can be done "once for all." Each genuine renewal of communion with God and dedication to Him makes us in a very real way new creatures. Sir William Osler, the great and beloved physician, was not indulging in fairy tale when he wrote, "At night, as I lay aside my clothes, I undress my soul, too, and lay aside my sin. In the presence of God, I lie down to rest and to waken a free man with a new life."

33.   THE GOSPEL IN ONE SENTENCE

God was in Christ reconciling the world to himself.   2 COR. 5:19.

Here is the Christian theology not for the theologian, except as he belongs to the family of man, but for every man. For we read of "the faith which was once for all delivered to the saints" (Jude 3). Note, the faith was not delivered to the theologians, but to the saints, to the company of Christ's men and women. No further delivery was needed.

Paul's words do not answer all the intricate questions of Christology. But they do put the imperishable gospel in a form so that he who runs from sin may read it. The affirmation declares that the things which Christ taught and for which he lived and gave his life are the very center of the universe.

This sentence cannot be used as a theological shibboleth, as so many great texts unfortunately have. It cannot be used as a fence.

It is too big and inclusive. We frequently see used in legal documents the phrase "act of God." Strangely enough, that tremendous phrase usually denotes some kind of calamity, such as hurricane, flood, or earthquake. Lift it up to its large meaning. It can mean *the act of God* in Christ, reconciling the world to himself, an act for man's redemption.

This affirmation, "God was in Christ," redeems our faith from any tendency to pantheism, a fate that in one degree or another has often taken hold of it. Nature and God are confused, or at least blended into a sort of misty cloud. About this Randall Stewart has written pungently,

In much romantic poetry nature worship and God worship seem a bit confused, one with the other. The basic theological error has been confusion of the creator with the thing created. The romantic poet is forever running the risk of mistaking God for a tree.

In Paul there was no risk of "mistaking God for a tree." God was in Christ. It is a mystery, but we are stewards, trustees, of that mystery of God. To us has been committed a ministry of reconciliation. But all too often Christians have not been forces for reconciliation between men. They have been sometimes too preoccupied with a "ministry" of denunciation or of segregation.

Where that ministry of reconciliation has been accepted, where God in Christ has reconciled us, a glory lights our whole life. A man in Colorado spoke of his love for his town, saying there were "blue mountains at the end of every street." In different language, but expressive of the same joy, was the remark of a man on the upper West Side of New York. He said that "at every sunset, there is a bonfire at the end of every street."

To the one who has found God in Christ, no matter how drab his surroundings may look to the casual view, there are blue mountains and bonfires at the end of every street.

There is an unintended but revealing picture of the way in which this high faith redeems life in some of the old Grimm fairy stories. In several stories a curse is lifted from a life when the right word is spoken. It is so in "The Sleeping Beauty" and in "Rumpelstiltskin."

There is more than a fairy tale in Christian faith. A curse is lifted when the right word, "God was in Christ," is spoken commandingly.

34. AMBASSADORS

So we are ambassadors for Christ, God making his appeal through us.
2 COR. 5:20.

Certainly there are two meanings to the word "we" in Paul's statement. First, it was Paul's role ever since his conversion. He wrote to
the Corinthian church, in this letter, "For what we preach is not
ourselves, but Jesus Christ as Lord" (2 Cor. 4:5). Always he was an
ambassador for Christ, even when he was "an ambassador in bonds"
(Eph. 6:20, AV), or when, on trial for his life before Agrippa, he was
an ambassador of Christ to his judge.

Also, the "we" is inclusive. Every disciple is called to be an ambassador. Each of us is faced with the question, Do we represent
anything or anyone beyond ourselves?

Being an ambassador is a high role. It has been pointed out by
many that there are really three roles which we can adopt in life.
The first is *strangers*. We all begin that way. We come into the
world as strangers.

> *I, a stranger and afraid*
> *In a world I never made.*

The words of Chronicles repeat the feeling: "We are strangers before thee, and sojourners, as all our fathers were" (1 Chron. 29:15).

Then there is a higher role—*pilgrims*. A pilgrim goes on a personal quest, seeking some spiritual good for himself. He is not a
stranger to faith in God or to God's mercy. He makes a pilgrimage
for himself.

The role of *ambassador* is a higher one. When we accept that
commission, we do not wander about the world as strangers, nor
casually loiter as tourists. We do not seek primarily our own security or advantage. We are representatives of another country, a Kingdom of God, and another Ruler, God. An ambassador is concerned
with more than himself. He represents the Ruler of another country, a heavenly country, to the world of men. He carries the message,
"Be reconciled to God" (2 Cor. 5:20). The whole impact of an
ambassador's life reveals the outreaching, forgiving love of God be-
seeching men. Also, a faithful ambassador must remember that his
message is not to be lost in a general urge to good conduct, but is
specific good news. There is no gospel in just urging "Try hard,"

even at the top of one's voice. His message is the good news of God's gift in Christ, of a forgiving and empowering God.

We are poor ambassadors when we do not really know the ruler we serve, or know his message of reconciliation. He who has never known in his own life reconciliation with God is a bungling, incompetent ambassador.

One of the commonest ways in which people fail as ambassadors is that they just become observers. God's cause is never carried to victory by lookers-on. There is an arresting suggestion in the title of John Van Druten's play *I Am a Camera*. It is a play about the anguish of Germany before and during World War II. Many of the scenes reported are heart-rending. But the author does not attempt to do anything about it. He is just a camera, taking pictures. That is often what is the matter; we become just a *camera*, observing, when we should be representatives. To be truly ambassadors, we must be participants, as God was a participant in Christ.

We may fail miserably as ambassadors by failing to identify ourselves with human need, by failing to plead the cause for men and women who are defeated and suffering. An ambassador of the love of God is an emissary to and for the least and the lost. John Masefield puts this beautifully and powerfully in his poem "Consecration," in which he chooses as his part as a poet to represent human need. His words might well be read at services of ordination to the Christian ministry.

To be an effective ambassador does not mean that we learn formulas by rote. Surely about that we can think of the Master saying something like "I had as lief the town crier spoke my lines." The effect is often the same. The King's message must come through the ambassador's whole personality, his mind, his heart, his God-given gift of himself. The role of representative is much like that of an interpreter of Shakespeare, as portrayed by Margaret Webster:

There is no one right "Hamlet" with all the others wrong. Shakespeare allows his actors a greater margin of interpretation than can possibly be pinioned by a single mind. He wrote to be interpreted, not to lay down a system of mathematics. The actor must use his own physical powers, his own mind, and his own personal quality, that essential flavor of the spirit which will insensibly pervade his performance despite miracles of make-up.

Also we fail as ambassadors when we do not really know the people to whom we are sent. We may know the formulas, but we must know the people, suffering and sinning, gay or gloomy, endearing or repulsive, all our brothers in Christ. Think of the people whom Jesus knew. He heard blind Bartimaeus when no one else heard him. He saw Zacchaeus when no one else saw him. It is a costly form of knowledge. It is not acquired by reading books. It calls for exposed nerves. Men and women also fail many times by "going native" among the people to whom they are sent. The ambassador forgets the homeland; he forgets the mission on which he was sent; the customs of the natives, which allow an easy sprawl, displace the standards of the power which sent them. They become religious and moral "beachcombers."

Remember the message we carry: "We beseech you, on behalf of Christ."

35. WASTED GRACE

We entreat you not to accept the grace of God in vain.   2 COR. 6:1

A monstrous waste! To accept the grace wherein we stand, the very air by which the spirit lives, and let it run to waste, and not accomplish that for which it is given! Some of the company of Christians at Corinth had done just that. Phillips translates Paul's plea, "We beg you, then, not to fail to use the grace of God." God's grace is given to be used. But sometimes it becomes like a picture on the wall, a decorative effect in life but never put to vital use. So the most precious gift of life is wasted. The people to whom Paul was directly appealing had lost the restraining and sustaining gift so freely given.

As we look steadily at this plea of Paul, it subtly becomes a mirror in which we can see ourselves. Ours is the danger of accepting the grace of God in vain. The free gift of God's forgiving love is to be used for a purpose. Poetry has been described as "the celebration of perennial things, and its task is to see the eternal through the prism of the here and now." In like language the Christian faith is the celebration of the eternal, and the grace of God enables us to see and accept the eternal in the here and now.

A picture which puts in an imaginative manner what the grace of God brings to life comes to us from Vermont. A widow's house had been burned to the ground and some generous neighbors volunteered to rebuild it. Someone suggested that it would be a good thing if they asked her first if there were any changes she wished to be made. "Yes," she said, "I would like a window over the sink."

Think of washing dishes for half a lifetime, looking into a blank wall! The vision of the grace of God puts a window over the sink. It opens a vista of God's love above our place of work, whatever our occupation may be. When that grace is not wasted but penetrates our whole life, we can say with Paul, "I have learned the secret of facing plenty and hunger, abundance and want" (Phil. 4:12). That is the disciple's great secret. It is life's great secret. Those who have learned it form the greatest secret society on earth.

An unforgettable picture of the waste of grace is found in the will of a man who lived on Cape Cod in the eighteenth century. He was John Barnstable, a man seemingly devoted to the scriptures, but who gave evidence of having the grace revealed in them wasted on him. He left this bequest:

[John Barnstable] bequeathed to his wife for her lifetime the "Use and improvement" of a slave-woman, Dinah. "If, at the death of my wife, Dinah be still living, I desire my executioners to sell her, and to use and improve the money for which she is sold in the purchase of Bibles, and distribute them equally among my said wife's and my grandchildren."

Could futility go further? A human being, a child of God and a sister in Christ, sold like a sack of coal to buy Bibles for distribution!

"We beg you, then, not to fail to use the grace of God!"

36. NOW IS THE TIME

Now is the day of salvation. 2 COR. 6:2

The word "now" is a tremendous word in the New Testament. We never get away from it. There is no dream world of procrastination. The New Testament moves to the drumbeat of now. That drum plays us up into the line of action.

Among the Hebrews up till the advent of Jesus, two principal words were "yesterday" and "tomorrow." The first recorded word of Jesus' ministry, his address at the synagogue at Nazareth, was the word "today." After reading from Isaiah he said, *"Today* this scripture has been fulfilled in your hearing" (Luke 4:21).

Those same two words which bulked so largely in the thought and speech of the Hebrews may be our pitfalls today. We may dwell in the confines of the word "yesterday," which may be like prison walls to us. Yesterday may have for us not the propelling power of a great tradition but a crippling kind of nostalgia. Ours may be merely a bondage to the details of a past. Jaurès, the Frenchman, warned against that when he said, "We should take from the past its fires, not its ashes."

Or we may live chiefly in the world of tomorrow. We can feel "disregard today, dream of tomorrow." That becomes a spiritual obituary. Great hosts of people have died of tomorrow, as far as any spiritual life is concerned.

The word "now" not only marks the day of salvation. It is a *word* of salvation. *Now* is the time to receive the grace of God. *Now* is the time to enlist in His service. *Now* is the time to live life to its fullest possibilities. There is a memorable word in Thornton Wilder's play, *Our Town,* which pictures the common failing to reach the limit of the possibilities of *now* as life rushes by. A young woman, dead at a very early age, returns from the cemetery to her birthday party of years ago and can be seen by her parents only as she was. As she leaves them she wonders whether people "ever realize life while they live it, every minute." She cries out, "Why don't we look at each other?" Robert Louis Stevenson wrote that "the obscurest epoch is today." That is true in many senses, especially whenever the imperative of the *now* drops out of life. The hour in which we are now living is the magic hour in the truest sense, for now is the day of salvation. We get easily into the blighting habit of reserving ourselves, our friendships, our participation, till we find better company or better opportunities, to which Emerson well asks, "Where?"

In a peculiar way, with a sharpness never before matched, *now* is the day of salvation in a world threatened with destruction. Our house, the house of our world, the only one we all have to live in, will be a slaughterhouse or a family house. One scientist said at the explosion of the atomic bomb at Los Alamos, New Mexico, that it was "the nearest thing to doomsday that one could possibly imagine." No wonder! It *was* doomsday! Yet, with a possible doomsday upon us, we so readily fall into a "business as usual" mentality. At the beginning of World War I, H. G. Wells prophesied the coming of the atomic bomb. In that foretelling he was right on the mark. But then he went on to prophesy that the revulsion of the peoples of the earth would be so strong that the bondage of war, from the days of the caveman, would be broken. He wrote,

Nothing could have been more obvious to the people of the early 20th century than the rapidity with which war was becoming impossible. And as certainly they did not see it. They did not see it until the atomic bombs burst in their fumbling hands. . . . It was a matter of common knowledge that a man could carry about in a handbag an amount of latent energy sufficient to wreck half a city. And yet the world still, as the Americans used to phrase it, "fooled around" with the paraphernalia and pretensions of war. . . .

The catastrophe of the atomic bombs which shook men out of cities and businesses and economic relations, shook them also out of their old-established habits of thought, and out of the lightly held beliefs and prejudices that came down to them from the past. To borrow a word from the old-fashioned chemists, men were made nascent; were ready for new associations. . . . the moral shock of the atomic bombs had been a profound one, and for a while the cunning side of the human animal was overpowered by its sincere realization of the vital necessity for reconstruction.

If Wells had only been right! But no such shaking free from the bonds of the past occurred, God pity us!

Now is the day of salvation.

37. WHATEVER WE HAVE TO GO THROUGH

We want to prove ourselves genuine ministers of God whatever we have to go through. 2 COR. 6:4 (Phillips)

A large order, *whatever!* It covers all the space there is!

All too often the minister is judged by the vulgar standard of *where he gets to.* Even in deluded hours men have used the phrase "princes of the church." How does that fit into the Carpenter of Galilee? Among some people who have lost their gospel-measuring tape, men have proved their ministry by getting to the seats of the mighty.

Paul here sets up a very different test. We are to be measured not by where we get to, but by *what we go through.* Our ministry is proved genuine by the ardors and endurances of the way.

This applies to the minister, using that word in its professional sense. It also applies just as truly to all disciples of Christ who in any way minister to people of the grace of God.

One main point is made here, in connection with the pertinent words that follow, describing what the servant of Christ has to go through. These words apply with a peculiar force to our day. For in our generation, so much of an inventive genius has been devoted to smoothing out all the bumps and hazards of life, in fact,

all the necessities which Paul lists in this paragraph as making up
whatever we have to go through. We are not confronted with written examinations; there is no quiz contest covering vast knowledge.
We must meet the tests of living. Look at Paul's list of tests. Live
without being all smoothed out. ". . . patient endurance of troubles
or even disasters, being flogged or imprisoned; being mobbed,
having to work like slaves, having to go without food or sleep"
(Phillips).

These tests loom up like barricades across our road in life. Some
we can consider and dismiss as not facing us, as the inevitable
parts of first-century pioneering in a pagan world. But others are
part of "whatever we have to go through," in the twentieth century as in the first.

Consider this test: "patient endurance of troubles." Patience is
never out of date, but it is not a popular virtue with a host of
people in this age of smoothing out all troubles. We easily get to
demanding that all troubles be cleared away, fast, fast, fast, like
aspirin for a headache. Many people (and we may well watch and
pray that we are not of their number), when there are any trials
and tribulations they cannot run from, but have to live with feel
unjustly treated by a universe in which they are not special pets.
John Keats confessed to a common failing when he wrote, "If I
stub my toe, in five minutes it becomes a theme for Sophocles."

We are to go through being "mobbed." Not, in this day, such
mobs as Paul met again and again, and by which he was almost
lynched. Yet, if we really stand for a sharply defined and highly
visible Christian faith and goal, we will be mobbed in ways that
can be felt, with pressure put upon us by those in opposition to
any threatened upsetting of comfortable ways of life. We must go
through mobs in the incessant demand for conformity. John
Wesley said to his preachers, "Always look a mob in the face."
That is a way of salvation. It will help us to say words that must
be at home on our tongue: "We must obey God rather than man."
We easily get to asking only good sailing weather,

> If on a quiet sea
> Toward heaven we calmly sail.

That is the way we like it!

Look at this major test—"work like slaves." Even in that, the
disciple of Christ may feel badly used if he actually has to *work*.
And worse still, like a *slave*. It is a strong word, but not too strong
for Paul. He accounted himself "a slave of Jesus Christ." But we
get so enamored of independence that we do not like slavery. A

woman told her pastor that she could not do any work in the church because she did not like to be "tied down." She went on with such emphasis and at such length that he finally said, "Strange, for we are the disciples of a Lord who was willing to be nailed down that he might be the saviour of many."

Examination day is here. It can also be coronation day.

38. ATTACK OR DEFENSE

With the weapons of integrity for attack or for defense. 2 COR. 6:8 (Moffatt)

The sentence in which these words are found is one of the great panoramas of the New Testament. It stretches out like the Alps with a distant view of blue water. It is one of the longest verses of the Bible (eighty-two words in the Revised Standard Version). But that is its least distinction. It takes in a wide range of Christian faith and experience. One could live with it fifty years and never circumnavigate it, nor walk around it. It takes in the life of the servant of God, its trials and triumphs, its enemies and allies, its imprisonments and liberations.

Dr. Moffatt translates the words rendered in the Revised Standard Version as "weapons of righteousness for the right hand and for the left" by the words "weapons of integrity for attack or for defense." Whatever the words "attack or defense" may lack as literal rendering, they are a true as well as a vivid picture of Christian living and fighting. The life of the Christian disciple is a matter of attack or defense, as this verse portrays it. The words "attack or defense" illuminate at least part of the meaning of this long, glorious sentence with its glimpses of many battlefields. The victory of Christ calls for two forms of warfare, offensive and defensive. In one list Paul gives the things to attack. In another there are the weapons of defense. In the things representing attack he lists nine enemies which we can think of in various forms: "afflictions, hardships, calamities, beatings, imprisonments, tumults, labors, watching, hunger." He gives in defense "purity, knowledge, forbearance, kindness, the Holy Spirit, genuine love, truthful speech, and the power of God." Paul presents these opposing forces on life's battlefields.

The point stressed here is that in the whole matter of Christian living, all too often the too exclusive attention has been given to defense against the evil liabilities of life. Now, of course, God as defense cannot be overstressed. It is a tremendous theme in the Old Testament; "God is a sun and shield" (Ps. 84:11). And in the New Testament, "above all, taking the shield of faith, wherewith ye shall be able to quench all the fiery darts of the wicked" (Eph. 6:16, AV).

Yet the whole conception of the Christian religion has often been too exclusively defensive. It has had too little quality of an attack on evil. So many prayers have been prayers for defense against mishap. Too few have been prayers for strength for struggle against wrong. That is often noticed in the *Book of Common Prayer*. There are so many prayers that follow the pattern of "defend us against all the evils of the coming night." Perhaps one reason is that the Prayer Book was composed in the latter part of the fifteenth century when there were far more dangers to personal security from all sorts of assault, such as highwaymen and disease. Life was precarious. The life of the Christian disciple should be conceived and lived as a battle, both as a defense of a beleaguered fortress, and as a sortie and an attack. Robert Louis Stevenson wrote that "life is an affair of cavalry." We should enlarge our personal hymnal to include "Who Is On the Lord's Side?" as well as "Hide Me, O My Saviour, Hide."

There are so many things that keep life from being on the attack. Ola Winslow writes of Roger Williams that "one of God's doves he could never be." There can be too many cooing doves, lovable creatures, but not much good in coming to the help of the Lord against the mighty.

Sometimes what keeps a person from attack on a fighting front is nothing more terrifying than respectability. John Dewey has not been widely accepted as an interpreter of the Christian faith. But he has put his finger on one of its dangerous threats. He wrote, "It seems to me that the chief danger to religion lies in the fact that it has become so respectable. It has become largely a sanction on what socially exists—a kind of gloss upon institutions and conventions. Primitive Christianity was devastating in its claims."

39.   BEING CALLED A NOBODY

Called "nobodies" we must be in the public eye.   2 COR. 6:9 (Phillips)

Among the charges that Paul had to bear from his enemies was that of being a "nobody." It was an easy way of undermining his authority and impairing his influence, to say with scorn, "He's a nobody."

The word has a special interest to our day. A great multitude of people today fear nothing so much as being regarded as a nobody. That is a dirty word today. The name does not set well in a publicity-drenched age. A young woman entitled the story of her life, *I Wanted To Be Somebody*. The title voices the deepest desire of many. There is a desperate, often a frantic effort to be "somebody." No matter what, so long as it is a somebody. Human sacrifices are being offered all the time on the altars of the great gods, Publicity and Notoriety. This host of worshipers has no sharing of the mood of Emily Dickinson:

> How dreary to be somebody
> How public like a frog.
> To tell your name the livelong day
> To an admiring bog!

Dreary? Not by a long shot, many will say. It is paradise, to be pointed out, photographed, written about! But life takes a strong revenge on the somebodies. Dr. Johnson, talking to Boswell, pointed it out. "Sir," he said, "a man may be so much of everything that he is nothing of anything." The career of the person determined to be somebody works out in a neat little equation: too much of everything = o.

For the refugee from being a nobody often gets so fascinated with himself that that absorbs all his attention. It frequently works out as it did with a child singing on television. Just before she sounded the first note her eye was caught by the little monitor in which she could see herself. She was so taken up with the sight that she was held voiceless, transfixed as a bird is reported to be by a snake. So the person in deadly fear of being a nobody gives up making any positive contribution to society. So in the fear of being nobody he becomes an authentic nobody in all the spiritual qualities of life and in all its possible services to humanity. The person who wants frantically to be a "figure" frequently ends up by becoming one—a zero.

But, with endless repetition, the world's nobody is God's somebody. For man looketh on the outward appearance, but God looketh upon the heart. It makes one of the greatest fascinations of history to trace that truth. Go back in your imagination to that day in Jerusalem when a poor widow dropped two coins into the alms box. She was the nobody of nobodies, the lowest of the low. The two little coins represented her whole living. No one could get lower in the social scale than that. But a Visitor to Jerusalem weighed her on a different scale. She was God's Somebody. The Visitor cried out, "This poor widow has put in more than all the others" (Mark 12:43, Phillips). History over the centuries has shown that that gift of two coins was in its influence one of the mightiest financial transactions that ever took place on the planet. Compared to the effect of that gift, all the financial assets of all the companies represented on the stock exchange are like the rattle of a few pennies in a tin cup. A nobody!

Once again, think of a whole company of unknowns. Sir Winston Churchill paid this tribute to the scholars who made the King James translation of the Bible: "The scholars who produced this masterpiece are mostly *unknown* and *unremembered*. But they forged an enduring link, religious and literary, between the English-speaking peoples of the world."

The italics are ours, *"unknown* and *unremembered"!* But God's Very Important Persons.

40.   ALIVE!

Never far from death, yet here we are alive.   2 COR. 6:9 (Phillips)

This exclamation records the astounding wonder of the Christian life. This amazing sentence of only nine words pictures a long journey which Paul took over rough roads, steep cliffs, and deep chasms that looked to be fatal; yet he came through all those hazards and here we are alive! It is like a man coming through nine critical operations, yet here he is alive! "Never far from death, yet here we are alive."

Paul does not ascribe his survival to his powers of endurance or resilience, but to the grace of God and the power of God (verses 6 and 7). Paul could say with the psalmist, "This is the Lord's doing; it is marvelous in our eyes." When we allow an overwhelming sense of the mystery of God and the mysterious operation of grace to drop out of our lives, we miss the true nature of Christian faith and experience. A minister affirmed in writing a few years ago that being a Christian was a good business proposition. The real bankruptcy of faith is revealed when it is commended as a good business deal. For that indicates that there is something higher than good—the market. To such a worshiper of our business culture, the gospel is not really an invitation from God. It is a tip from Dun and Bradstreet. It is not a letter from Christ, but something resembling a letter on the stock market.

In true Christian faith and experience, the mysterious factor in life is God's grace. The equation is $X = God$. Phillips' translation of a part of this marvelous sentence pictures this glowingly and exultantly: "always 'going through it' yet never 'going under.'" The Christian's preposition is *through,* not under! There are many reasons for coming through instead of going under the hazards of life. Look at two of them.

The big reason for survival is *a living relationship to God.* When firsthand religion gives way to secondhand hearsay, the living faith has died. Edwin Arlington Robinson said of an early work by George Santayana that it seemed "like something by a highly sophisticated corpse." However true or false that might be as a judgment on a philosopher, the words well describe a faith from which living relationship with God has dropped out. It is either a ghost or a corpse.

A physical symbol of Paul's triumphant "here we are alive" is found in a common, and always stirring, sight, a tree growing out of a stony crag. Frequently it grows where there does not seem to be one chance in a thousand for a tree to grow. But the tree does not grow out of the stones. It has sunk its root down to the living earth and here it is alive. Relationship! Jesus said it about seeds, "and since they had no root they withered away" (Matt. 13:6). For the preservation of spiritual life, we need what is so often left out of a busy life, solitude. A novelist of present-day life in the suburbs has described "that peculiarly suburban breed of lithe, tanned, middle-aged golfing suburban wives, running parallel to the lives of men, they do not touch the quiet ground of solitude from the moment of their 'coming out' as girls to the moment they themselves are laid to rest." They never hear the words, "Enter into thy closet . . . and shut thy door" (Matt. 6:6, AV).

Wordsworth wrote of "the deep power of joy." The joy of the Lord is power, life-giving power. Christian joy is not just an exuberance; it is a dynamo.

41. THE WIDE HEART

Widen your hearts.   2 COR. 6:13

Paul is appealing to those in the church in Corinth to give him as much love as he has given them. His heart has been wide. There is no restriction in his affection for them. He appeals to them to widen their hearts.

Lift that plea up beyond the immediate occasion of its use. Of course, it did apply there in force. A "wide" heart is a divine instrument for bringing harmony out of conflict. It is also true that the deep need of our world is for wide hearts. One forbidding barrier on all the roads leading to a better world is the narrow heart. It stands as a road block, with the sign "No Thoroughfare."

Jesus widened the hearts of his disciples. He turned the lust for calling down fire into the outreach of brotherhood. The influence of Christ has been bringing the same power to widen hearts ever since.

Ortega y Gasset has said that a novelist "must see to it that the reader is cut off from his real horizon and imprisoned in a small, hermetically sealed universe. He must make a 'villager out of him' and interest him in the inhabitants of this realm." That is a good prescription for a novel. Jane Austen did it superbly in *Pride and Prejudice*. She has been rebuked by some people because she did not look out the window and see the French Revolution which was going on. But we are grateful that she *did* see the Bennett family. All well for a novel. But the words make a terribly true description when the narrow heart cuts us off from our real horizon and makes "villagers" out of us, when the great need of the world is for men who are not imprisoned in a cell, but are world citizens. The world cries out for wide hearts.

The blight of a narrow heart in our immediate surroundings was well and bitterly pictured in a cartoon which appeared a few years ago. A mink-coated dowager was approached on a snowy winter day by a poor woman. The mink woman was greatly annoyed. She put on her best "Why-don't-they-eat-cake" manner and said, "I thought the *New York Times* took care of all you people." A very wide heart!

Aldous Huxley has ventured into a classification of the virtues which resulted in his putting two virtues of love and awareness at the top of the list. That is in accord with the Christian tradition. He gives more than the mere classification of virtues into minor and major. He roundly affirms that temperance, prudence, and courage without love and intelligence may be merely instruments for doing evil more efficiently. Love and awareness are forms of loving God with the heart and mind.

The direction "Widen your hearts" comes with peculiar pertinence and force to the church. When the church has a narrow heart, it becomes an unrivaled obstacle to the progress of the Christian gospel. Shakespeare, in vivid phrase, has left a simile of the church door being wide. When in *Romeo and Juliet* Mercutio is wounded in a street brawl and is asked about his wound, he answers, ". . . 'tis not so deep as a well, nor so wide as a church door; but 'tis enough, 'twill serve." No doubt Shakespeare had in mind the door of a cathedral or a large church. The door of a church of Christ ought to be wide enough to admit all God's children. But so many times the door of the church has been as narrow as the prejudices and the hatreds of the people within, who claimed Christ's name but disdained his spirit. Color tests, money tests, tests of accent, have been set up to malign the Master who said, "Come unto me, all ye that labour and are heavy laden" (Matt. 11:28, AV).

One of the many societies of reform which flourished in Boston in the 1830's had a name that should be rescued from oblivion. It was, "Meeting of gentlemen friendly to new and worthier views of God and man." If that were only a true description of every church! God could use such a "meeting."

42. PORTRAIT OF A GENERATION

Fighting without and fear within. 2 COR. 7:5

In these words Paul describes his outer and inner state as he journeyed into Macedonia. They do not cover any larger physical and emotional territory. Yet the words serve, when taken into our imagination, as a rather vivid picture of a generation. We in our time do have that personal landscape, "fighting without and fear within." Of course, it can be truly said that those words portray the landscape of every generation. Man has a heritage of fighting and fear. But Paul's words, used in a self-picture, do draw a startling likeness of our own generation. Moffatt's translation, "wrangling all round me, fears in my own mind," makes the picture even sharper. Great hosts of people find no place to hide from turmoil outside and anxiety inside.

We are entangled in such varieties of fighting: the long wars of competition, the clash of ideologies, wars of resistance to the forces which break down the sense of personal significance, the world conflicts in which cold war threatens to become hot. Charles Lamb felt that we should have grace before books as well as grace before meals. In a different sense of the word, we need a special grace before newspapers, a grace of fortification which enables us to face the ordeal of reading the morning paper every day. In the world arena wranglings grow more fearsome with each invention which was first hailed as a maker of peace. Here are the words of Orville Wright in 1917: "When my brother and I built and flew the first man-carrying flying machine, we thought we were introducing into the world an invention which would make further wars impossible. That we were not alone in the thought is shown by the fact that the French Peace Society presented us with medals on account of our invention." When Alfred Nobel invented dynamite in 1866, he felt that it would put an end to war. No doubt the subhuman warrior who devised that "instrument of peace," the first stone club, thought the same.

Fears and anxieties seem to multiply with the increasing complexities of life. Ancient geographers filled their maps of unknown portions of the earth with frightening animals. Dean Swift described the process:

> So, geographers in Afric maps
> With savage pictures filled their gaps,
> And o'er uninhabited downs,
> Placed elephants instead of towns.

In like manner, people not very "ancient" today fill the unknown future with looming disasters.

The spirit is filled with apprehension and fears and often gets into a state of fidgets. Worries can, and do, shackle a life. We get a good picture of the effect of common worries in *Gulliver's Travels*. Gulliver, a giant among pigmies, is securely tied down flat on the earth by a thousand little strings. A life can be tied down flat by the stout strings of a score of worries. One widely felt worry strong in America, as noted by a British visitor, is "that hysterical fear which besets prosperous society when it feels its way of living to be threatened and finds itself bankrupt of the moral and spiritual resources needed to restore courage and a cool judgment."

Notice the two words which follow the "fighting without and fear within," the tremendous words "But God." Now the plot thickens. Words for daily remembrance! God comes into the harassed soul if the door is opened. The defense takes over. Faith brings stout props to life: "If God be for us, who can be against us?" (Rom. 8:31, AV). "Casting all your care upon him; for he careth for you" (I Pet. 5:7, AV).

The soul that on Jesus hath leaned for repose finds power against outside and inside turmoil. "My peace I give to you"

(John 14:27). The peace which comes with trust in God does not mean indifference. It does not mean a sort of comatose condition of spirit. That is the *rigor mortis* of the soul. It does not mean a gushing sentimentalism, which really never sees evils clearly, looking out on life through a fog darkly. There is no salvation in fog, any more than there is in a nervous breakdown from worry. But in a living trust in God there is a central peace. Wordsworth describes our gospel:

> *Authentic tidings of invisible things,*
> *Of ebb and flow, and ever-enduring powers,*
> *And central peace, subsisting at the heart*
> *Of endless agitation.*

"For he will hide me in his shelter in the day of trouble" (Ps. 27:5).

43. GUIDED GRIEF

Godly grief. 2 COR. 7:9
Pain God is allowed to guide. (Moffatt)

Most of the human family could say to Paul, or to anyone else, If you have anything to say about grief, other than shopworn commonplaces, we will listen. For we are all men "acquainted with grief." George Eliot once wrote to a friend, "My address is Grief Castle." We have lived there for a time.

In this passage Paul specifically rejoices that the group in the church at Corinth, whom he has severely reproved for condoning flagrant evil, has shown grief for sin and that grief has led to repentance. But the contrast in life between worldly and godly grief covers far more than that specific kind of grief. The contrast is a valid one, and between the two kinds of grief there is a great gulf fixed.

There is another attitude, assumed by many, which tries to put grief of every sort out of life entirely. Grief, in that view, is something for weaklings. The feeling is, "Trouble happens to all. Don't take it too hard." So, human feelings are blunted in the effort to be "hard boiled." The result is always a blunted and blighted mind and heart.

But beyond that futile effort to shut grief out of life, there are the two kinds, worldly and godly grief. J. B. Phillips further defines godly grief as "the sorrow which God uses." Moffatt's translation is similar: "the pain God is allowed to guide."

Worldly grief is grief unrelated to God. There are so many kinds of worldly grief. It is often regarded as just "hard luck." That is indicated by the frequently used phrase, "It came to grief." Much grief comes under the head of the phrase which Disraeli used: "the hell of failure." It is the collapse of some ambition on which the heart has been set with a frantic determination. It was said of Napoleon that he had no technique for failure. So many lives also have no technique for failure. There must be success or grievous disaster. There is no pain which "God is allowed to guide." Because sorrow is not put into God's hands to be used by him, a life is defeated. One sad instance of that is found in the autobiography of a great American teacher, Professor John M. Mecklin. He describes the tragic experience, with which we can all deeply sympathize, of watching his wife dying with an incurable disease. He writes,

As I watched her tender and sympathetic spirit fade out of my life, in the midst of unparalleled and unjustifiable physical agony, I rejected forever the traditional conception of a Heavenly Father.

No grief guided by God.

In a less poignant and painful manner worldly grief comes from the feeling that suffering ought not to happen to *us*. To other people, perhaps, but not to *us*. Floods in China,, but not in our town. Tornadoes in some places, Oklahoma, perhaps, but not to us. As John Betjeman, the English poet, writes sardonically in World War II, many British people prayed, "Gracious Lord, Oh bomb the Germans, but don't let anyone bomb me." Worldly grief has no living issue.

Turn to godly grief. Grief need not be a lonesome torture. It can be guided and used for a spiritual result. Grief, no matter how painful, can have a partner. The God of all comfort comes in if we allow Him. The most wonderful of all stage directions is "Enter God." This inscription in one of Leslie Weatherhead's books gives a picture of guided grief, used by God, which applies to innumerable life experiences:

This book is dedicated in unfailing remembrance to Elizabeth Mary Weatherhead, my mother, and to Muriel Weatherhead, my sister, whose bodies were defeated in the battle against painful disease, but who from that defeat, wrested a spiritual victory which challenged and inspired all who knew them, and made glad the heart of God.

That was God-guided grief.

Paul rejoices especially that the group in the Corinth church have experienced godly grief over sin, which "produces a repentance that leads to salvation" (2 Cor. 7:10). Deep-felt grief over wrongdoing flings open the doors of a prison and sets the prisoner free. For such grief is a saving power. It moves one to action. Much of the beatitude which declares "Blessed are those who mourn" is included in the mourning over sin. We trace it clearly in the plight of the Prodigal Son in the pig pen: "I will arise and go to my father, and I will say to him, 'Father, I have sinned'" (Luke 15:18). Grief over sin, followed by action, "I will arise." It was grief leading to action by Zacchaeus: "I restore it fourfold" (Luke 19:8). It was grief over failure that became a saving force in the life of Peter: "And he went out and wept bitterly" (Matt. 26:75). It has been the experience of countless numbers who have blundered and failed, and been lifted to their feet again.

Grief over the loss of loved ones, so universal and so painful, can become a grief that God uses. A godly grief sees through the darkest dark to God.

Grief over the tragedy of our world and over its threatened destruction in war can be a godly grief, and not merely a worldly grief, consisting mainly of hand-wringing by a wailing wall. We often are given the superficial advice about an agitated sorrow over the world, "Don't let it get you down." That is good advice only so far as it may mean, "Don't let it paralyze you." But as far as a deep grief and concern over the world's danger and calamity are concerned, the only good advice is, "*Do* let it get you down." That is an indispensable step toward world survival. Our present tragedy and threat is that there is not enough grief that leads to action, not enough people who care desperately enough to think and act. There is too much of the attitude of "Business as usual," business with military hardware, and too little godly grief of a sort.

44.   NEVER LET ME DOWN

You have not let me down.   2 cor. 7:14 (Phillips)

That is a high accolade of praise. It is the distinguished service medal in human relations and in a man's relations to God.

This is a vivid picture in words. For the same high tribute in a picture of people who did not let their faith or their God down, it is hard to find a more impressive picture than that called "The Return of the Mayflower." A company of the Pilgrim settlers at Plymouth, Massachusetts, who had survived the first terrible winter, are standing and gazing wistfully at the *Mayflower* setting sail for the trip back to England. That ship represented so much to them: going home, the better chance of survival. But here is the record of history. When the *Mayflower* returned to England, only the sailors were on board. The remaining Pilgrims did not let their faith or their purpose down. No one had said, "Let's call it a day. There's no use to stay here and die." They stayed.

Paul pays tribute to some of those in the church at Corinth: "I was not put to shame." The people who have been the creating and sustaining powers in the church have been those who have not let their Master down. Philip Hone, the mayor of New York in the early part of the nineteenth century, wrote about the city of Washington, D. C., that "there were many great folk, some clever folk, and a fair proportion of queer folk." That could be said of the churches. We are grateful for the clever folk. There will always be a need for them. We are familiar with the "queer folk" on the roll of the church. If the church is a cross section of the population, of course there will be folk labeled "queer." But the *great* folk, the absolutely essential folk, are those who never let their Master down, no matter how threatening the demand of the world about them to do so.

It is often a dangerous and costly role to play. A member of the French Resistance used a phrase in the dark days of the German conquest of France in 1941 which fits the demand on the Christian disciple today. He said, "This is not the time to change all my old dreams, or all the images of my faith, but rather to remain dangerously faithful." This is the call "to remain dangerously faithful to old dreams,"

> *That in the name of Jesus*
> *The world shall be reborn!*

"Poetry," wrote Santayana, "is religion which is no longer believed." That is a very inadequate description of poetry. But one aspect of religion is true, that faithfulness marks religion that *is* true.

Consider three ways by which we *do not* let our Master and our fellow Christians, past and present, down.

1. We can witness with our *feet*. We witness forcibly with our feet when they take us regularly to church. We can say, "How beautiful upon the sidewalk are the feet of those who come to the

church with loyalty and dedication."

2. We can witness with our *faces*. A glow in the face witnesses that we are happy in our choice as disciples. It proclaims, "I have a secret."

3. We can witness with our *hands*. "Establish thou the work of our hands" (Ps. 90:17). We can so fill all our varied handiwork with Christ's spirit that, in the sight of all, we do not let him down.

45. DOWN TO THE LAST PENNY

Their joy and the fact of being down to their last penny themselves, produced a magnificent concern for other people. 2 cor. 8:2 (Phillips) *Their abundance of joy and their extreme poverty have overflowed in a wealth of liberality on their part.*

Paul, in these words, pays high tribute to the churches of Macedonia for their generosity as shown by their "last penny" giving. Jesus was not deeply impressed with giving out of a comfortable surplus. "For they all contributed out of their abundance" (Luke 21:4). What deeply stirred him was the gift from poverty, the "last penny" giving.

But when one gives down to the last penny, Paul declares here, that is not the end of the story. It is just the beginning. For then the plot thickens. Out of poverty comes an overflow, "in a wealth of liberality." Today, when people are down to their last penny, that is usually considered an honorable discharge. They hear the last penny saying to them, as they look at it, "You are excused from doing anything." God's way is different. It is a matter of history that the treasury of the churches has been made up largely of last pennies. There have been large financial gifts from rich givers. Thank God for their generosity. But in overwhelming amount the work of the churches has been carried on by gifts of the poor. Comparatively, they are literally "pennies from heaven." For from those down to the last penny, there has been an overflow of liberality. It can be put into an equation, $A + P = L$: affliction plus the last penny equals liberality. This applies equally to any gift to the work of God, the last pennies, the last hour of time in a busy, often overloaded life, the last ounce of strength, the last bit of endurance. These are the real capital funds of the church.

Life is justly measured by its overflow. Madame Schumann-Heink was once asked how to sing. She said, "You just fill your lungs with air and let it slop over." There must be more to it than that; for many people have tried that without notable results! But it is true that great music is an overflow. Great living is an overflow. It is the overflow of a filled heart. The very word comes into the next chapter of this epistle, "For the rendering of this service not only supplies the wants of the saints but also *overflows* in many thanksgivings to God" (2 Cor. 9:12).

A common trouble is that we live too near spiritual penury, so that we have no "last penny" overflow. We are not financially bankrupt, but often there is an approach to bankrupt enthusiasm. Dick Sheppard has given an amusing etching of a churchman over the cliff of spiritual bankruptcy: "Our old church warden (a diehard Colonel) is having a fearful row with a man who called him 'religious,' and when furiously asked why, said because he was a church warden. The Colonel said, 'That's damned unfair.'" To him, religion was not a proud word, but a fighting word.

If we have never had any "last penny" overflow, we have not lived the life which is life indeed.

46. CARRY IT THROUGH

Now, carry it through, so that your readines to take it up may be equalled by the way you carry it through.   2 COR. 8:11 (Moffatt)
That your readiness in desiring it may be matched by your completing it.

To match the start by the finish—aye, that's the rub! We all have readiness in desiring some good result. We are like the English troops before battle, as King Henry V saw them, "straining at the leash." It is a great moment when we start a new enterprise, a new way of life, a new venture of faith, a new commitment of service. But it is hard to carry it through "with as much efficiency as you showed readiness to begin" (Phillips).

Of course, one reason is always "the long, hard pull." But there is a more subtle danger than that. When we desire a thing, and talk about it, there is a strange illusion that we have finished it. Or at least we rest back languidly on the less-than-half truth that "well begun is half done." Many writers fear this illusion and its deadly deception so much that they will never talk about a work in process.

We need, at every step in life, the "grace of continuance." One prayer preserved in the English heritage is the one written by Sir Francis Drake, on that April morning, 1587, just before he pushed into the Bay of Cadiz to "singe the beard" of the Spanish king. It is a prayer of "continuance" without which all effort is vain. Here it is: "O Lord God, when Thou givest to Thy servants to endeavor any great matter, grant us also to know that it is not the beginning, but the continuing of the same until it be thoroughly finished; that yieldeth the true glory; through Him that for the finishing of Thy work, laid down His life, Amen."

Continuance yields the true glory! This is true in the spiritual life and work. Consider this in relation to the title given to Christ in the Epistle to the Hebrews, "looking unto Jesus the author and finisher of our faith" (AV). A word to look at a second time and at all times is "finisher." Jesus was the "author" of our faith, the divine beginner. But he was also the "finisher" of our faith. He said from the cross, "It is finished." How badly we need finishers in individual life and the life and work of the church. That is, the need to finish what we undertake, not just quitting, but in the high and thrilling sense of carrying an undertaking to its successful conclusion with the verdict "Mission accomplished."

A life can be made up of quick starts and equally quick finishes. Such a life lacks coherence, lacks the going-on quality. Part of the trouble is premature assurance. A striking example of that is found in Matthew 13:51 (AV). Jesus said to his disciples, "Have ye understood all these things?" They confidently answered, "Yea." They were sadly mistaken. Here was a particularly difficult and involved parable. Yet they gave a quick affirmative answer. In the same way we may suffer from misplaced confidence. We start without preparing for the long pull in which our strength and endurance will be tested.

Another snare is the alluring chance to get out of the undertaking when the going gets tough. We often succumb to the temptation to call it off. This follows rather closely the arrangement which banks call "revocable trust." This can be used as a scheme for dodging taxes. A man creates a trust which he can revoke at any time. Meanwhile, he saves taxes because his money is tied up in a trust. The trust document instructs the bank to hold investments as trustee, to keep them properly invested, and to pay the income and eventually the principal to certain persons. The point stressed is that this arrangement can be revoked at any time, bringing it to an end and taking back the property.

This is a disturbing phrase, "revocable trust," when we keep in mind our religious commitment and religious trust. It raises the question we may well face, "Is my religious dedication a 'revocable trust'?" We read the fine words of scripture (AV), "Trust ye in the Lord for ever" (Isa. 26:4) and "I trust in the mercy of God (Ps. 52:8) and "What time I am afraid, I will trust in thee" (Ps. 56:3). But there come times when we are tempted to revoke that trust and put our trust in something that seems more tangible. So, we read, "Casting all your care upon him; for he careth for you" (I Pet. 5:7). That is beautiful, but we make our high trust a temporary one, and we often put into the place of a calm trust in the love and care of God a strained anxiety and fear which break down the mind and spirit.

There are three great stages in the act of continuing. They are outlined by Edward Gibbon in describing the work of writing *The Decline and Fall of the Roman Empire*. He says that from the wish to the hope, from the hope to the design, from the design to the execution. We can count on God's help at each stage if we ask earnestly enough for it. If we are to continue in difficulty there must be continual renewal. There stands our need. Eternal reliance is this: "They that wait upon the Lord shall renew their strength" (Isa. 40:31, AV).

47.   LIVING SPARINGLY

The point is this: he who sows sparingly will also reap sparingly.
2 COR. 9:6

There are equations as true in the moral or spiritual world as in that of mathematics. It is not a theme for debate, except by belated high school students who follow Euclid afar off, that the sum of the angles of a triangle is two right angles.

The text above is, likewise, one of life's axioms. A sparing sower reaps a sparse harvest. This is true in agriculture. We have the traditional image of a sower—a man taking giant steps over a plowed field as though he had in mind the counsel, "Fear not to sow on account of the birds." But the man who sows sparingly makes a very different picture. Instead of the bountiful scattering, it is as though the sower deposits each seed in a little hole with as much caution as he would use in depositing the Hope Diamond in a safe-deposit box. Not much of a harvest! So with the man who lives sparingly. The grudging planter wins a grudging return from the earth.

Every power of a life, every capacity, every gift, is precious seed. The wonder of seed, the amazing potential, is described lyrically in O. E. Rölvaag's novel *Giants in the Earth*. The pioneer who broke the sod, the man with the heart of an old Viking, Per Hansa, had acres to sow.

With what zest he broke the tough-fibered prairie sod, which had never been broken before since the beginning of time. . . . And with what reverence he held up the beautiful seed which he was to sow on his own ground. The plump kernels appeared to glow with some inner golden light as the warm rays of the sun struck full across them, and they seemed to be squirming in the hand that grasped them as if they were charged with a life, suddenly roused from slumber, that was seeking release there.

Every seed is a miracle. It should be handled as Per Hansa handled the wheat seed, with reverence.

This is tragically true of a person who sows with a niggardly financial "let go." He who sows the seeds in his pocketbook, be there many or few, will reap a scrimpy harvest. A true picture of the life reduced to a firm clutch on the coins is that lava-encrusted body taken from the ruins of Pompeii, a man holding grimly to a bag of coins. He had a firm grasp of the coins, and was dead. So the spirit becomes petrified when life is lived sparingly. A warped idea of life results. An extreme picture of that, but sadly true, was given in a recent cartoon showing two men in a London club about one hundred years ago. One had a book in his hand and explained, "It's a new story by that Dickens fellow—about a worthy banker named Scrooge, who finally degenerates into a sentimental weakling." The milk of human kindness was frozen solid.

A sparing harvest is yielded to those who give sparingly of themselves. There are many people who, in their personal relations, have all the fine warmth of a cigar store Indian, or of one of Madame Tussaud's waxworks. Perversely, you want to stick them with a pin to see if they will bleed or even jump. Harriet Beecher Stowe once wrote that she had been out at a party where everyone seemed to have left himself at home. That often happens. Such people have cast no bread upon the waters. The tide brings nothing back. As Emerson writes in his Journal, some people preserve themselves, hoarding their outgo of personality for some better occasion or more fitting place. He asks, where or when?

When we spend the emotions sparingly, we get in return a crop of life's enrichments and joys, like the yield of a garden in the Sahara desert. John Stuart Mill's father, James Mill, trained his boy on a stiff program of emotional scrimping. He said, "The youthful brain should not be cluttered with emotions. That should be prevented. Nor should the brain be cluttered with dramas, or recreations. It should be tied down to the strict development of the faculties."

How carefully James Mill kept his son's mind from being "cluttered" with the emotions of poetry is seen in his definitions. "Prose," he wrote, "is where all the lines except the last, go on to the end. Poetry is when some of the lines fall short of it." Probably James Mill never had any feeling that there might be more to poetry than that. The contrast to emotional withholding is this: "Owe no man anything, except to love one another" (Rom. 13:8).

Abundant sowing brings a quantitative measurement of life, instead of any mere quantitative measure. This contrast is expressed beautifully in Psalm 4:7: "Thou hast put more joy in my heart than they have when their grain and wine abound."

In a cemetery in Scotland there is engraved on the tombstone of a man who died many years ago the words, "He died opulent." Just what was meant by that engimatic inscription is hard to tell. Perhaps it merely records the fact, rather irrelevant in the presence of eternity, that he died having a lot of money. The words may mean much more. When we live unsparingly, with an open hand and heart, we can not only die opulent but live opulently.

48. IN THE WORLD, BUT NOT OF IT

Though we live in the world we are not carrying on a worldly war.
2 COR. 10:3

Here is one of the great challenges to the Christian—to live *in* the world, and yet not be *of* it. It is remarkable how much of life depends on the right use of prepositions! Some people fall on one side of this alternative, and some on another. Some people, often very pious people, do not really live *in* the world. They get a balcony view of life, something they see remotely, looking down. For one thing, some people have little or no awareness of beauty. They are disciples of Him who said, "Consider the lilies." But they do not deign to consider men lilies or anything equally unimportant. They are not in that world, and they are not *in* the world of evil and suffering. We see many statues of saints carved with blind eyes. There are too many blind saints! Jesus was *in* the world of need. On his approach to Jerusalem, with all the issues of his life before him, he could hear the roadside plea of blind Bartimaeus, "Jesus, Son of David, have mercy on me!" (Mark 10:47). Catherine Fry and John Howard actually lived in England with its cruel and murderous prisons. Jane Addams lived in the world around Hull House in Chicago. Walter

Rauschenbusch lived in the world of Hell's Kitchen on the West Side of New York. It is not an easy trick, but it can be done by God's grace.

We can be in the world but not *of* it, in that we do not fight an earthly war. We need not accept the goals of those who fight an earthly war, or adopt their methods. In England, the days of the queues have made necessary laws forbidding the misuse of elbows. That is a problem for the whole world, and much of our tragic woe has come from the misuse of elbows. In an earthly war, elbows are used for jabbing one another. In the Christian war, elbows are to be linked together in friendship.

A question comes down to us from the first century. The great struggle between Roman power and Christianity centered around the cult of the emperor, around the Caesars. When Christians refused to worship the image of the emperor, they faced the sword and flame. That is still a major battlefield of the struggle against the aggression of our day. Will the Christians bow down before the ultimate power in our society, a new emperor, finance?

Emerson met this problem, *in* but not *of* it, memorably. He wrote, "It is easy to live by the opinion of the world. It is easy in solitude to be self-centered. But the finished man is he who in the midst of a crowd keeps the perfect sweetness, the independence of solitude." By God's grace we can do it. Jesus prayed, "I do not pray that thou shouldst take them out of the world, but that thou shouldst keep them from the evil one. They are not of the world, even as I am not of the world (John 17:15-16).

49. WEAPONS OF OUR WARFARE

For the weapons of our warfare are not worldly but have divine power to destroy strongholds. 2 COR. 10:4

For more than eighteen centuries the reply to this claim, by the wielders of worldly weapons, has been, "That's what *you* think!" This is reflected in a sneer of Stalin, "How many divisions has the Pope?" To the confirmed militant, the Christian weapons, such as love, seem like pieces in an historical museum. They are, so some assume, curiosities in this world of electronics, intercontinental missiles, and atomic submarines.

Christ's weapons are *all* old-fashioned, as old-fashioned as humanity, as sin, as God. The temptation in our day is to try some new weapons.

on which to rely chiefly. The danger is that we shall discard the Word of God. For it is tragically clear that the mightiest weapons are only agencies for destroying our world. If the world is to be saved, it will not be by any sort of military hardware, but by different weapons, by love, by the application of intelligent good will. The weapons of love, which are those of law, of brotherhood, are the only weapons which have power to save the world.

A French artist of the last century, Daumier, said, "One must be of one's time." Another artist answered that with a question, "What if one's time is wrong?" The ruling ideas of other times have been tragically wrong. The ruling ideas of this world, the ideas of billions and bombs, are abysmally wrong as far as preserving the world from the final bonfire is concerned.

At a recent anniversary of the birth of Alexander Graham Bell, the Telephone Company used large advertisements proclaiming that "he gave the world a new voice." True. And a tremendous achievement and gift to the world. But the world needs more than a new voice. The telephone gave Hitler a new voice. It provides a new voice to every distorted idea in the world. The world needs a new word, rather, an old word, with a contemporary accent and application, *love*. As Walter Millis has said:

Any society which pins its hope of survival upon its technical ability to massacre scores of millions of the enemy's innocent noncombatants, which is at the same time reckless of its responsibility for poisoning, in the name of self-defense, the atmosphere and food-bearing soil of the whole earth, has accepted a moral degradation which denies it any title to freedom within itself. It has accepted a brutalization of its foreign policy which must inevitably brutalize and poison its internal life as well. It has taken a position which necessarily undermines all its highest protestations on the world stage, and at the same time undermines— as did the slaughters at Hiroshima and Nagasaki—all its most deeply held beliefs.

50.   SUSPENSE STORY

We . . . take every thought captive to obey Christ.   2 COR. 10:5

This is the age of the suspense story. A large part of the television offering has been for the titillation of the nerves of the viewer. Will the horse thief escape the noose, or will the sleuth get his man, dead or alive? The very name conveys the suspense: "Trackdown," "Climax," and others aimed at the nerves. The early movies were essentially a chase of some kind; that heritage lives on.

The project pictured in Phillips' translation of this verse of Paul, taking "every thought captive to obey Christ," is an amazing "trackdown," a "fight to capture every thought." The size of the battle and chase is extensive, it is as big as all life, as big as the world. It is comparatively easy to make one affirmation of belief in Christ. It is a lifelong fight and pursuit to bring every thought under his obedience to give a truly Christian quality to all our actions, a truly Christian accent to all our speech.

In the first place, we have to fight to keep a Christian mind among all the influences about us which would weaken or change that Christian mind. In one of the remarkable prison stories to come out of World War II is that of a British naval officer who, while in a Japanese prison, made a desperate and winning fight to retain his mind. The emptiness of the days, the filth, the torture, all combined to break down his mind and his control of it. He took extreme and desperate measures:

> To avoid going crazy during the long torturous months in prison, Commander Smith tried to remember poems he had once memorized, and his adventures as a champion snake collector in Florida. He thought of books he had once read. It took him a week to think of the second line of "Bingen on the Rhine" and he recalled "War and Peace" with the assiduity of a critic deploring the trend in modern novels.

He literally dragged his mind for everything in it. He kept the mind active and alive. He saved it.

It is a similar desperate effort we need to keep a Christian mind against all the forces which can wear it down. The goal of a Christian's commitment is that the mind shall be one undivided country, that there should be one allegiance. That means suspense, fight, that we go after the thoughts which have not come under the obedience to Christ. A mind that has not been completely captured is often like Thomas Hardy's description of his own mind: "I have no philosophy —merely what I have often explained to be only a heap of confused impressions, like those of a bewildered child at a conjuring show."

For instance, what a long chase it was to capture for Christ the mind that approved slavery! Many pretentious books were written, showing that slavery was a distinctly Christian institution, the proof running all the way from Ham, the son of Noah, to Onesimus, the slave of Philemon, whom Paul sent back to his master. Poor Onesimus! He has had to carry a weight of argument that would crush a herd of elephants! It has been a long, long struggle, not yet at its end, to capture thoughts on labor for a Christian quality. A quaint picture of the problem and the distance we have come is seen in the life of Samuel J. Tilden, a highly regarded Christain, a candidate for President of the United States. He was a "soft touch" for beggars, very generous, but when one of the clerks in his law office asked for a week's vacation with pay, Tilden fired him on the spot. The mind had not captured the thought of justice. So, even today, there are those who, when greatly needed moves are made to curb the gross evils of some labor leaders and unions, seize the hue and cry and opportunity to break the power of *all* unions, no matter what social achievements they accomplish. The great need is to go out on the chase and capture every realm of life for the obedience to Christ. It was said of one man, "His reaction to an episode had behind it a reaction to the universe." A good model. Our reaction to any episode of life should have behind it the reaction to God's revelation in Christ. Thoughts are elusive things. Go out and capture them.

51.   RIGHT BEFORE YOUR EYES

Look at what is before your eyes.   2 COR. 10:7

There are things we are so apt to miss—the things right before our eyes. As Phillips translates it, even more accusingly, "Do look at things which stare you in the face!"

Paul, as usual, was not discussing a general proposition, but an immediate, concrete situation. This verse occurs in a section of the second epistle to the Corinthians, which is often regarded as a separate letter, sometimes called "the stern letter," in which he rebukes the group in the church who condoned immorality. But the warning against what stares us in the eyes has a much wider application.

It is profoundly true that the obvious often escapes our attention. We look at it with glazed eyes. G. K. Chesterton has capitalized on this trait of human nature in a convincing way. In one of his stories the criminal for whom everyone, including the police, is searching, escaped notice because he was *right before their eyes.* He was disguised as a postman, and of course no one noticed him.

This tragedy—for it is often tragic, missing the things right in front of us—spreads from the home to the far reaches of the world and its future. It is very common, alas, for a person to miss the joys of a home, the wonders of its fellowship, as completely as if it were a picture on the wall which a householder never sees. He—it is usually he—takes it all for granted. One man has written vividly of the things that make up the joys of leisure and which can count so much in life, and yet we miss them so constantly: "The time with the family, the walk before breakfast, the use of our hands, the limbering of our minds, the making of love, the mystery of music, the plastic arts, past and present, the endless realm of reading, fishing in the spring, laughter, the religious experience, the sea from the ship, really looked at." We should pray for anointed eyes. Samuel Johnson remarked truly that there are men who see more in a coach to Hampstead, than others do on a grand tour of Europe.

In Frances Ridley Havergal's hymn, "Take My Life, and Let It Be," there is listed the offering for the Lord's use: hands, feet, the lips, the intellect, practically everything except one's eyes. All gifts to God without the gifts of eyes that see are impaired. We should pray that 'the eyes of the heart" be opened.

In the civil life one question in our minds and on our lips must be "What goes on here?" We are prone to let it pass because it is too much trouble to ask it. But in doing so we often allow festering evil to grow. General James Oglethorpe asked it about the English prisons of the Eighteenth Century. Few people paid any attention to it. In 1729 he asked it thunderingly about the horrors of the Fleet Debtor's Prison where jailers tormented debtors to death. Lillian Wald asked it about the lower East Side. Good words to learn—not only "Thy kingdom come," but its corollary, "What goes on here?"

It is true also in the wide world of our international affairs. Many have not really seen the atomic bomb and all its improvements. It stares us in the eyes as an instrument of world destruction. Yet we do not really see it to the extent of making changes necessary to live *with* it, instead of dying *by* it. Bertrand Russell asks an extreme question, probably in order to try, at least, to stab us broad awake. He asks whether we would prefer to live under a tyranny or have our whole world burned to an ash heap!

The trouble is, as Conan Doyle writes through the words of his sharp-seeing hero, Sherlock Holmes. "We see but we do not observe." God needs observers. Life is not a game of blindman's buff.

More than carelessness is the evil of seeing without imagination. That is a real meaning of the New Testament phrase, "the eyes of your heart" (Eph. 1:18). We have a common expression, frequently used as an exclamation, "Imagine that!" It often means nothing but "For goodness' sake!" But take it seriously, "Do imagine what you see." That will mean eyes plus mind and heart, and that in life is the winning combination.

We need the eyes of the heart in personal relations at home, where we are most prone to look without seeing. Henry van Dyke asks, "Are you willing to stoop down and consider the needs of little children; to remember the weakness and loneliness of people who are growing old?" There is also the imagination which sharpens eyesight in large affairs. An English short-story writer, William Sansom, when asked to give his recreation for the British *Who's Who,* put down simply, "Watching." It's a great recreation—none better, if we really watch what is in front of us.

52. HOW TO MEASURE YOURSELF

They measure themselves by one another, and compare themselves with one another. 2 COR. 10:12

This description by Paul of some of the church members at Corinth is rather frighteningly timely to us today. Indeed, it is contemporary in any age. It is notable for two reasons, among others. One reason is that it is one of the commonest habits to fall into, and most persons take a stumble and fall into it. The other reason is that it is one of the most destructive habits that fasten upon one. It brings the blight and mildew of self-satisfaction upon one. A person goes into the comforting dialogue with himself, "Well, I guess I'm doing pretty well. I'm just as good as others and a lot better than some." Then follows a pat on the back. Phillips translates it, "Comparisons within their own circle."

Many people have no absolute standard of measurement for their lives. All of us tend to ease the strain of moral and spiritual effort by measuring ourselves against an easy comparison. It is hard to bring a high standard, one which is inflexible and does not condone our weakness or laziness. What every life needs is a yardstick, one which has an unchangeable measure; a yard is thirty-six inches, not twenty-two or even thirty-two."

It is always easy to find someone near us, against whom we show up pretty well. That is undoubtedly the psychological reason why some of us choose certain people for associates. It is a comfort to have someone beside whom we tower. A little girl was once found by her mother dissolved in tears because a Polish family in the neighborhood had moved away. The mother said in surprise, "Why, I didn't know you cared so much for those children." The child explained, "Now there is nobody that I am better than." We are not so frank, but many of us feel the same way!

One great service which Jesus Christ does for the race is to furnish a true standard of measurement. For, as Phillips translates, measurement by one another "doesn't make for accurate estimation, you may be sure." Here is the true standard for us to measure by. "Until we all attain . . . to mature manhood, to the measure of the stature of the fullness of Christ" (Eph. 4:13). We should measure our smallness against his greatness, our selfishness against his love, our faithlessness against his doing the will of his Father.

53.   WRITING OUR OWN TESTIMONIALS

Those who write their own testimonials.   2 COR. 10:12 (Phillips)
Not that we venture to class or compare ourselves with some of those who commend themselves.

A young girl in England was applying for a position as a housemaid. She showed her recommendations to her prospective employer. After reading them, the woman said to the applicant, "You certainly have some fine recommendations here." The girl replied, much pleased, "I am glad you like them. I wrote them myself."

She may have been a relative of ours. Surely she showed the family traits which most of us possess. We are good at commending ourselves. Sometimes, it is a mild sort of unconscious commending ourselves. Such was the case of a Hollywood actor who confided to some friends. He said, "I used to be quite conceited. But my analyst cured me of that, and now I am one of the nicest guys in town." We can readily commend ourselves as one of the nicest people in town!

Paul was rebuking his enemies in the Corinthian church for extolling themselves. We all need salvation from self-commendation which comes from Christian humility. History has not been kind to those who commend themselves. A few verses further on, Paul declares that the person who commends himself is not accepted by the Lord (2 Cor. 10:18). But the man who writes his own testimonials is not accepted by history, either. The author of the life of one of the greatest braggarts of his time, or any time, the great George Villiers, Duke of Buckingham, chemist, fiddler, statesman, and buffoon, notes that the Duke of Buckingham has "shrunk to a footnote." Those who swell in the head have a way of shrinking to a footnote. Without the saving grace of humility, we are in danger of complacency. That is fatal to the spirit. It is dangerous to the soul as it has proved to be dangerous to a society and nation. Indeed, the historian of Rome, Samuel Dill, claims that the decline of the Roman

Empire was due to complacency. He writes, "The decline of the Roman Empire was due, not to the disruptive influence of Christianity, not to sheer moral weakness, but to an intellectual complacency that froze the life blood." That is a phrase to remember. Do not let complacency "freeze" the life blood of your soul. That is something to pray about!

We should commend ourselves, but by our actions, not by our words about ourselves. Timothy is urged, "Do your best to present yourself to God as one approved, a workman who has no need to be ashamed" (2 Tim. 2:15). In other words, commend yourself as a *workman!* Jesus made clear the only kind of commendation which counts with God, that of commending by deed. "Not every one who says to me, 'Lord, Lord,' shall enter the kingdom of heaven, but he who does the will of my Father who is in heaven" (Matt. 7:21).

54.   DO BEAR WITH ME

Do bear with me!   2 COR. 11:1
I wish you could put up with a little of my foolishness—please try!
(Phillips)

This is not a plea we make very often—"Do bear with me!" Yet it is a prayer that fits every day. Paul is asking humbly of his critics and enemies in the church at Corinth to put up with what he called his foolishness. That amounted to his denunciation of evil running wild, and his unyielding claim to be an apostle by the call of God. Paul was genuinely humble as far as his own gifts and powers were concerned. He was as uncompromising as granite in his conviction of the word of God and the service of Christ.

Two remembrances come from these words, which originated in a church split but which apply to all time and to all people. One is the need of a continuous sense of how much people have had to bear with us. We could well use the words of the communion service, "The rememberance of them is grievous unto us." Just review our lives, not only the sins we commit so readily, but the times when we shone with a bright light and said, with little Jack Horner, "What a good boy am I!" But think of all the other times when even our dearest friends have had to put up with us patiently. Most of what we do seems exactly right to us. We need a good deal of self-confidence to keep going. But most of us have too much blessed forgetfulness of our stupidities, our blindness, our blind cruelties. Make a list sometime, for the good of your soul, of quotations, not of the world's wisdom but of your own stupidities, things about which later you feel that you had better have cut your tongue out. Edward Rowland Sill's poem *"The Fool's Prayer"* was written for all of us:

> O Lord,
> Be merciful to me, a fool!
> . . . .
> These clumsy feet, still in the mire,
>   Go crushing blossoms without end;
> These hard, well-meaning hands we thrust
>   Among the heart-strings of a friend.
>
> The ill-timed truth we might have kept—
>   Who knows how sharp it pierced and stung?
> The word we had not sense to say—
>   Who knows how grandly it had rung?

That remark which seemed so bright at the time, but which cut so painfully, the times when we sacrificed truth to an epigram, the time when we preferred an epithet about another person, instead of any understanding kindness—these are the things to remember.

Second, some unblinking self-knowledge will help to make us more generous in our judgment of others. Often the things which we criticize most savagely in others are the very things which are our own faults. The man who has never said, "God, be merciful to me, a sinner," becomes hard and inflexible to others who need mercy. And the man who has never said, "God, be merciful to me, a fool," is most likely to need to say, "Do bear with me!" The crowning word on this is, "Forgive us our trespasses, as we forgive those who trespass against us."

55. ACCEPTING ANOTHER GOSPEL

For if some one comes and preaches another Jesus than the one we preached, or if you receive a different spirit from the one you received, or if you accept a different gospel from the one you accepted, you submit to it readily enough.   2 COR. 11:4

Apparently you cheerfully accept a man who comes to you preaching a different Jesus. (Phillips)

This happened in Corinth, and it has also happened in New York, in Rome, in Melbourne, and in Cornfield Corners everywhere. The old charge can be made over and over again, "You have accepted another gospel and a different Jesus from the one Paul told you about."

How easily and frequently a multitude have been persuaded to take another Christ than the Christ of the gospels. Paul refers sarcastically to the preachers of some different Jesus and different gospel as "superlative aspostles." These "extraspecial messengers," as Phillips translates their title, have been peddling their wares ever since some of them reached Corinth. Since somewhere about A.D. 60, over and over, it has been necessary to say to these peddlers of new gospels what was said of Alexander Pope's translation of Homer, "A very pretty poem, Mr. Pope, but it is not Homer."

There has been in other years, and today, great popular acceptance for an "easy Christ." Many self-appointed evangelists and also many regularly ordained ministers have, in their preaching of the gospel, played the part of the wicked steward in Jesus' parable, who "preached" a very easy gospel. "He said to the first [debtor], 'How much do you owe my master?' He said, 'A hundred measures of oil.' And he said to him, 'Take your bill, and sit down quickly and write fifty' " (Luke 16:5-6). In like manner, some dividers of the word divide it viciously. They reduce it more than half. They often say, "How much owest thou unto my Lord? And the True answer is, "Undivided allegiance. 'Enter ye in at the strait gate.' Take up his cross and follow me." And the divider will say, "That is old-fashioned. Just relax and cut that amount in half. I offer you an easy Christ." Some people, according to this different gospel, sing an old song:

> His yoke is easy,
> His burden is light,
> I've found it so.

Now, those old words have had a profound meaning. They are, of course, the words of Jesus, "My yoke is easy, and my burden is light" (Matt. 11:30). But the words are so often taken superficially. They describe a "different Jesus" from the one we meet in the gospels.

Many people have accepted a legalized Christ. Their Christ is one who has adopted all the legalisms against which he fought all his life. Or they have accepted a towering theological structure hanging in the sky without any foundation in fact, without any visible means of support in actual history, as belonging to mere tradition and old wives' tales. Then there is always the seductive talk of those who pretend to have a private line to the Almighty, the holy roller sects, the fraudulent healers. There are others, alas, who have rejoiced to accept, at the hand of rabble rousers, a Christ of racial hatred and conflict, yet he is the Christ in whom there is neither Greek nor Jew, but all are one in him. We are all in danger of accepting a *diluted Jesus*. Many can readily accept a Christ who proposes some less complete action in the present situation than love. They do not accept the complete Jesus, for the present day, presented in the line of W. H. Auden, "We must love each other or die!"

That, truly, is our only alternative.

56. THE MASQUERADE BALL

Even Satan disguises himself as an angel of light. 2 COR. 11:14
How Satan himself masquerades. (Phillips)

All through history, the great Masquerade Ball has been going on— Satan, or Evil, disguised as an angel of light. It began with the dawn of mind in man. The spiritual geniuses who tell the story in the third chapter of Genesis put this masquerade which deludes men and women at the very dawn of time. The soft-spoken serpent tricks Eve into accepting him as a bringer of light, Evil's most dazzling costume. It is a crowning symbol of the deceitfulness of sin. "I will enlighten you. You shall be as gods."

In all these disguises no glimpse is ever given of the tragic hour of unmasking, like midnight for Cinderella, when all the horses change into mice and the gilded coach becomes a pumpkin. Every promissory note of evil falls due and light turns into darkness.

This masquerade of Satan deceives our *faith and conviction*. It claims to bring us out of the darkness of our old faith into new light. It argues to us that, having become a man, we should put away childish things such as faith in God.

The disguise of Evil comes to our *ideas of conduct*. Satan promises to be our guide into an age of enlightenment, throwing over the rigid control of appetite and conduct. Evil says, "Leave the darkness of old narrow controls and step out into the light of freedom." It speaks persuading words *to ourselves*. It appeals to our ambition. It insinuates, 'Make a name for yourself. Be important."

One of the supreme figures of speech in the Bible is that of light. "God is light and in him is no darkness at all" (1 John 1:5). Against this masquerade, Christ is "the true light that enlightens every man" (John 1:9).

57.   THE TEST OF SERVICE

Are they servants of Christ? I am a better one.   2 COR. 11:23

Paul, all through this passage, admits that he is boasting. But his boasting is in the interests of truth and the puncturing of strutting pretension. It is striking to note that all the tests which he uses for allegiance to Christ are tests of service. The crowning proof is not race or descent, though he does not yield on these ratings, but the toil and endurances, the sacrifices, the actual services rendered his master. That is all that counts!

That list of services should hold our attention while we bow in deep humility. Today our place in the Christian discipleship is not marked by degrees, not by any laying on of hands, not by any position, though often a procession of ecclesiastics in gowns and hoods provokes the comment, "Solomon in all his glory was not arrayed like one of these" (Matt. 7:29).

Paul's credentials are all those of service. So it must be with any disciple. And what a list follows! It begins, "Far greater labors, far more imprisonments, with countless beatings." And he goes on in verses 11:23-28. Surely the most moving autobiography ever condensed into a few words!

The question confronts us, What would be our list of services? No lashes, of course, or imprisonments, but could we name anything comparable to them, or service to be justly named sacrificial? Our idea of Christian rating has been violently corrupted by confusion about what counts with God. Let Paul put us straight. One phrase which deserves complete retirement is "Prince of the Church." Harvard University, at its 1959 commencement, gave an honorary degree to a Catholic archbishop. But the citation insisted on calling him a "Prince of the Church." Why not give him the much higher honor, "a servant of his master, Christ?" What a contradiction—a "prince" following in the company of One who had not where to lay his head, and who left as his entire material legacy to the world one robe! One shudders at the old-fashioned phrase, "princes of the pulpit," now fortunately discarded into the wastebasket. For the "prince" conception may be so corrupting that discipleship comes to resemble that of Pilate, of all people. At least he expressed admiration. He said plainly, "I find no fault in this man" (Luke 23:4, AV). But he would not lift a finger to serve him in any way.

Again the insistent question, What is your list of services?

58. DANGER IN THE CITY

I have been in danger in the city. 2 COR. 11:26

Paul's list of dangers, familiar to us as perils in the Authorized Version, make a suggestive and formidable list of the hazards of life. They were very real dangers to Paul. To read the list with an active imagination makes the blood run cold. No wonder Paul could exclaim, after going through some of them, "Here we are alive!" They were real perils, from the Jews who fought the Christian evangel, from Paul's implacable enemies, riots, beatings, dangers from both bandits and pirates. Not only was Paul one of the finest minds ever loosed on earth, but he was also one of the toughest men who ever went through an almost incredible endurance race. The drama of his life would make some of the popular "westerns" look and sound like an afternoon tea of the women's garden club.

He speaks of "danger in the city." This we can understand, for the danger of the city comes close to our time and situation. So many of us live and move and have what being we can manage in cities. Our city life presents very real dangers to the life of the spirit. This does not mean, of course, that cities have been entirely antagonistic to the growth of Christianity. Some of the greatest seed plots of Christianity have been, and are today, in great cities. We have only to think of Rome, Geneva, London, Edinburgh, Boston. Nor is the old adage at all true,

> God made the country
> And the man made the town.

Both God and the devil are found in rural lanes as well as in city streets. Yet there is need for strong fortification of spirit, and what the Scots have called "bonny fighting," to carry on a vigorous and triumphant Christian life in cities. John Newton, the clergyman and hymn writer of Olney, England, has a good phrase for this need. When he moved to London from his village in the north of England, he made a fervent prayer for "London grace." He explained that by "London grace" he meant grace in a very high degree, "grace to enable one to live as a Christian even in London." We need a kind of "New York grace," or "Chicago grace," or "Denver grace," to live as a Christian where all the tides of every sort are running. That would be grace in a very high degree, would it not? "Grace abounding," to use John Bunyan's phrase.

Among the dangers in the city in our day is the intensified pressure to conformity. Many people in our cities look and act as though they had been stamped by a giant biscuit cutter, making them all the same shape and size. There is need for a thundering echo of the old plea, fitted to the city, "Come out from them, and be separate" (2 COR. 6:17). Not for the sake of being different, but for the sake of keeping a Christian quality in our life. A recent book has told the sad story of Everyman Gary Gray, who forgot how to say "I." It is the familiar story of group pressures in job, housing, car ownership, and the uses of leisure, if any. A great many people are in that mournful state. It is interesting, and also disturbing, to note that a hearing clinic at Northwestern University has discovered by experiment that one of the very hard words to be heard is the word "No." That is a sort of sinister symbol of the sad truth that very often the word "No" is not heard at all from some people in the city. Many people seem to spend their lives "window shopping," and their great response is "I want that." In cities, individuality is pounded by agencies such as the newspaper, advertising, radio, television. They wield a mighty hammer. From the jungles of Africa, Dr. Schweitzer describes it:

The man of today is exposed to influences which are bent on robbing him of all confidence in his own thinking. He is called to surrender his spiritual independence by so much that he reads and hears. Parties and associations claim him for their own. Over and over convictions are forced upon him in the same way, by means of large electrical signs which flare in the streets of the city, and persuade him to buy shoe polish or soup.

J. B. Priestley makes the same observation on "mass living":

People in the mass are not only losing their independence, but are losing any desire to be independent, and active-minded, sharply differentiated individuals. They prefer a mass existence, mass standards, with which they feel more comfortable in their circles.

One risk of life in a city is that of losing the sense of personal value and significance. Feeling rises in a city of two million, or in a city such as New York or London with eight million, "What does one person count?" The effect of a great crowd is that the individual seems lost. A woman looking down from the top of the Empire State Building, and seeing people on the street below, said, "I guess that is the way people look to God." The gospel declares, that is *not* the way people look to God. Here is the way people look to God: "If a man has a hundred sheep, and one of them has gone astray, does

he not leave the ninety-nine on the hills and go in search of the one
that went astray?" (Matt. 18:12).

Another danger of living in the mass of cities is that of losing the
sense of personal relationship with people. There is a deadly sense
of the anonymous in cities. In the city we are protected from having
our feelings lacerated with sympathy and concern because we do
not know the people concerned. We do not have such vulnerable
hearts. When a person dies on the next floor of the apartment, only
a few feet away, as a rule we do not know the family. The sorrow is
anonymous. If the milkman falls down and breaks his hip, we do not
know him, at least not well, and the most we can summon is an
exclamation, "Tough break!" But in the country or small town we
would know him, for he lives down the road. Our nerves are exposed
painfully.

A task for everyone is to keep alive the sense of life in personal
terms. There is a "London grace," a grace for city living. "My grace
is sufficient for thee" (2 Cor. 12:9, AV).

59.   THE WILDERNESS ROAD

Danger in the wilderness.   2 COR. 11:26

This long sentence is one of the most vivid and impressive in the
New Testament. What a thrilling scenario for a technicolor movie!
It carries us back to pioneering days of Christianity in the Mediterranean world. It is a drama, not only of the life of Paul, but of
of the life of the Christian disciple of any time.

The present dangers of the Christian are not exact physical
duplicates of those which Paul went through. But the very words
are suggestive of parallel perils which the Christian disciple under-
goes.

The danger of the wilderness, in one sense, is that in wilderness
solitude man may miss the relationship for which he was created.
Henry Howard, the Australian preacher who was for some time in
his later years pastor of the Fifth Avenue Presbyterian Church, New
York, used to describe a single brick. This brick was badly
frustrated; made for relationship on six sides, it was nevertheless a
solitary brick, and bricks are not meant to be solitary. Dr. Howard
would have audiences in tears over the pitiful brick! Man is made
for relationships, and without them his life never has high meaning.

In a literal sense, a large number of Christians in the first three
centuries of the church tried the wilderness. Many men were so

afraid of the sins of the city and what they considered the dangers of life in families and groups, that they became hermits and lived a frugal and abnormal life in the desert. As Paul Hutchinson describes the cult,

Some earnest spirits thought that since Christians were still a despised minority of the pure in a pagan world, they were perforce living in an environment utterly hostile to their principles and practices. Why not get entirely away from a corrupt society the sins of which were—as sins often are—alternately revolting and tempting? The desert was safer for the soul than the city.

But they found that the desert was not safe. There were perils in the wilderness for the hermits who tried it. The hermits lost a large part of their human heritage. The solitude of the desert mangled the soul. They overlooked entirely the psychic health of Jesus, revealed in his prayer for his disciples, "I do not pray that thou shouldst take them out of the world, but that thou shouldst keep them from the evil one" (John 17:15).

But sometimes we are forced, by the very circumstances, to go through a wilderness, to survive in a place where no nourishment springs up. We seem to tramp on a wilderness road, and it is hard to keep going. The prayer fits us exactly:

> Guide me, O Thou great Jehovah
> Pilgrim through this barren land.

A danger of a wilderness march, through which we are forced to journey, is that its aridity is such that we may come to feel deserted by God. We may feel with the Ancient Mariner,

> So lonely 'twas, that God himself
> Scarce seeméd there to be.

The 73rd Psalm is the record of a trudge through a dark wilderness. But God is on the wilderness road and can be found in the desert. W. K. Clifford said somewhat jauntily back in the nineteenth century, "The great companion is dead." Multitudes find, in the twentieth century, "the great companion" alive. A different sort of a wilderness, one with great dangers, is the self-made desert. There is danger in the wilderness when a person lives in self-centered isolation from any relation of fellowship with people, and insists on tramping a desert road. Ties of helpful relationship have liabilities of demands on life, but they do not end up in a lonesome grave of the spirit. A life of brotherly burdens does have what Alan Parsons calls "radiant discomfort." Instead of danger in a wilderness of lonely aloofness, many people have this prayer answered:

> O Master, let me walk with thee
> In lowly paths of service free.

60. DANGER FROM MY OWN PEOPLE

[I have been in] danger from my own people. 2 COR. 11:26

Paul is referring, of course, to his own countrymen, the Jews. There was real danger from his own people which he met at practically every step of his life. In verse 24 of this chapter, he mentions that five times he had been given "forty lashes less one" by the Jews. All through his journeys over the Mediterranean world he met bitter opposition from his fellow Jews. These blows from his own people were the hardest to take.

In our day we do not face any such danger from our own people. These words of Paul sound like echoes of battles long ago. Yet, we all stand in danger from our own people. It is very different but very real. Two dangers in particular face us in our relation to family and near relatives. One is the danger of being enclosed by provincialism. It is the danger of shrinking the world to the dimensions of our own home. Our own people become the universe. Jesus met this danger in words that sometimes seem harsh and unloving. Jesus was told that his mother and brothers were waiting for him. They had really come to protect him, for there had been rumors that he was "beside himself" (Mark 3:21). But Jesus said, " 'Who is my mother, and who are my brothers?' And stretching out his hand toward his disciples, he said, 'Here are my mother and my brothers! For whoever does the will of my father in heaven is my brother, and sister, and mother' " (Matt. 12:48-50). The family of God was his family. He refused to be shut up in the enclosure of his immediate family.

We face the danger from our own people of being imprisoned by *possessive love*. We can be cuddled to death by our loved ones. It is terribly true, in that sense, that "a man's foes will be those of his own household" (Matt. 10:36). The precautions which love urges may be a dirge of the spirit, a death toll. We hear the seductive charms being wound, "Don't take any risks, dear. Play it safe. Don't forget your overshoes. Watch out for yourself!"

Danger from my own people!

61. WHAT IS YOUR LIST OF ENDURANCES?

I have been beaten times without number.   2 COR. 11:23-27 (Phillips)

Here is a thrilling passage—and it makes the mind tingle just to read it with lively imagination. Paul sets down his life, his toils and tribulations, his turmoils, his fightings, his costly sacrifies. Suppose that, following his example, we undertook to set down the credentials of our own discipleship as Paul here sets down his, what could we enter? Go over Paul's record of blood, sweat, and tears as translated by Phillips:

> I have worked harder than any of them. I have served more prison sentences! I have been beaten times without number. I have faced death again and again. I have been beaten by the regulation thirty-nine stripes by the Jews five times. I have been beaten with rods three times. I have been stoned once. I have been shipwrecked three times. I have been twenty-four hours in the open sea. In my travels I have been in constant danger from rivers and floods, from bandits, from my own countrymen, and from pagans. I have faced danger in city streets, danger in the desert, danger on the high seas, danger among false Christians. I have known exhaustion, pain, long vigils, hunger and thirst, doing without meals, cold and lack of clothing.

No wonder Paul could say with grateful amazement, "Here we are alive (2 Cor. 6:9, Phillips). What is our list of expenditures? Discipleship is an expenditure of life, of labor, of sacrifice. How would it seem if the most we have to write down is something like this: "Five times have I been to church in six months. Nearly every Sunday I have driven the children to Sunday School, before going to the golf club. I gave one hundred dollars in a year to the church and fifty dollars to the Community Chest"?

What is our list of the costs of discipleship?

62. A SAVING ANXIETY

And, apart from other things, there is the daily pressure upon me of my anxiety for all the churches.   2 COR. 11:28

This is an amazing statement which adds cubits to our measure of Paul's stature. It comes as a climax to his prodigious list of dangers.

He has just recorded one of the most remarkable summaries of the risks taken and dangers undergone that has ever been compiled. Lashings and stonings, robberies and shipwrecks, were only a few costs of his apostleship. Then on top of everything else, there was the continual pressure of anxiety for the churches that played on his mind like a trip hammer. He might have been excused for writing, "Then there was the pressure of anxiety for my own skin." But Paul never mentions his skin. That was not the most important thing about him; not a word of anxiety about himself but about the churches. It was a heavy anxiety, but it was a saving one, carrying him beyond his own bruises and sufferings.

We feel the cost of carrying the churches, in the head, on the heart, and in the hands. Paul's anxiety is well worth considering in the light of today, when anxiety is such a familiar state. Our time has been bapitized an "age of anxiety." But the word "anxiety" did not mean to Paul what it means to hosts of people today—the fraying of nerves, the wearing down of the spirit, the jerky, fidgety turmoil of the mind. It meant a deep concern for the welfare of the churches, an empathy, an outreach of mind which Phillips translates as "the daily burden of responsibility." He cries, "Who is weak, and I am not weak?" It was a costly but blessed identification.

In the Middle Ages, it was sometimes forbidden for a church to be erected and dedicated unless it had in it some "bones of the saints." Every church always needs, not bones, but what Paul here calls anxiety, the pressing business of a consuming concern for the welfare of the fellowship. Without it, a church becomes a thing of stone or broken lumber. Anxiety of that sort is the animating soul of a church.

It was no casual attention, no sparse gift of oneself, which we know so well, but the soul's expenditure which went into Paul's churches. That was an anxiety that saved a church.

It is a saving anxiety for everyone, an anxiety that carries us out of ourselves. We are, in our time, a prey to anxiety. But about what? About ourselves, about our skin, about our neck? Or is it an outgoing responsibility for others, a pressure of concern for something other and bigger than ourselves? We are truly measured by our anxieties.

63.   SOMEBODY MADE A GOOD ROPE

I was let down in a basket through a window in the wall, and escaped.
2 COR. 11:33

Paul has just finished giving a list of deadly perils which he met.
Here is another, a big one. He went over the walls of Damascus in a
basket. Put your imagination to work on that bit of history, biography,
and drama.

What if the rope had broken? How much it meant to the world,
then and for us, that Paul escaped! We are all familiar with the line
from Longfellow's poem on Paul Revere, "the fate of a nation was
riding that night." There was more than the fate of a nation riding
in the basket that carried Paul. There was the fate of so much of the
world's welfare. How crucially important it was that someone made
a good rope! Who the workman was we do not know. He did not
know at all what a part in the world's history his rope was to play.
We know this: he did a sound, dependable job! The picture of Paul
hanging from a rope at Damascus is a sharply etched picture of the
importance of doing a good job of workmanship. That is our first
responsibility, to turn out or to turn in a good job, no matter what the
job is, if it is worth doing at all. No amount of sentimental rhapsody
or mooning can ever make up for poor or sloppy work. The gospels
have many instances of Jesus' scorn for tawdry and careless workmanship—the foolish young women who wasted oil, a torn garment poorly
sewed, a builder who erected a house on the sands.

Every life ought to have the equivalent of this tribute, "He made a
good rope."

64.   SAVED FROM ELATION

*A thorn was given me in the flesh, a messenger of Satan, . . . to keep
me from being too elated.*   2 COR. 12:7

In this vale of tears, many of us would say that the danger of being
too elated is not an acute one. The danger so often seems to come from
the other direction. We need a messenger to save us from being too
despondent, sometimes too despairing. We do not have wings strong
enough to carry our load. We are well-grounded, heavily weighted.
There is no lift like that of an airplane leaving the ground.

Yet there is need for elation in life—the right kind of elation, not the kind which Paul refers to here, that of being too cocksure of himself. The elation that life needs is defined in one dictionary as "exaltation of spirit as from joy." That elation is pictured in the words, "that your joy may be full." That does not mean wearing a perpetual grin. It is not pleasure or even happiness in the superficial sense. It is a lift of spirit, a peculiar gift of Christian faith and experience. There is a glimpse of it in the remark of a woman watching a gorgeous sunset from a small village in India. She exclaimed with appreciation, "What a wonderful sunset, especially for such a little place!" So we can exclaim over the glorious light that comes into a life however ordinary and routine its setting, if the sun of God has been allowed to illuminate the life. The brightest illumination of life, its highest elation, is this: "Beloved, now are we the sons of God" (I John 3:2, AV). Charles Hartshorne thus describes the elation: "To say that Jesus was God, then, ought to mean that God himself is one with us, that divine love is not essentially benevolence,—external well-wishing—but sympathy, taking into itself our very grief."

But Paul means another kind of elation, on an infinitely lower level and from another source. Phillips translates elation from which Paul was saved as being "conceited." Moffatt translates it "puffed up," a tragedy from which most of us need saving desperately. We have that kind of elation when we are puffed up like a pouter pigeon. The word "saved" is used with precise meaning, for, in such puffed-up conceit, in such an attack of self-satisfaction, the fine possibility of a soul is truly lost. We do not explore here the mystery of Paul's affliction. There are many medical and psychological diagnoses. But we have Paul's word that his thorn kept him in touch with reality, brought a saving humility, brought a new dependence on God. It can happen in any life. So, "welcome such rebuff, that turns earth's smoothness rough."

65. CONTENT WITH INSULTS

For the sake of Christ, then, I am content with weakness, insults, hardship, persecutions, and calamaties.   2 COR. 12:10

Strange language! Content with insults! That sounds like an abject lying down and letting people walk all over a person. Strangely enough, that is exactly what it does mean; what is left out is the shining goal, "For the sake of Christ." But leave that out of Paul's life and what remained would be like the world with the sun left out of the sky. "For the sake of Christ," to be content with insults and hardship was not weakness but strength in the highest degree. It is the same strength from the same root as Paul's proud declaration, "in any and all circumstances I have learned the secret of facing plenty and hunger, abundance and want. I can do all things in him who strengths me" (Phil. 4:12-13).

A stirring example of a man who, for the sake of a great cause, was "content" with insults is Abraham Lincoln. Here are a few of the insults paid him by the opposition press—"ape, gorilla, fool, filthy storyteller, despot, liar, thief, braggart, buffoon, usurper, monster, tortoise, ignoramus." But the high goal, the saving of the Union, made him well content with all insults and hardship. For the sake of Christ, Paul could enjoy insults. With Paul's word in mind, think of the different meanings that can be put into that word "content"—one is shamefully selfish; the other is gloriously dedicated. Join two phrases together in the mind, phrases which use identical words, but with a difference in meaning that is almost measureless. One is a line from the hymn "Beneath the Cross of Jesus!" It is "Content to let the world go by." The other is a line from a popular song of a few years ago, "Let the rest of the world go by." The same words, but what utterly different meaning! In the popular song, written as a so-called love song, the words are the perfect expression of complete selfishness. They mean, "Just you and I get away somewhere, wrap ourselves up in a cocoon of our own affairs, and let the rest of the world go by."

But how different in attitude are the words of the hymn:

> Content to let the world go by,
> To know no gain nor loss,
> My sinful self my only shame,
> My glory all the cross.

The words mean, "We will not be disturbed by joining the feverish chase of the things of the world, money, comfort, or fame." All these we will be content to let go by because of the higher prize of the "excellency . . . of Christ Jesus" (Phil. 3:8 AV) and of being a part of God's love to a world in need.

Tremendous words, "I am content."

66. GETTING INTO THE PASSIVE VOICE

I will most gladly spend and be spent for your souls.   2 COR. 12:15

Here is a fine lesson in New Testament grammar, in the active and passive voice. Paul knew both. His life was a thrust of tremendous activity. He moved into difficulties with the energy of a battering ram. In a consuming ambition for Christ he cries, "I must also see Rome" (Acts 19:21). But in much of his life he was in the passive voice, not only acting but acted upon. In his famous list of perils, given in the preceding chapter, 2 Cor. 11:24-27, he is definitely and dangerously in the passive voice. He was "beaten with rods . . . stoned . . . shipwrecked." In that long list he was "being spent," acted upon.

Of course, the Christian life begins in the passive voice. We are redeemed, possessed. It was not that we loved Him, but we were loved by Him. We were called out of our darkness into His marvelous light. When there is no deep experience of the passive voice, life becomes thin. It is an affair of a person's own effort and activity. It does not have the passive voice of "I am persuaded" with its saving humility of being acted upon.

Yet life calls for the active voice. It is an affair of great verbs in the active voice—come, go, be, strive, give. The Christian life demands energy, what William James calls "a heave of the will." Henry James has given some sharp and often bitter pictures of people who seem to have no active voice, people who are devoted to nothing. Of one character, Mrs. St. George, he writes, "She looked as though she had put on her best clothes to go to church and then decided that they were too good for that, and stayed at home." Of another woman he writes, "She arched her neck in disdain like a cat whose nap by the fire had been interrupted." Not much active voice there! Jesus calls for the active—ask, seek, knock.

Jacques Barzun in his book *Teacher in America* comments on a teacher's life in active and passive voices:

Ours is a calling in which after effort we feel like the limp moist clothes which drop from a wringer at the side of a laundry tub. We know not only what it is to spend—which is not unpleasant when you initiate and control the outlay—but also to be spent when others take it out of you. But there is a satisfaction in both when one recalls the divine purpose for which we are being used up.

All true. But there is no question that the life of the disciple must know the passive voice as well as the active, "be spent" as well as spend. And there can be no question that to get into the passive voice is very often far more difficult than the active. To spend, we can drive right along; there is often the exhilaration of energetic activity. But then to be spent calls for first standing and taking things. There is no zest of active battle. We are acted upon by such "slings and arrows of outrageous fortune" as we are attacked by. That calls for restraint, endurance, patience, self-control. Look at this contrast as seen in the last week of Jesus' life. He had his achievements in the active voice. He drove the money-changers out of the temple. But the last hours of his life were in the passive voice. He was arrested, he was scourged, he was deserted. All the steps of the way up to "He was crucified."

There is no great achievement for others or for ourselves without being spent as well as spending. "He was wounded for our transgressions, . . . and with his stripes we are healed." (Isa. 53:5).

When life goes into the passive voice, when we are spent, welcome a healing and redeeming force of God.

67.   THE RISKS OF A CHURCH

I fear that perhaps I may come and find you not what I wish; . . . that perhaps there may be quarreling, jealousy, anger, selfishness, slander, gossip, conceit, and disorder.   2 COR. 12:20

Are these the risks of a church? It is a truly terrible list of calamities that may happen to a church. At any rate, they are the risks of the church at Corinth to which Paul is writing. (Incidentally, if any pastor gets downhearted about his church, he can at least remember that no matter what its condition, it is at least not so bad as the church Paul had to deal with at Corinth.)

Paul's fears of what he might find when he came again to the church at Corinth did not arise from any critical disparagement of the church. To Paul the church was a divine institution, the body of Christ, the church of the living God. To this very church he writes, "To the church of God which is at Corinth" (1 Cor. 1:2). That very high conception of the church made him feel all the more deeply the calamity of evils in the church such as he names—quarreling, jealousy, anger, and all the corruptions he mentions. How could a church spotted and honeycombed with such evils ever persuade a world to renounce them? The church should be the agency of life, the life of God in men's souls. If it has within it the seeds of death, it has lost its own life. J. L. Henderson contended that the world is biocentric, that is, it is centering about the production of life. So a church of Christ must be biocentric, centering about the production of the life that is life indeed.

Some sources of these evils in a church, which are evils lying in wait for any group or society of people, are easily seen.

One great source of infection was present among the first group of twelve disciples and has appeared ever since. It is the presence of the question "Who shall be greatest?" Whenever that question is raised, we can cry, "Mischief, thou art afoot." Mischief has been afoot again and again in churches, letting loose jealousy, anger, quarreling, gossip, and the whole deadly list that Paul gives. That particular devil cometh out only by prayer and fasting.

Slander and gossip are deadly poisons to the body of Christ. They are met when a church has lost its great commanding faith and devotion and goal, and hence drop down to the vicious level of personal conflicts. When the unity of the spirit is lost sight of, then the bond of peace is broken.

In like manner, a church becomes a prey to divisive and conflicting evils when it loses its horizon. When the far horizon of "Go ye into all the world" is lost in a cloud, a church can be imprisoned in its own provincialism. The church can become a small thing instead of a God-sized thing, with no dimension like the wideness of God's mercy, like the wideness of God's sea. Every few months we read of the claims of a church to be "the smallest church in the world." In January, 1959, newspapers described one of the latest entries for that dubious distinction, at Drumheller, Alberta, Canada, which seats six persons—too small even for the twelve disciples to worship there! A church at Warm Springs, Georgia, is a one-room family "kirk," eight by ten feet and sixteen feet high. But in the deeper sense of the church as a fellowship rather than a building, there are smaller churches than that. A church which does not recognize all men as sons of God, a church which does not know and live the truth that all are one in Christ Jesus, a "one class church" guarded by high fences of division of wealth and position or race, is too small to be a church of the living God.

Another cause of evils in the church is like that of the theater, where Shakespeare has often been crowded off the stage by the scenery. It becomes no longer true that "the play's the thing." The scenery is the thing and Hamlet or Romeo and Juliet come in a poor second to the eye-catching stage setting. So the stage setting of a church has often driven Christ off the stage, with the result that he is no longer the dominating factor in the church.

It calls for deep and dedicated fellowship around one living center, Christ, if any church is to keep out those things Paul feared he might find at Corinth.

68.   HOLDING TO THE FAITH

Examine yourselves, to see whether you are holding to your faith.
2 COR. 13:5
You should be looking at yourselves to make sure that you are really Christ's. (Phillips)

Do we really still deserve the name Christian? That is what Paul asks us to examine. A publisher once made the suggestion that every college graduate ought to be examined every five years to see if he still deserved his B.A. degree. That would be rough on the graduates, almost as bad as requiring members of a college faculty to pass the entrance examinations every few years!

Paul pleads here that we look at ourselves carefully to see whether we are still really Christ's, that he really rules in our lives. Without self-examination it is easy to assume complacently that we are holding to the faith. Lady Mary Wortley Montagu wrote to her daughter, "It is eleven years since I have seen my face or my figure in a glass. The last reflection I saw there was so disagreeable that I resolved to spare myself such mortification in the future." Alexander Pope noted later that the results of not looking in the mirror were definitely not good!

How long since we have really looked at ourselves to know if we are really Christ's? We have a commonly used, but very deceptive, phrase, "once and for all." In the Christian life there is no "once and for all." We can respond to Christ's invitation, "Come unto me," and grandly begin. But it is a matter of renewal. If we regard it as a "once-and-for-all" affair, we soon are not holding to the faith. The weather bureau has recently announced that it will give a new statistic, "the evaporation index." It records how much "free water" evaporates on any given day. This suggests that there can be, and frequently is, evaporation in our spiritual life. There are "showers of blessings." But they evaporate unless renewed. Remember Paul's companion, Demas, "having loved this present world" (2 Tim. 4:10, AV). William Graham Sumner, the Episcopal clergyman who became a professor at Yale, wrote that when he began his research in sociology he put his religious faith away in a drawer, and when he looked for it a few years later, there was nothing left. Evaporated!

It is always hard to know ourselves. A sharp and amusing statement of that was Schopenhauer's reply to the question, "Who are you?" He replied, "How I wish I knew!" When Tristram Shandy was asked the same question by a customs officer, he said pleadingly, "Don't confuse me."

It takes real humility to see ourselves, to measure ourselves by the stature of the man Christ Jesus. One reason why we may not hold to the faith is that the faith may be hazy, a sort of dim cloud effect instead of the God and Father of our Lord Jesus Christ! William Morris entitled a book *News from Nowhere*. That is what faith becomes to a number of people. It is just news from nowhere specifically. But Christian faith is founded on "news from *Somewhere!*"— good news to all people from the God who has revealed Himself. When faith is just belief in a fog, God becomes dim, much more dim than the things we see before us.

Another reason for losing hold on faith is the habit, today as in other days, of making faith too easy to be the real thing. Often it becomes an affair of words, of easy subscription to a collection of words, dimly understood. Often faith appears to be something one can pick up without any great price attached to it. Such was the idea of Cecil Rhodes. He was speaking of William Booth, the founder of the Salvation Army. On being asked one day whether he was happy, Rhodes answered, "Happy? Good God no! I would give all that I possess to believe what that old man believes." Rhodes was mistaken. He did not realize that William Booth's belief and faith was the achievement of a lifetime. Into it went years of sacrificial and dedicated living.

Faith is not something easy, to be snapped on or off. Faith is the acceptance of God's grace. It is the dedication of heart and mind and hand to His service. Hold on to that by the renewal of your mind.

The Epistle of Paul
to the Galatians

69. THE BOOK OF GRACE

Grace to you and peace from God the Father and our Lord Jesus Christ. GAL. 1:3

It is fitting that at the very heart of the Epistle to the Galatians is the word "grace." For truly this is the Book of Grace. Grace was the very foundation of Paul's thinking. It is the core of the Christian faith that we are saved by the free gift of God, unearned and undeserved. It is the unearned increment of our lives. Paul's thought and words in this letter free men from all efforts to earn their own salvation by their own doing, by acts, ceremonies, or obedience to laws.

The only way to please God is to throw oneself on the mercy of the court, to trust the free gift of God's love and to give up trying to build up a bank reserve of good acts. "By grace are [we] saved" (Eph. 2:8, AV). In no other epistle is this central theme stated and orchestrated as powerfully as in this one. What we do not deserve and do not earn, God gives freely—that is grace. The only way to God's favor is faith in that grace and acceptance of it. The whole song of the Christian life is full of grace notes. Grace notes sing of God's forgiving love in Jesus Christ.

No wonder Martin Luther loved this epistle and lived in it. It was a mighty fortress of his faith, a bulwark never failing. It was the foundation of the Reformation, the central core of Christian faith, an Emancipation Proclamation of God's free gift. It brought to the Galatians who first received it, who were being pushed back to servitude to laws and ceremonies, to the restrictions of obedience to traditional laws, the declaration of faith in God's forgiving love in Christ. This could strike the shackles of such slavery from all men. There is a warmth and urgency about this letter felt all the way through. To miss it would be like standing on the seashore and miss seeing the ocean.

We are not in any danger today of being persuaded back into the bonds of the Jewish legalism of Paul's time. That has gone into history. But we are in very real danger of losing our sense of the magnitude of God's grace, of minimizing it, and of putting it into

a second place in our thinking and living. "Grace" is likely to become just a word, a familiar word in the benediction, "The grace
of our Lord Jesus Christ," but not meaning much except that the
service is over. The free gift of God's forgiving love must be continually illuminated as the light of our life. We tend to trust in
something else, our own achievements in goodness, what we have
done. A caricature of that feeling is the remark of a man in the
eighteenth century about a prominent rake who had died: "God
will think twice before damning a man of his quality." We would
not feel or say anything so crude, but we do at times have a vague
feeling that our quality has earned God's favor. We are likely to
rest our faith on our own obedience to law, on our own doings.

Remember the grace wherein we stand. We stand in that grace
or we do not stand at all.

> *Were the whole realm of nature mine*
> *That were a present far too small.*

In the communion service in the *Book of Common Prayer,* there
is a prayer of humble access. That is our fitting response, humble
access to the grace of God.

70. THIS PRESENT EVIL AGE

*Our Lord Jesus Christ who gave himself for our sins to deliver us from the
present evil age.* GAL. 1:4

"The present evil age" was a familiar phrase to Paul. No matter
how suggestive we find the words as descriptive of our own time as
evil, as well as good, we should never overlook or forget what the
words meant to Paul. To Paul, "the present age," "the present world
order" as Phillips translates it, was "evil". The Christians of Paul's
time expected a speedy end of this present age. They hoped for a
second coming of Christ. Paul's letter to the Galatians is a proclamation of freedom not only for the individual from bondage to legalisms
and tradition, but also for the present evil age into the Kingdom
of God. In Christ men were to be made fit for a new age, for
"there's a great day coming" (cf. Mal. 4:5, AV).

With the meaning of the words to Paul kept firmly in mind, let
us remember that the words, first, have the same meaning for us.
We do not have the same expectation of a literal second coming, but
our faith is in a redeemed age, that "the kingdom of the world
[shall] become the kingdom of our Lord and of his Christ, and he

shall reign for ever and ever" (Rev. 11:15). We are lifted up by the faith in the redemption of an evil world order into the Kingdom of God.

Beyond that primary meaning, the words suggest a present-day meaning: that we may have the eyes of our heart enlightened in order to see the extent and the particulars in which our age is evil. We need a Christian criticism of our time.

We stand confronting two dangers. There is the danger of despising our age too much. That is an easy and an evil blunder. We read in Proverbs that "the eyes of a fool are in the ends of the earth" (17:24, AV). The eyes of a fool are also in the ends of the calendar, when he finds other ages better than this one, and harps eternally on this evil age. We must not be blind to the assets of this age and to its possibilities of becoming a Kingdom of our God.

The other blunder is at the other end of the scale. It is the danger of having too little perception of the evils of our present time and culture. We cannot be redeeming agents in our time unless we clearly see what is the matter with it, measured on God's scale. One striking instance of such "holy blindness" is found in a letter of Julia Ward Howe written in 1909: "Don't you think that the best things are clearly in view, the opportunities for women, the growing toleration and sympathy in religion, the sacred cause of peace? I have lived like Moses to see the entrance of the Promised Land!" Julia Ward Howe Moses on Mount Nebo! The Promised Land, just five years before there burst on the world the most evil holocaust it had ever known, the first World War! We risk the same danger of failing to see vividly the threat to world survival in our time. That is the colossal evil of our time, yet, while admitting the danger, the attitude of far too many is "business as usual." Henry Adams made a prophecy of doom away back in 1902 in words that still hang over us. He wrote to his brother Brooks Adams,

I apprehend for the next hundred years an ultimate, colossal cosmic collapse, but not on any of our old lines. My belief is that science will wreck us, and that we are like monkeys monkeying with a loaded shell. We don't in the least know or care where our practically infinite energies come from or will bring us to.

One wide-spreading evil of this age is our concentration on material progress and possession. There is a consequent lack of spiritual and moral understanding and interest. Years ago, William James called this scramble for material things "the great American frenzy." We live in the midst of plenty of frenzied finance and frenzied accumulation. Margaret Halsey puts the evil age in this indictment:

There are other business societies, England, Holland, Belgium and France, for instance. But ours is the only culture now extant in which business so competely dominates the national scene that sports, death, philanthropy, and Easter Sunday are money-making propositions.

We come back to Paul's words. This evil age must be redeemed and brought into a Kingdom of God. In his Gifford Lectures, 1953, Arnold Toynbee uses the very words, "redeemed from sin." He thus makes a prayer for redemption:

Today the time has come for us to follow this seventeenth-century example of jumping clear in our turn from the mathematical-physical standpoint that has armed mankind with deadly weapons without having redeemed it from Original Sin. We need once again to make a new start—and this time by returning to the spiritual outlook that was abandoned in the seventeenth century. But in doing this we must take care not to repeat our seventeenth-century ancestors' mistake. They threw away religion itself in their anxiety to get rid of the evils of religious strife and warfare. In now seeking to retrieve the religion they discarded, we do not have to throw away the technological and scientific achievements of the last quarter of a millennium. We merely need to realize that technology is not either a cure for sin or a key to the mystery of the universe.

71. TURNING TO A DIFFERENT GOSPEL

I am astonished that you are so quickly deserting him who called you in the grace of Christ and turning to a different gospel. GAL. 1:6

This is both a story of long, long ago and one as new as today's sunrise. Some of the Christians in Galatia to whom Paul is writing have proved to be quick deserters from the freedom into which they have been led by the faith in Christ, and they have turned to a very different, contrary gospel, "that of supplementing the grace of God by law, by slavish devotion to Jewish legalism." They were exchanging freedom in Christ for the old jail in which they had been confined. Jesus, quoting from Isaiah, had declared, "He has sent me to proclaim release to the captives" (Luke 4:18). He released the captives from Jewish laws, but some were deserting the one who released them to freedom and were going back to prison.

Today also there is much "transfer of allegiance." There are competitive and contrary "gospels" which turn people away from the Gospel of Christ. In our day, of course, the contrary religion is not a relapse into Judaism. It is not Mohammedanism or Buddhism. It is rather an "adjusted gospel," adjusted to a way of life much easier, and often more fashionable, for men love to be "in fashion." The blessed word in many circles today is the word "adjustment." In some places it is the supreme aim of education not to teach the child to think but to get him "adjusted" to his surroundings. The religious adjustment is so often a downward one—a degrading of the Gospel of Christ.

In a comment earlier on Galatians 1:3, this epistle was called the core of the Christian faith. We can parallel the words of the American Declaration: "We hold this truth to be self-evident; that man is and of a right ought to be free, freed by God's grace in Jesus Christ, freed from sin and freed from legalistic compulsions." That declaration needs to be made strongly today. There are so many popular ways of quickly or gradually deserting to a gospel diluted to fit the world's taste.

The gospel is often adjusted to mammon. To the forthright declaration of Jesus, "You cannot serve God and mammon" (Matt. 7:24), the answer of many could be put into words like this: "Oh, let's not be fanatical." (Fanatical is very often the word used to describe an undivided allegiance to Christ.) We can make the best of both words in this world and the world to come by a judicious mixture of mammon and God. Lord Chesterfield in his letters gave some advice of a sophisticated worldling: "Learn to shrink yourself to the size of the company you are in." Too many people make that advice to apply to the gospel. They shrink it to the size of the company they are in. In the hands of worshipers in the temple of mammon, the gospel gets to be a terribly shrunken thing. It is, as Paul calls it, a "different" gospel, very different.

Another contrary gospel is that which is adjusted to ease. The word to Timothy, "Take your share of suffering as a good soldier of Jesus Christ" (2 Tim. 2:3), is changed and softened into the familiar advice, "Take it easy." Many do take it very easy, with the hard commands of Christ put into an easier form.

The call, "Take up [your] cross and follow me" (Mark 8:34), becomes strangely transformed into something more attractive. "Pull up your upholstered chair and sit in it." Into "a different gospel"!

72. MAY HE BE DAMNED!

If I, or an angel from Heaven, were to preach to you any other gospel than the one you have heard, may he be damned! GAL. 1:8 (Phillips)
God's curse be on him! (Moffatt)

These are terrible words, and a terrible curse. The word "damned" means substantially the same as the word "accursed," which is found in the Revised Standard Version and King James Version. But there is more of an air of profanity about them. They are by no means profanity. They form a strong expression of the enormous wickedness of teaching a different gospel, a contrary substitute for the true Gospel of Christ.

Teaching a different gospel is quite literally a damnable business. In music there are many compositions which are variations, often very skillfully done, on other themes or compositions. There is a very well-known composition, "Variations on a Theme," by Haydn. There is a notable one by Weinberger entitled "Variations and Fugue on Under a Chestnut Tree." There are many variations on a theme by Jesus, variations of his gospel. They are often so varied that from them one could not tell what the original melody was. In Christian history there have been monstrous variations such as the Spanish Inquisition, for instance, variations in which the thumbscrew and the rack, the executioner's block, and the stake and faggots had a place. They were agonizing variations in which the original was totally lost. War has been a ghastly variation of the gospel, a perversion of the Gospel of Christ.

But we do not need to go back into history or to the ends of the earth in our search for variations of the gospel theme. We have them all around us. A segregated gospel is a variation far, far from the central theme of brothers in Christ. It is as bad a caricature as a variation of the Hallelujah Chorus which comes out sounding like Yankee Doodle. Sometimes we wonder if some professed exponents of the Gospel of Christ ever really knew what the original gospel was and is. In many respects they are like King Canute. It has been pointed out that the tragedy of King Canute was not that he told the waves to stop. Holland and her sea walls had done that. His tragic ignorance was that he had no recognition of the true force at work, the tides. So the people who accept and put forth such imitation gospels have little conception, in spite of memory of a flood of words, of what the gospel is really all about.

The fatal variation of the gospel is not only the denial of God's revelation in Christ, but the denial of brotherhood in Christ. That denial of brotherhood is arrestingly illustrated by the words used by the elder brother of the Prodigal Son to his father. He called him, "Your son." He would not say the name, "My brother." We are in a world of calamity because men have refused to say those life-saving words, "My brother." It is as though a demon with a flaming bomb stands over us and commands, "Now say, Brother." We had better hear.

Those are strong words of Paul—"May anybody who preaches any other gospel than the one you have already heard be a damned soul!" They are not too strong, for it is a question of salvation or damnation. The saving words to pronounce in a threatened world are these, "In God's name, my brother."

73. OUT OF THIS WORLD

The gospel which was preached by me is not man's gospel. GAL. 1:11
No human invention. (Phillips)
Not a human affair. (Moffatt)

Paul affirms here that the gospel is from out of this world. It did not originate in man's wit or wisdom or fancy but in the revelation of God in Jesus Christ our Lord. Paul parallels the 100th Psalm, "It is he that made us, and not we ourselves." So it is God who has made the gospel and not man. It is not a human invention. Therefore, to the Galatians who were quickly deserting the gospel of which Paul had been the preacher, Paul declares with all his energy that they were forsaking God's gospel, and not a mere human invention.

Today this passionate declaration of Paul is greatly needed, lest our gospel be so accommodated to present styles and forms of thinking that it becomes a merely human affair. When the gospel is exchanged for a much praised "common-sense religion," the awe and mystery and wonder of the gospel is gone, and a God out of this world is gone. Denis De Rougemont writes of this tendency, "Psychoanalysis, considered in its entirety and in its general tendency, no doubt unconscious, may be defined as an attempt to reduce sin and evil to subjective mechanisms which a doctor will be able to control. Each age has its own utopia."

Man is put at the center when God is exiled to the fringe of life, if not dropped from life altogether. A religion of common sense is a human affair, and has small place for a God out of this world.

But to what disastrous loneliness does such "common sense" lead, never more than in the twentieth century with its two world wars? Man's need of God at the center of life is vividly expressed in the words, strangely enough, of H. G. Wells. Without recognizing it, he merely illustrates man's helplessness. He wrote of man's scientific advances, "Man has enormously extended his powers, become a creature that can see through a stone wall, jump across an ocean, hear a pin drop on the other side of the world, but still goes on being the quarrelsome little ape he used to be." But all that Wells could do was to shout at humanity in book after book, "Stop being an ape." Good advice, surely! But it is hardly good enough. What is needed is a gospel of power by which man can become a new creature. Our world needs something out of this world, "If any man be in Christ, he is a new creature" (2 Cor. 5:17, AV).

Man's need of God is pictured forcefully by Gamaliel Bradford, who wrote,

I have long been convinced that the greatest need of American civilization today is the need of God, and the kernel of the matter lies precisely in what you allude to, the utter lack of religious education. Strange that we do not stop to think that never before in the history of civilized man has there been a people who did not make God the first principle and basic stay of all its elementary education.

Only a gospel that is God's affair will meet man's need. That need was memorably put by Walter Scott in the words of Bessie MacLine in *Old Mortality*: "Many a hungry starving creature when he sits down on a Sunday morning to get something that might warm him for great work, has a dry clutter of morality about his lugs."

A "dry clutter of morality" is not enough. The gospel is not a human affair.

74. THE LONELY DECISION

I did not confer with flesh and blood. GAL. 1:16
Instead of consulting with any human being, . . . I went off at once to Arabia. (Moffatt)

This might well be called a text for an age of conferences. Our characteristic word is not Paul's—"I did not confer with flesh and blood"; we might say, "I consulted with everybody I met, including a panel of psychological counselors."

Of course, counseling is a great asset of our age. "Iron sharpens iron, and one man sharpens another" (Prov. 27:17). There is wisdom in skilled counselors, wisdom in the voice of experience. Paul was no recluse. He took counsel many times. Here we read that "for several days he was with the disciples at Damascus" (Act 9:19). He went up to critical councils at Jerusalem. Again and again we see him strengthened by fellowship.

Yet the crucial decision of his life was a lonely decision. He went to a lonely place, Arabia. There in his own mind and soul he made the great decision. It was a lonely one. The great decisions of life are always lonely ones. People who live in crowds—and that means most of us in this huddled age—find it hard to have a great dialogue with themselves. There is no solitary world. It becomes harder and harder to make turning decisions by themselves. So many lives are thin because they have no Arabia in which to find sanctuary for making the crucial decisions. They have just asked a lot of people their opinion. The true symbol of so many people is not Rodin's statue of solitary turmoil, "The Thinker," but a photograph of a crowd.

In launching a life that has any carrying power, there must be the propulsive power of the individual soul. Paul launched his world-shaping life as an Apostle after lonely thinking in Arabia. Jesus launched his public ministry in the crucial—and lonely—decisions in the desert. They both knew well that great word "alone." Jesus, all during his life, well knew the "lonely place." It was so in the beginning, "he rose and went out to a lonely place, and there he prayed" (Mark 1:35). It was so at the end. In Gethsemane he said to his disciples, "Sit here, while I go yonder and pray" (Matt. 26:36). The final decision he made alone.

Today we have so much "togetherness" that we are losing our aloneness. Someone wrote a penetrating story of a person who disappeared into thin air whenever all the other people left the room. He had no separate existence alone. It often happens. The mind becomes merely a can of echoes. Admittedly, it is hard to draw the line. We have to walk a difficult tightrope. On the one hand, there is the glory of "I conferred not with flesh and blood" (AV). On the other hand, there is the needed reinforcement of other minds and lives.

Yet, we must face the great issues of life alone. Our fight must be a chance to be "by ourselves." The world seems to be in a conspiracy to prevent us from being alone. There is the ever-present newspaper, the radio, the television. Now we have the transistor radio to ward off any danger of our being alone with our thoughts.

We can make room for everyone in our minds—the butcher, the baker, the candlestick maker—everyone but ourselves. Time when we are not prodded by someone else is regarded as empty and blank. Hosts of us are "other-directed people."

A striking modern story has been written about a man who could not say "I." That might be written about any of us. It has been well said that our greatest problem today is learning to say "we." True. But we must learn to say "I" and have it stand for something stout and rich, if the "we" is not to be a collection of zeroes. No number of zeros ever adds up to anything but zero. If a church is to be an enriched "we," there must be in it people who have learned to say "I," people who have been to Arabia. Someone has well said, "The streams that turn the machinery of the world take their rise in solitary places." It is true of rivers. It is true of men and women. Paul and Jesus went out to lonely places. They were places of power.

75. NOT AN INCH

We did not give those men an inch. GAL. 2:5 (Phillips)
To them we did not yield submission even for a moment.

Paul was at a crucial point in his own life and in the future of the Christian gospel and church. He had to decide where to make a last-ditch stand. He had to choose what inch was worth staking all for. It is so much pleasanter to make a compromise. But Paul did not yield a single inch, for the goal at stake was the very nature of the Christian gospel and the church. It was the issue of the surrender of freedom in Jesus Christ for bondage to Jewish legalism (Gal. 2:4). That compelled Paul to a granitelike stand, for if he had yielded the inch, the Christian gospel would have become the mark of a little Jewish sect soon forgotten.

This pictures a tremendous problem which in one form or other we all face, or ought to face. It is this: Where is the point in controversy which demands an absolutely unyielding resistance? Some people make a last-ditch stand at every inch. Every inch is holy ground to them. Life is an unending bitter-end fight on all fronts. There are those who seem to have made the sign seen at road junctions, "Yield right of way," the motto for every action. Usually it is every lack of action. It is a difficult and supremely important concern to choose the battlefield where we stand. It is important to have the insight to know the right place at which to say the words pronounced on the Lexington Green at the beginning of the American Revolution: "If they mean to have a fight, let it begin here."

What consideriton should enter into the "not yield an inch" stand? Here are a few that deserve a place.

1. *Be sure of your goal.* Is the power you are standing for like Paul's, a defense of the gospel at its very center, or is it a fight on some little outpost? Does this thing you are unyielding on make a supreme difference to people? In church life and ecclesiastical affairs, it is imperative to make sure that you are not contending for every inch of some ecclesiastical form, which has been endowed with an undeserved sanctity. That last sentence covers nearly all the road blocks on the road to reunion of Christ's church. Often our tragedy is that we have great convictions about little things. All too often our stand may not truly represent Paul's stand at this controversy at Jerusalem, a stand for the very essence of the Christian gospel, so much as a battle twixt Tweedledum and Tweedledee.

2. *Be sure your "not yield an inch" stand is not for some merely personal gain.* Ask yourself if you are pugnacious and love a fight for a fight's sake. Paul was by no means pugnacious. He was courteous to many officials, willing to subordinate himself for the sake of the shining goal of the furtherance of the gospel. As yourself, Is it a personal victory that motivates my unyielding stand, or something infinitely larger? Often in a church conflict, some people may say rejoicingly, "Well, he earned it." They may have carried the vote, but they lost the big thing, the total welfare and love of Christ's church.

3. *Do you hold back from an out-and-out struggle with evil, on account of ease and safety, when you ought to be unyielding?* Do you surrender by "adjustment" to things which you have no right to get adjusted to? Is your tolerance, on which you are so apt to flatter yourself, made up largely of indifference? Someone once confessed that his backbone was made up of macaroni. Do you give the right of way to the gospel, come what may? Sometimes people deceive themselves by friendly courtesy. We all sometimes think, although we would be ashamed to put it in articulate words, "Better pipe down on social issues. These people do not like it, and it is not too important." So the course of Christ is often yielded not an inch but a mile.

Good words to remember, "Having done all, to stand" (Eph. 6:13).

76. NO LONGER I

It is no longer I who live, but Christ who lives in me; and the life I now live in the flesh I live by faith in the Son of God, who loved me and gave himself for me. GAL. 2:20

Here is the beating heart of the gospel. Here is the good news to all people. In Christ a man can be a new creature. Christ lives in him. That is the great charter of the Christian faith. The good news of the gospel is not "Try real hard to be good." That is laudable advice. But there is no saving gospel in that. A living power comes into life, making a change in the personality. It is no longer the old "I," but Christ on the throne of a life, directing and empowering it.

Man needs the entrance of a new power into his life. There is a moving portrait which acquires the quality of a symbol in Hermann Hagedorn's biography of Edwin Arlington Robinson, that strangely repressed personality. Hagedorn describes Robinson's lonely years in New York, in his room on the fourth floor back. "Seeing him in his narrow room, sitting with his back to the window, facing the door, it seemed that Robinson was waiting for someone to come in by that door, someone who would change everything." When Christ comes in by the open door of our life, he changes everything. "No longer I." The wonder is described in Revelation, "Behold, I stand at the door and knock; if anyone hears my voice and opens the door, I will come in to him and eat with him, and he with me" (Rev. 3:20). It is the glory of the Christian faith that Christ does come in.

But the words "in Christ" must be given a concrete and not a metaphorical meaning. Christ must be enthroned if he is to live in us. It is not enough to make him merely one of a number of interests, and very often not even first. If it is to be "Christ liveth in me," he must be elevated above all.

Notice that preceding the words "Christ liveth in me" are other words, "I am crucified with Christ" (AV). Remember that that is both the preface and the conclusion of Christ living with us. There are two aspects of being "crucified with Christ." It means participating in all the gifts of God in Christ—forgiveness, sonship, and reconciliation. It means also a tremendous thing, to share the motives, and the purposes of Christ, and the way of life that led Jesus to the cross. That is part of the cost of being crucified with Christ. Its high reward is to have Christ live in us.

77. WITCHCRAFT

O foolish Galatians! Who has bewitched you, before whose eyes Jesus Christ was publicly portrayed as crucified?   GAL. 3:1

Witchcraft was the only figure of speech strong enough to convey Paul's feeling about the foolishness of the Galatians. They had begun their Christian discipleship with faith in Christ, and now they had retreated to reliance on observances. Phillips translates the word "foolish" as "dear idiots." They were idiots to Paul. They were making a trade like that of Esau, giving up a priceless heritage for a mess of pottage. Today we might describe the witchcraft of the Judaizers who seduced them away from faith in Christ to reliance on observances as like the magic of the Pied Piper of Hamlein. It was an evil spell put upon them.

Part of the spell was the reliance on some kind of a prop for their feeling of religious security. Often freedom is a burden. It proved true in Nazi Germany. Freedom and responsibility became a burden. A strange power of dictators is that they take all the responsibility of thinking and tell their followers what to do. The old Jewish legal requirements were a security against which some Galatians were willing to lean.

A similar evil spell was what might be called the "enchantment of bookkeeping." Those are strange words, but for many people there was, and is, a strong spell about it. There is a satisfaction to many people—and was to some of the Galatians—a great satisfaction in having their religious credits in a form in which they could be counted. It was like having a pocketful of money. It was something visual and countable. Benjamin Franklin made it visible in his little cards with the virtues listed upon them. So that when he did an act he regarded as virtuous, he punched the appropriate virtue. A person knew how he stood, and that was more tangible than a vague thing like faith in Christ. It gave the thrill of a good Boy Scout who could feel, "I've done my good deed for today!"

Then of course for some, perhaps for the majority of the Galatians, there was the allure of the crowd. To discard every legalistic demand and rely on faith in Christ meant that one stood out alone. For a Jew to become a Christian was a hard thing. It meant often leaving the snug and dear family group and fellowship of neighbors and kinsmen. Paul suffered it, "danger from my own people." It was hard to lose the easy feeling of being one of a crowd, not a lonely figure looked at with scorn.

What bewitches *us*? For Paul's word, bewitchment is not too strong a word. Many of our strong seductions away from faith in Christ parallel those of the Galatians.

We feel the *lure of ceremonies*. It is so much easier to go through ceremonies than to make a definite and lasting commitment to the gospel. A great many people do just that, going through religious motions rather than giving undivided allegiance to the gospel. It is much easier to take part in a church parade than to make such a commitment as

> *Take my life, and let it be*
> *Consecrated, Lord, to thee.*

There is the bewitchment of *measuring life by material*. We tend to measure life by what we have. It is our bewitchment. For us, witchcraft is not a matter of gaunt women riding broomsticks in the sky. It is the lure of things on the earth, motor cars and houses and mink coats, and things of far less material value. We are lured to take the cash and let the credit go. Browning put this allure memorably:

> *Just for a handful of silver he left us,*
> *Just for a riband to stick in his coat.*

The *enchantment of the crowd* bewitches us as it did the Galatians. We have a fear of open places. It is a comfort to be surrounded by a crowd. The command of Paul, "Come out from them, and be separate from them" (2 Cor. 6:17), is a hard one to follow. Many would far rather get lost in the crowd. Like the white winter coats of some animals, it is safer not to be noticed.

The word "witchcraft" takes us a long way back in history. But we do not have to go back as far as the Salem, Massachusetts witchcraft hysteria to encounter bewitchment. We can hear the alluring voice of the crowd whispering, "Come over here, stand with us. You will be safe." This allurement has been vividly pictured by Dr. Schweitzer from the African jungle.

The man of today is exposed to influences which are bent on robbing him of all confidence in his own thinking. The spirit of spiritual dependence to which he is called on to surrender is in everything that he hears or reads; it is in the people whom he meets every day; it is in the parties and associations which have claimed him as their own; it pervades all the circumstances of his life.

Over and over again convictions are forced upon him in the same way as, by means of the electric advertisements which flare in the streets of every large town, any company which has sufficient capital to get itself securely established exercises pressure on him at every step he takes to induce him to buy their boot polish or their soup tablets.

God save us from being "idiots." May we get away from the bewitchment of the crowd to a greater allure, commitment to Christ.

78.   ANTICLIMAX

Having begun with the Spirit, are you now ending with the flesh?
GAL. 3:3

Going down! The Galatians were reproved for beginning high and then falling downstairs to end in an anticlimax. After beginning with faith in Christ they slid down to reliance on outward observances.

A downward drop is tragically common. An echo of such a drop appeared in a newspaper account of a church anniversary service a few years ago. The First Parish Church of York, Maine, celebrated its three hundredth anniversary. Many of the parishioners were in colonial costume. The minister impersonated an earlier pastor, the Rev. Samuel Moody, who served as pastor from 1697 to 1747. Part of one of Mr. Moody's sermons, preached in 1710, was read. The title of the sermon was regarded as very "quaint." It was "The Doleful State of the Damned, especially such as go to Hell from under the Gospel." It was by no means "quaint." For to slip from a great beginning to a depth is always a doleful history. It was with the Galatians, dropping from faith to works of the flesh.

It is our danger, before which we must watch and pray. We can drop in so many ways. Many fall just as the Galatians did. We need an alert guard against complacency, against trusting for our spiritual welfare to acts we have done, instead of confessing,

> *Nothing in my hands I bring,*
> *Simply to thy cross I cling.*

Look at just one kind of downward slide, common in our day, the conquest of Christianity by a gentlemanly secularism. The characteristic anticlimax of our day is not to be subdued to the sins of the flesh. That happens, and needs a vigilant guard. But another conquest is far more common: that of dropping from a life of faith and dedication to Christ's way and his cross, to an easier way, quite refined and quite spiritually dead. A distinguished Jewish author, Maurice Samuel, has given his sharp impression of this common substitution of a well-bred secularism for an out-and-out Christian discipleship. He writes,

This I found in the world of Christendom: A universal alternative ideal which is respectable but profoundly pagan and immoral. In Christendom, side by side with the world of the New Testament, "The Consolations of Philosophy," "The Imitation of Christ," and St. Francis of Assisi, there is a rival world, a rival literature, a rival pantheon, pagan, playful, and destructive, but with universal and coeval status, and of wider acceptance. On the upper intellectual levels Plato is the teacher; on the lower intellectual levels Kipling and the Union Jack. One could escape from Christ to these without incurring conscious censure.

On guard against the rival religion—the gentlemanly secularism. "Let him that thinketh he standeth take heed lest he fall" (1 Cor. 10:12, AV).

Indeed, we face the same situation in religion that is so familiar in politics, in the tired or played-out liberal. It has been a common sight. That firebrand Samuel Adams became a reactionary in his latest years. So did Thomas Paine and John Randolph. As someone has written, "The political quarter horse who burned up the track in the first 400 yards, but couldn't stay the course and fell out in the gruelling backstretch, may develop into almost anything." He may even become "a frozen monument to dead ideas."

It can happen in Christian religion. It can happen to us.

79. THE FAMILY LIKENESS OF CHRIST

There is neither Jew nor Greek, there is neither slave nor free, there is neither male nor female; for you are all one in Christ Jesus. GAL. 3:28

These repetitions gather power as they follow one another—"There is neither . . . nor; there is neither . . . nor, there is neither . . . nor." No doubt we owe part of the wonderful cadence of this verse to the genius of the translator who produced the King James Version of the Bible in 1611. The words reveal the power and beauty of English prose. But the substance belongs to Paul and it is the very substance of Christ and the gospel. These repetitions, as with massive hammer strokes, drive home the truth of the universalism of the Christian church.

The church of Christ was the first great internationalism. There had been previous internationalisms, that of Alexander the Great and of Rome, the one world of force and conquest, the effort to bind the world together by a band of cold iron. But this was a new internationalism, "all one in Christ Jesus." There were foregleams of it in Isaiah. It burst full on the world in Christ.

And yet, as we search through history and look about our world today, it would seem as though this were a missing verse in the Bible, as though it had never been included or printed. There is so little trace of the "neither slave nor free, . . . for you are all one" in the story of the centuries, and so little trace of that oneness in our world divided by sharp picket fences today. That glorious vision of oneness has cast its light on the world in spots, but its fullness is still to be achieved. We are told that the Confucian Ballet of the Imperial City of Hue has rehearsed for ten years behind closed doors, without a public performance! So the great divine drama of "all one in Christ Jesus" still waits for a complete public performance.

We talk so much about "catching up to tomorrow." Our true task is "catching up to yesterday," the yesterday of the New Testament. We have not yet caught up to Christ, so that we see in him "one great fellowship of love, close-binding all mankind." When we do not see Christ, we do not really see our neighbors. Robert St. John says that that is what has happened in South Africa. He shows what most whites in South Africa never see, how the nonwhites live. Here is one example:

Twelve miles from Johannesburg there is a suburb called Alexandra, where 90,000 Africans live in 600 acres of jerry-built shacks, and from which they commute by bus to work in the city. The bus service is not good. Queues start forming at 3:30 A.M. for the buses, which leave every five minutes. If someone wants to avoid an hour and a half standing in line, then he takes the four o'clock bus, which lands him in town about three hours before he is due at work. Queues form at the other end, too, and the man who got up at 3:30 will be lucky if he gets back home by 8:30 P.M.

Here is Lillian Smith asking the white men of the world to look steadily into the mirror:

No studies have been made of the white man's infantile desire always to be first, always to sit in the front seat, always to have the biggest and best of everything—a desire that makes a nuisance of a child but makes a menace of a man who has the power to get what he wants.

It must seem to people watching us a strange and curious thing that when we in America study race relations we study the Negro—not the white man. . . . No surveys have been made to determine the cause of that desperate feeling of inferiority which drives white men to shout aloud to the whole world that their skin color gives them priority over other human beings.

Still out in the future: neither Jew nor Greek, Negro nor white, but one! The *Dictionary of Hard Words* should prove a useful volume; there are plenty of difficult words. But in any language the hardest words to pronounce correctly, in the fullest sense, are not the long words guaranteed to break any jaw, but the short words. In English, words men have found hardest to pronounce, firmly and with conviction, are the words "we" and "brother." What on earth can a segregated church say persuasively to a segregated world?

80. SLAVE AND SON

So through God you are no longer a slave but a son. GAL. 4:7

All through the New Testament the difference between a slave and a son is stressed as the perfect figure of speech indicating the gift of God's love in Christ. We find it in the story of the Prodigal Son. The Prodigal is received by the father, not as a servant but as a son. We find the stress in the Epistle to the Hebrews. It is central in this letter. The Galatians are no longer in bondage to legal observances, which they have to obey as a slave, but are sons of God, given the love and freedom that are the heritage of a son.

The primary meaning of Paul's words—that we are redeemed from slavery to law to sonship to God—is relevant to us in our day as in every day. That is our inheritance, that is the gift of freedom which faith in God's grace brings. We never get over the need for that stress, for it is tragically easy to become working slaves to law and have little or none of the joy a son has in his father. That happens, alas, often to the church. There are people who are busy at the Father's work, but there is no radiant outgoing love to the Father or any great sharing of the Father's love to His other children. That was the trouble with the elder son, in the Parable of the Prodigal Son. He was busy about the father's work. He boasted, bitterly, "Lo, these many years I have served you" (Luke 15:29). He was a slave and not a son. He served but he did not love, either his father or the boy whom he refused to call brother. So there can be in the church people who will "work their fingers to the bone," but in the spirit of a slave and not knowing or returning the Father's love or sharing it with others.

We need to hear and accept this assurance of Paul that we are not slaves of the law but sons of the Father. This assurance of son-ship reaches out in ways beyond what Paul had immediately in mind. We need the assurance of sonship in these days when there is such a dominance of impersonal forces. Our chief fear of slavery is not from natural forces, but from man. It is man's long dark shadow which lies across the world. There is constant tremendous pressure to make us slaves of the machine, whether it be a conveyor belt or a missile of an atomic bomb. In the story of Aladdin, the jinni was the slave of the lamp. In today's story of man in this industrial world, man is the slave of the machine. Our world is something like Ezekiel's vision of wheels. We are a world on wheels, little ones in a bewilder-ing variety of business machines, and gigantic ones like those of a giant dynamo. The demon of today is not the old one of classic imagination, a monster breathing out fire, but a mechanized man who looks as though he was made out of stovepipes. He threatens to make a slave out of man. These are timely words in our world of today, "No longer a slave but a son."

The deep need of man in a mechanical world is an old need, the need of a family order, an assurance that he is not a cog in a machine, not an interchangeable part, but a son in a family, God's family. That is what the Gospel of Christ does for a man; it makes a possible nonentity into something—more than a something; into a someone, a son in God's family.

81.   A RELIGION OF OBSERVANCES

You observe days, and months, and seasons, and years! I am afraid I have labored over you in vain.   GAL. 4:10-11

Your religion is beginning to be a matter of observing certain days or months or seasons or years. Frankly, you stagger me, you make we won-der if all my efforts over you have been wasted!   (Phillips)

Paul is condemning a religion which has dwindled down to ob-serving certain days. That becomes a form without the substance.

But in order to focus on Paul's real meaning, let us remember that in the Christian religion there has been a great high value to ob-servances. The words of Jesus, "This do in remembrance of me" (Luke 22:19, AV), calls for an observance. We are asked to observe the first day of the week by giving a portion of our means. Every

Sunday is an observance of the resurrection of Christ. If there is no high and holy observance, life loses a dimension, that of the past. It becomes thin. Phillips Brooks put this memorably. He wrote, "If there is no reverence for the sublimities of the past, there will be no perception of the hidden triumphs of tomorrow."

That kind of observances was not, of course, what Paul had in mind. He meant the ceremonies which were a substitution of forms for the realities of religious experience. In marriage, there can be a similar drop into a succession of anniversary observances. A man, for instance, may always remember a wedding anniversary, and observe it with a gift, while the reality that ought to be behind the anniversary, that of love "up to the level of each day's most quiet need," has disappeared.

What Paul lists as a dreary succession of days and months and years is no substitute for the soul of religion, that of receiving the grace of God and showing love to men. There is a searing picture of the Christian religion gone into a bankruptcy in Edward Gibbon's account of the Greek scholars in tenth-century Constantinople:

They held in their lifeless hands the riches of their fathers, without inheriting the spirit which had created and improved that sacred patrimony: They read, they praised, they compiled, but their languid souls seemed alike incapable of thought and action. . . . A succession of patient disciples became in their turn the dogmatic teachers of the next servile generation.

But we can be sure they did not miss any anniversary observances! When that happens we can ask, "Where is the life we have lost in living?"

It is not routine observances and ceremonies which the Christian religion needs, but genuine renewals of great experience. Without renewals, the substance of Christianity is gone. Oliver Wendell Holmes compares the renewal of the mind to making deposits in a bank. He writes,

. . . that the human mind and human life are like a checking account. So long as you keep putting enough money in the bank, your check book is the most magic book in the world. All you have to do is to dip your pen in ink, make a few flourishes, and your check becomes the open sesame to your heart's desires. But just stop making ample deposits and the magic evaporates with a curt and imperious message from the bank, "No Funds."

The spirit and the religious life and experience need renewal or we may hear the same doom, "No Funds."

82. LIFE'S HINDRANCES

You were running well; who hindered you from obeying the truth?
GAL. 5:7
Who put you off the course?   (Phillips)

This is as real and tormenting a question today as when Paul asked the Galatians what happened that their Christian faith, which began so well, was lost. What happens when life goes downhill? High beginnings which go into a decline. Somerset Maugham recognizes this downward slide in regard to fiction. He said, "It is the mark of an inexpert novelist to pose a powerful situation at the beginning of his story, and then to fail to realize, or at least, examine, the ineviable implications." The novel starts off well but it runs downhill. It is the mark of inexpert living as well. We all face the danger of downhill living. We can ask of ourselves and of others, "You were running well; what happened that the sunrise was clouded over?"

Paul gives in this epistle some suggestion of what hindered the Galatians. Three verses earlier, Galatians 5:4, he gives the central reason: "You are severed from Christ." The first attachment was weakened. As they went their way the vision splendid was not attended. The going got hard, and when difficulties arose the backward look stole in. There was the absence of familiar reliances, the observances of the law, and the close fellowship of people, much of which was broken off by their taking the Christian gospel. There was evidence of the failure of renewal of faith. Faith without renewal is diluted and weakened.

From this question about the Galatians, we are compelled to go on to the same question about ourselves. Why do we swerve from a brave beginning and go downhill? As Phillips translates, "Who put you off the course?"

Our faith is worn down by attrition. Faith is not lost by any dramatic betrayal, but by wearing down by compromises. As Stephen Vincent Benét writes truly,

> *Life is not lost by dying! Life is lost*
> *Minute by minute, day by dragging day.*
> *In all the thousand small, uncaring ways,*
> *The smooth appeasing compromises of time.*
> *. . . Life can be . . .*
> *Lost without vision but not lost by death,*
> *Lost by not caring.*

We all know "the smooth appeasing compromises of time." The downhill slide is found in many lives, in aspects other than religious. Some liberals become conservatives, radicals become reactionaries. Thus, Lewis Browne writes of William Wilberforce that he "devoted most of his adult life to grieving over the lot of the downtrodden. Yet when he was a member of Parliament in 1799, he was among the most eloquent supporters of the bill which made it a crime for workers to strike." We see Samuel Adams, a flaming firebrand in his early days, called by many "the father of the American Revolution," becoming an arch conservative. Stewart Holbrook writes of his attitude to the demand for reform in the Massachusetts administion. "Even Samuel Adams, now grown old and conservative, was against any reform. He thought things about right as they were. His arteries were hardening."

The process of grinding down by attrition, a wearing away by friction, is a constant danger of one's religious faith.

The means of the religious life may become the ends. That happens over and over and is one of the risks of the spiritual life. What is designed as a help to the life of the spirit becomes a substitute for it. In other realms we see evil means start by corrupting good ends and end by replacing them. That was one thing that happened to the Jewish legalizers. The laws and customs became not the help of the religious life but its substitute. Often it is the tragedy of business, which is a means of supporting life, but then becomes the end of life. So the church, which is a means of aiding the religious life, can easily become the end. That often has been a spiritual tragedy of the church. It has supplanted the life of God in the soul which it was designed to aid. That possibility calls for unending watchfulness.

Our spiritual life is hindered by lack of renewal. The vision of life can go under a cloud. Wordsworth has traced it in unforgettable lines:

> The youth . . . by the vision splendid
> Is on his way attended;
> At length the man perceives it die away,
> And fade into the light of common day.

"You were running well. Who hindered you?" All too often it is that the vision is lost. As Paul writes, "You are severed from Christ" (Gal. 5:4). Keep the vision of Christ before the eyes of the heart.

83.   LEAVEN OF EVIL

A little yeast leavens the whole lump.   GAL. 5:9

Jesus' parable of the leaven has established the idea of leaven as good. Under the impress of that parable we forget that leaven or yeast may be either evil or good. Jesus himself made the distinction. He said, "The kingdom of heaven is like leaven" (Matt. 13:33). But he also warned his disciples, solemnly, "Beware of the leaven of the Pharisees and the Sadducees" (Matt. 16:6). Leaven is something that spreads. It may be evil or good.

Here Paul is warning against the leaven of malice and evil by which the Galatians were being persuaded. This leaven was spreading among them, and, like all kinds of evil, threatened to infect their whole discipleship. He urged them to beware of the yeast of evil, and turning to the appropriate figure of bread, urged them to use only the unleavened bread of truth and sincerity and obedience.

We need to keep from being befuddled about the innocence of evil. There is a tendency to condone evil if there seems to be only a small amount. We tend to forget what Paul was reminding the Galatians of: that evil in a small amount spreads. It is infectious, even when the evil itself, compared to major sins such as murder and robbery, looks like a small thing. Still, "A little yeast leavens the whole lump." It is a warning against evils of attitude and spirit which spread through our nature and life.

Look at some evil sorts of leaven which we may discount on the ground that they are trivial.

There is the evil leaven of vanity. When mixed in with a person's whole nature, it may spoil the effect of much good. When the passion for display lays hold of a person, it gets in the way of other and better qualities. It leavens the whole lump. We see it at work in the reported confidential remark of a preacher to a friend: "I preached a powerful sermon on humility." He preached it. Too bad he didn't hear it! There is much sharp point, about which we should watch and pray, in the remark of a little girl in England about a bishop who had preached in her church. She said to her father, greatly surprising him, "It's too bad the bishop was never baptized." Her father asked her what she meant. She replied, searching her memory, "When a person is baptized he renounces the vainglory of the world, and the bishop is the most vainglorious person I ever saw." No doubt she was extremely unfair, but from her words one gets a picture of a golden cross dangling from a chest thrown out like a pouter pigeon. A little leaven of vanity leavens the whole lump.

So it is with the spirit of complaint. There are worse sins if we are to grade sins, certainly, but there is none which grows more steadily. The habit of complaint grows and swells like a deadly and rapidly spreading infection. Paul recognized its deadly character. For he thanks God that he has been enabled to kill the spirit of whining complaint: "I have learned, in whatever state I am, to be content" (Phil. 4:11). No swelling complaint, no sniveling self-pity, no envy.

Archbishop Richard Chenevix Trench has expressed that difference between a howl of complaint and grateful acceptance of God's mercy:

> Some murmur when their sky is clear
> And wholly bright to view,
> If one small speck of dark appear
> In their great heaven of blue:
> And some with thankful love are filled,
> If but one streak of light,
> One ray of God's good mercy, gild
> The darkness of their night.

A spreading yeast is also the habit of indecision. When that takes hold, it leavens the whole personality. Some people live in a valley of hesitations—postponements. Rarely the glad confident morning of a total commitment. When the habit of indecision spreads like leaven, the most forthright utterance they will risk is that ascribed to a Hollywood movie producer: "I'll give you a definite maybe."

A little evil leaven can spread and corrupt.

84. FREE FOR WHAT?

Do not use your freedom as an opportunity for the flesh, but through love be servants of one another. GAL. 5:13

Again and again Paul stresses the truth, as in this passage, that freedom is always given for a purpose. He never allows the Christian to whom he writes freedom for its own sake—an end in itself. It is not merely freedom from the bondage of the law, but freedom for serving in love. Freedom without a positive goal gives an echo of Southey's question:

> *"But what good came of it at last?"*
> *Little Peterkin asked.*
> *"Why that I cannot tell," said he,*
> *"But 'twas a famous victory."*

Freedom without a positive purpose of service is an empty boon.

A notable comment on this truth, a central idea of Galatians, is that made by T. S. Eliot. He may not have had this verse in mind, but he makes a memorable comment on it. He writes,

> If one is going to theorize about liberty, then one must go on from political and economic liberty to moral liberty. . . . What, in short, is the ultimate nature and reason for liberty? To me, the notion of *liberty* is meaningless without the further notion of *liberation*. One lives, not to be free, but to be freed. And to be *freed from* is meaningless unless one has some notion of what one is to be *freed for*.

Paul had in mind, in this verse and in the whole epistle, freedom from bondage to the law, including circumcision and dietary laws. But the idea of freedom through Christ and in Christ inevitably has windows that look out on other freedoms which are the gift of Christ. A few of them that come into view through the vision of Christ's gift may be barely mentioned.

There is the freedom from fear. That is, freedom from a low terrifying fear of an angry judge. We frequently see words painted on rocks and other dangerous spots along a road, "Prepare to meet thy God." Men ought to prepare to meet their God not in cringing fear of punishment but in expectation and joy, to meet Him in reverence, in faith and in fellowship. "We are fellow workmen for God" (I Cor. 3:9). This is freedom from the lower level of fear to the highest level of the fear of God, which is the beginning of wisdom. We can be set free from the compulsion of the mass, of the crowd, which threatens our individual personality and tends to stamp it out. Christ's gift of freedom carries one up to the spirit of the apostles who said, "We must obey God rather than men" (Acts 5:29).

Freedom in Christ includes also freedom from the provincialism of time and space. There is a bondage which can hold a person in chains, bondage to the illusion that this particular time in which we live is the only one that counts, that the fashions of this present hour are the supreme laws of the universe. That makes us creatures of the day, shutting out both the past and the future. An equally galling provincialism is provincialism of space—the bondage of thinking that our immediate space, town, state, nation, is the only space that counts or has a demand on us, shutting out all else of God's creation and all its need.

The great end of all freedoms is, as Paul declares, to serve one another in love. "Life's final goal is brotherhood." Look at that goal of life as it stands out in contrast. First, here are the words of Henry Ford:

I do not believe that man can ever leave his business. He ought to think of it by day and dream of it by night. . . . Thinking men know that work is the salvation of the race, morally, physically, socially. Work does more than gets us a living; it gets us a life.

Contrast with that narrow view the wider vision of a well-known man, the late Jacob Marley, the ghost in Dickens' *Christmas Carol*. Here is what he saw, though he had to look back from another world to see it:

Business! cried the Ghost, wringing his hands again. Mankind was my business. The common welfare was my business; charity, mercy, forbearance, and benevolence were my business. The dealings of my trade were but a drop of water in the comprehensive ocean of my business.

Free to serve each other in love.

85. BITE AND DEVOUR

But if you bite and devour one another take heed that you are not consumed by one another. GAL. 5:15
If you snap at each other and prey upon each other. (Moffatt)

This is quite a zoological verse. It pictures a jungle mode of living together, and killing off each other. The RSV "bite and devour" suggests tigers and lions; Moffatt's translation "snap at each other" brings a picture of a genial company of snapping turtles. Paul gives in effect the advice and plea, "Don't live in a zoo. Live in a home." If life is resolved into a biting and devouring contest, both parties will be killed off as members of Christ's company. If we bite and devour, and enjoy swift snapping, we will be sure to receive similar action in return; we will experience the passive voice as well as the active, we will be bitten and devoured.

These are the marks of brutes. When we indulge these qualities we go down in the biological scale. Tennyson writes, "Let the ape and tiger die." The trouble is that they do not die readily. They are long lived. They do not respond easily to the command, "Lie down and die." They have to be chained. The strong chains of God's love, as it is expressed in our love to our fellow men, are needed to control the snap and the bite of our nature.

Paul is not discussing physical murder or injury but the swift stroke of the paws with the sharp claws extended, claws that are so often hidden beneath as velvet a covering as that of a kitten's foot. Here is a sharp picture of the "claw" in conversation, as scratched by Edmund Gosse. We read that when some literary aspirants would send a book to the great critic, Gosse,

whose heart was always of the warmest, who, moreover, was forever needing reassurances from his friends, [he] would write a most complimentary letter in return, saying he found the book a most proper masterpiece. But in a gay and merry after-dinner conversation the same book would be mentioned, and out would come Gosse's claw; the witty thing would be said—and the next day repeated.

How sharply we can snap! It is a habit that grows by employment, the sarcastic bite, the veiled innuendo, the sting of criticism without any love or kindness. Sometimes such love as a person has is given in an airy form to humanity in general, but rarely condensed into love for a particular person. Phyllis McGinley has pictured this arrestingly in an epitaph entitled "The Old Reformer":

> Few friends he kept that pleased his mind.
> His marriage failed when it began,
> Who worked unceasing for mankind,
> But loathed his fellow man.

Alfred Tennyson once declared that it was his ambition to "take the hiss out of the English language." By that he meant to eliminate the "ss"; whenever possible the liquid "ms" and "ls." He succeeded to a very large degree. There are very few geese and snakes in Tennyson's poetry. It does not hiss.

It should, it must, be our ambition to take the hiss out of our lips and teeth, to take the bite and the snappish disposition out of our minds and hearts. The one sure way to do it is to see people in a new light, in the light of our brothers.

86. PARTY SPIRIT

Now the works of the flesh are . . . party spirit. GAL. 5:19-20

It is passing strange to have this trait, party spirit, listed among the most ferocious and distinctive qualities of brute nature, such as impurity, licentiousness, strife, drunkenness, and carousing. The RSV also notes that "other ancient authorities add *murder*." The list, as we have it, often leads to murder.

Party spirit, even when extreme, is frequently thought of by us as a sort of peccadillo, sometimes amusing, not to be put in with such strange bedfellows as lust and murder.

But party spirit, as Paul has it in mind here, is a work of the flesh to be condemned and overcome. Such party spirit is no minor affair to be indulgently passed over. It corrupts the spirit and kills by freezing the fruit of the spirit. We can take every one of the fruits of the spirit—love, joy, peace, and all nine of them—and see clearly that party spirit can wither every one of them. What an inflamed party spirit, such as that had by the Judaizers who were bringing the Galatians back into bondage to the law, can do and does do to love! Blind party spirit has no love for those outside of the party. It ruins peace, makes patience impossible, turns goodness into hate, and makes gentleness out-of-bounds.

What a list of evils has sprung from vicious party spirit—frantic sectionalism, nationalism, white supremacy, adamant denominationalism. The prejudice of factionalism blocks the mind against the entrance of new ideas and freezes all "the genial currents of the soul." These are a few results of a violent and blind party spirit.

This does not mean that we should go through life as innocuous neutrals. The neutral, without strong connections of any sort, has retired from the battle of life. He is like the donkey which starved to death standing between two mounds of hay, unable to decide which to eat first. The complete neutral is as lively and effective as a stone statue.

The true alternative to the neutral is not the man of vicious party spirit, but the man of conviction who can look out on the world with unbandaged eyes, whose mind is still supple enough to learn from experience, who sets human welfare above every party spirit. Paul was writing to a group of Christian converts among whom party spirit had wrought havoc. In the church, party spirit has worked terrible damage and loss. In the church the resource against destructive and competitive party spirit is the commitment which puts the cause of Christ and the spirit of Christ above all else.

87. THE DOOR WAS SHUT

Those who do such things shall not inherit the kingdom of God. GAL.
5:21

The preceding verses list the things which keep a person from inheriting the kingdom. It is immediately obvious why some of these should be mentioned: immorality, licentiousness, idolatry, drunkenness, and carousing. But other actions and traits much less obvious are also included in Paul's list of evils which shut the door on the Kingdom of God. As we look at them, it seems incredible that such familiar things as jealousy, envy, anger, and selfishness should exact such a heavy price. They seem such small failings compared to physical vice. But there they stand. Paul says it seriously, "I warn you" (Gal. 5:21). Such traits of mind and heart will prevent the inheritance of the Kingdom.

The insight is sure. Jealousy, anger, and selfishness are all results of the cardinal sin of lovelessness. God is love. The mark of the members of His Kingdom is love. If love is smothered by such traits, the door to the Kingdom is closed.

Jealousy is an active form of the lack of love. It focuses the spotlight on ourselves. Jealousy is like the action of a child who goes about crying "Someone has my balloon" till he is purple in the face. Envy also springs from inordinate self-regard. The person afflicted with envy cannot see another person have anything fine, be it possessions, position, or appearance, without pushing himself into the center of the picture and feeling bitter over the vast injustice that he does not have it. It corrodes the whole being and displaces love.

Anger is a natural product of lovelessness. It cries, "Somebody has dared to cross my will." Anger is like a wild horse without any rein on it. The phrase "righteous indignation," while it has a real and genuine meaning, has a way of becoming for many people a high-sounding excuse for any outburst of anger. Indignation is not anger. Righteous indignation comes, in a great majority of cases, from a deep concern for a cause beyond oneself. A petulant self-concern, a giving away to bad temper, ready to fly off the handle when a person gets "mad" without any notice, is a long distance away from righteous indignation. Anger is an emotional explosion usually turned on by an aroused egoism. It shuts one out of the true inheritance of spirit which marks the Kingdom of God.

Selfishness is the general attitude by which one erects fences around himself. Self is the beginning and end of one's thought. It is a general name for lovelessness. We sometimes use the phrase "the cancer of selfishness." But we rarely realize how terribly fitting the metaphor is. Cancer is an abnormal and uncontrolled growth. That is exactly what selfishness is: an abnormal growth of the self, out of place in a member of the Kingdom of God.

88. AMBITIOUS FOR REPUTATIONS

Let us not be ambitious for our own reputations. (Phillips) GAL. 5:26
Let us not be desirous of vain glory. (AV)

This is one of the most subtle of all temptations a man can face— ambition for reputation. And many there be that go down before it. Men may be free from greed and avarice; they may be free from gross appetites; but they go down before ambition for their own reputation. A person ambitious for his own reputation is concerned for appearance rather than for reality, more interested in the glare of his own reputation than in his contribution to human welfare. Paul is here warning the Galatians against that calamity. He pleads with them not to glory in the things that are empty.

Tennyson wrote of "the fierce light that beats about a throne." There is a fierce light that beats about a person's reputation, like a klieg light in the movies. It has a deceptive allure about it, for it puts a person in the center of the glare. To many people their highest pleasure is to bask in that light. To resist that lure is a major enterprise of the spirit.

Emerson warns that a symbol may be a prison, once it gets too definite and rigid a meaning. Thus a wedding ring, one of life's most beautiful symbols, may be a prison if it symbolizes, as it sometimes does, the four walls of the home, while the wife complacently lets the rest of the world go by. An ecclesiastical gown may be a symbol that becomes a prison, confining its wearer to an interest only in ecclesiastical affairs, putting God's great world of service and need far away, until they are seen only dimly through the cell windows. In like manner, a laurel, the symbol of achievement and victory in a race, may be a prison, shutting up a person to contemplate his own beloved reputation. For reputation in itself can become an *idol* whose worship requires costly human sacrifices. Some wise man has said that the cost of possessiveness is that it requires the sacrifice of the qualities that should render possessions worthwhile. The same can be said of the cost of ambition for reputation; it demands an absorption in itself. Ambition for "my reputation" confines one in a stout prison, lined with mirrors, in which the soul shrivels while the person looks at reflections of himself.

There is a high place for ambition in life, and in the whole Christian ideal of life. There is a high place for ambition to create something of value, to make a contribution to human welfare. But reputation is always a by-product. Paul had an ambition. He cried, "I must also see Rome" (Acts 19:21). He was ambitious to inaugurate evangelistic work when no foundation had been laid. He made in his service a reputation that no man has ever matched. But he did not aim at a reputation. That was not a motive power in his life. It was an unintended and incidental by-product. It is true of a small reputation, as men count size, as well as of a great one. There was a woman, Dorcas by name, who had quite a reputation in the town of Joppa in Asia Minor. That was not her ambition, but a far higher one: to clothe the needy.

It is hard to eradicate vainglorious ambition, for it takes strong hold of our self-regard. Paul, in a tribute to Jesus, wrote that he "made himself of no reputation" (Phil. 2:7, AV). That to many is the supreme sacrifice—to become of no reputation—giving up the beloved idol of self.

The escape from ambition for reputation is by a higher ambition, not ambition for my reputation, but ambition for the God and Father of our Lord Jesus Christ and His service. Whittier has put it memorably in four lines:

> *What matters, I or they*
> *Mine or another's day,*
> *So the right word be said*
> *And life the sweeter made?*

89.   THE ARTS OF BURDEN-BEARING

Bear one another's burdens, and so fulfil the law of Christ.   GAL. 6:2
For each man will have to bear his own load.   GAL. 6:5
For every man must "shoulder his own pack."   (Phillips)

These two texts belong together for many reasons. One reason is that if we are to bear another's burden we must be fitted for it by bearing our own. If we have not learned to carry our own load, there is small chance of being an effective burden-bearer for others. The motive for bearing burdens of others is clearly stated here. It is to fulfill the law of Christ. That law is love, the law of him who came to give his life a ransom for many. Without a deep and genuine love, being concerned with other people's burdens may turn into a fussy interference with other people's business.

The love which is the law of Christ uses many instruments in bearing the burdens of others. One of the most powerful is *imagination*. It is the inward eye which sees the burdens that others carry. It fulfills what General Charles Gordon called the sovereign duty of crawling under another person's skin. We are all likely to be afflicted with "skin trouble." That is the danger of never getting out of our skin. One man who was surprised by a friend coming up behind him said, "You made me jump out of my skin." The other man said quickly, "That might be a good idea." It is a good idea for all of us. We need to get out of our skin into the skins of others. In these days of racial conflict and burdens of dark-colored races, we need to get under skins of another color. As Shelley wrote,"A man to be greatly good, must imagine intensely and comprehensively; he must put himself in place of another, and of many others. The pains and pleasures of his species must become his own. The great instrument of moral good is the imagination."

Another great instrument of love is *curiosity*. Not, of course, curiosity in the form of an idle meddlesomeness, but an earnest effort to find out what the situation with another person is. In the Parable of the Last Judgment, the people whom the king condemned for failing to feed the hungry and visit the sick had one excuse, "I did not know." That was not good enough. It is our business to find out. So, a consecration of curiosity in the service of need is of the essence of burden-bearing. Desmond MacCarthy once said that curiosity was of the essence of literature and that the first aim of a writer should be to excite it. Curiosity is also a first aim of bearing others' burdens.

James Stephens has a very thoughtful six-line poem entitled "Secrets." He writes that when he was young he thought that every eye peered through a chink, and that every man had around him a wall of self behind which none could find him. Then he writes that though he is older he still sees "in every face a mystery." To the mystery of a human life which we confront, we must bring a Christ-directed curiosity to penetrate behind the wall.

With these agencies there is also the continual need of the employment of *encouragment*. This does not mean that we become chirping Pollyannas. A man who had had all he could take of "everything-is-for-the-best" syrup said that if it came to a choice between Pollyanna and Scrooge, he would take Scrooge every time. We can all understand that. It might be less of a painful irritation. Encouragement is made of sterner stuff. It is a surgical operation by which a heartening takes place; part of one's heart is transplanted to another's heart. The role of Barnabas, "the son of encouragement," is one of the highest roles in the whole drama of life. All these traits blend into one another. Sometimes we fail to be "hearteners" because we fail really to see another person in his need of encouraged heart. William James writes of the "great cloud bank of ancestral blindness weighing down on us, only transiently riven here and there by fitful revelations of the truth." He goes on to say that most of us are so limited in our insight into the true nature of others that we go on through life appreciating only a few of the personalities we meet. We might say also, encouraging only a few of those who need a part of our heart.

Life's experience also shows us that bearing others' burdens helps us to bear our own. Strange paradox—that taking on additional burdens should diminish our own burden! But it is one of the paradoxes of Jesus, eternally true. "He that loseth his life for my sake shall find it" (Matt. 10:39, AV). It can be proved in our own life if we will make the venture. At a dinner where guests were being entertained, the hostess, a woman deep in many social causes, was called to the phone three times during the meal. She returned to the table after the third call, slightly irritated. She said with impatience, "There is nothing worse than being bothered all the time." Her guest said quietly, "There is one thing worse. That is, not to be bothered at all." For that means a terrible thing. It means that we do not count, that no one expects us to lift any burden.

There is one thing always to remember about bearing our own burden. That is, we do not have to bear it alone, for sometimes it is distressingly heavy. One of the beautiful conceptions of the God and Father of our Lord Jesus Christ is that of the Burden-Bearer. In our trust and faith we share our burden. "Cast thy burden upon the Lord" (Ps. 55:22, AV). "Cast all your anxieties on him, for he cares about you" (1 Pet. 5:7).

90.   TRYING TO BE "SOMEBODY"

If anyone thinks he is something, when he is nothing, he deceives himself. GAL. 6:3
If a man thinks he is "somebody."   (Phillips)

It is a common affliction, trying to be "somebody"! The aim is not to accomplish something of value primarily, but to swell up like a grandfather frog and to force the illusion that he is a great person, a V.I.P., a Very Important Person. Some of the Galatians to whom Paul writes have been seduced away from their first attachment to Christ, in which they received his grace in humility, and have been deceived into thinking of themselves as important in their own right, a "somebody" on account of their observance of the Jewish laws.

The swelling up to be a "somebody" is not just a matter for amusement, though it frequently is that. It not only makes a person a ridiculous figure but it is a source of deadly evil. It throws a whole life out of focus—this effort to get into the limelight or to climb up on a pedestal. It has been the cause of measureless disaster to society. H. G. Wells recorded that the chief enemies of the human race were the smart alecks, sharp, clever opportunists. In other words, the "somebodies."

Now, of course, there is a big basic human value in the desire to be something or somebody. It is a human right to have individual significance and dignity. The denial of value to an individual is one of the greatest evils of our world. It is a source of race oppression and conflict, a cause of slavery, of human revolt against exploiting powers. Our society must be constructed more and more to gratify the legitimate desire of a person to count.

But that basic human desire to count for something is a very different thing from the desire for mere prominence or high position. That high desire is pictured in the request of Mazzini in a letter to a friend: "Pray for me that, before I die, I may be good for something."

"I will show you a still more excellent way" (I Cor. 12:31). There is a more excellent way to be "somebody," in the highest sense, a member of the true aristocracy of earth. Faith in God through Christ can make us a servant, the highest nobility. "Whoever would be great among you must be your servant" (Matt. 20:26). We can be sons—"See what love the Father has given us, that we should be called children of God; and so we are" (1 John 3:1).

91. SELF-MEASUREMENT

Let each one test his own work. GAL. 6:4

Self-measurement and testing is a highly difficult task, and many there be that fail therein. We are all adept at testing the work of other people, but measuring the worth of our own work and testing it is a very difficult thing. It is hard to see our own work clearly without illusion. The fact that it is ourselves under scrutiny bandages the eyes and clouds the judgment.

The first necessity in this understanding is really to look at our-selves. The opening words of Daphne Du Maurier's novel *Scapegoat* are memorable:

Someone jolted my elbow, and said, "I beg your pardon," and as I moved to give him space, he turned and stared at me and I at him. And I realized, with a strong sense of shock and fear and nausea all combined, that his face was known to me only too well. I was looking at myself.

James describes the experience all too common with us: "He is like a man who observes his natural face in a mirror; for he observes him-self and goes away and at once forgets what he was like" (James 1:23-24). We do not really see ourselves. We take a hasty look and conveniently forget it.

Consider some basic rules for self-examination. What is effective?

1. *We must be pitilessly objective in our self-measurement and testing.* We all like ourselves too well and that makes it hard to get a true test. Few of us are so shamefully self-congratulatory as James Boswell, but his words of self-satisfaction point out the yawning pit that lies in front of us. He writes in his London *Journal* on December 11, 1762,

I am at least living happily, I am seeing the world, studying men and manners, and fitting myself for a pleasing, quiet life in old age, by lay-ing up agreeable ideas to feast upon in recollection. I have an honest mind and warm friendships. Upon my soul, not a bad specimen of a man!

Again, he writes on February 9, 1763,

How easily and cleverly do I write just now! I am really pleased with my self; words come skipping to me like lambs, upon Moffatt Hill; . . . in short I am at present a genius!

Boswell certainly likes himself. In that respect we are all standing in the need of prayer. To be really objective calls for some rough and cruel treatment of ourselves.

A writer, an artist, a musical composer, for instance, must be a bit of Herod, slaughtering his own children. He must say, "This, in spite of the fact that I wrote it myself, is insufferably dull." Then he should reach for the sword. In our whole character and way of life we should see all and see objectively.

2. *We should strive to keep a strong sense of humility.* A con-ceited person cannot measure truly his own work or his own self. Paul warns in the preceding verses against the deceiving delusion that we are "somebody" when we are nobody. A true sense of humility is

good for the eyesight; indeed it is essential to clear sight when we look at ourselves.

3. *We should look at our own acts and thoughts as though we had never seen them before.* What do we really think of them? A merchandising expert was called in by a store proprietor to evaluate the efficiency of his store. One thing the consultant told the proprietor was, "Look at your store as though you had never seen it before. From the standpoint of a possible customer, how would you like what you see?" In like manner we should look at our lives as though we had never seen them before. How do they appear to a searching first look?

4. *We ought not to accept alibis or easy excuses for our failures.* A man quoting the Bible question, "If thou, Lord, shouldest mark iniquities, O Lord, who shall stand?" (Ps. 130:3, AV), said that we might well also ask, "If thou shouldest accept alibis, who would be condemned?" We make excuses for things all the time. It would be well if we kept clear of the contagion of what Abraham Lincoln once called the "can't-help-its." He said of an unsavory character that he had the "can't-help-its" in that he was always blaming his moral failures on things over which he had no control.

5. *We must apply God's measurements to ourselves.* How do we stand that test? We will find these measurements for a life in the Bible, specifically in the Ten Commandments and the prophets, in the Gospels, and above all in the person of Jesus. Oliver Wendell Holmes in his old age, in his walks around Cambridge, Massachusetts, usually carried with him a compass and a measuring tape with which to measure the girth of his beloved trees. That is what we get from Christ. We get a compass to show the direction of our goal and in what direction we are moving—away from our goal in Christ or near to it. We also get a measuring standard that we can apply to our life. We also get God's measurement of the things on earth that we may not have mistaken magnitudes.

6. *In testing ourselves we will watch out for slow suffocation of spirit by a devotion to things.* Irwin Edman has described this calamity as it comes to a teacher:

> I have seen spirits destroyed, youthful lovers of literature turned into pedants, some of them quite respectable in academic circles; passionate revolutionaries turned into reactionaries, or perhaps more sadly passionate liberals. I have seen the soul become deadened by the flesh, and the letter kill the spirit.

In other words, the soul has been suffocated.

In life, as in teaching, the soul can be slowly suffocated by things, as a city may be covered with desert sand.

92. YOU CAN'T MAKE A FOOL OF GOD

*Do not be deceived; God is not mocked, for whatever a man sows, that
he will also reap.* GAL. 6:7
You cannot make a fool of God! (Phillips)

Here is agricultural law in the spiritual world, the law of identical
harvest. Paul is warning the Galatians against a common delusion,
that good harvest can be grown from bad seed. Altogether opposed
to the stern realism of the spiritual world, this sentimental delusion
nevertheless hangs on through the centuries. Jesus made the application of physical law to the world of spirit in his withering question,
"Are grapes gathered from thorns, or figs from thistles?" (Matt. 7:16).
Paul is warning against the ruinous delusion that by such actions as
boasting, grasping, pushing, and envying—all things opposed to the
meekness and gentleness of the Christian faith and life—the fruits
of the spirit could be harvested. As the farmer cannot outwit seed,
soil, and sun, no more can a person outwit God. The things of the
flesh cannot produce a spiritual nature. One of the meanings of the
verb translated "mocked" is "to turn up the nose." We cannot "turn
up the nose" to God with impunity. We are deceived if we think we
do not live in an orderly world where bad seed bears bad fruit. There
is a strange delusion which has quite a wide acceptance, that the
mere passage of time into old age makes a person sweet and mellow.
It does nothing of the kind. People who have lived a sour and crabbed
middle age will have a sour old age, as sour as a green plum.

But many still expect good fruit from bad seed. The law of identical
harvest is covered up by the illusion that it does not exist. A large
number of people are still engaged at the hopeless enterprise of what
Phillips calls making "a fool of God." Here are a few of the strange
crops we look for.

People who sow to the flesh, who devote themselves to the gratifica-
tion of appetite, expect to reap high-minded character. It can't be
done. There is a law of God against it.

Some people sow the seeds of a merely casual attention to the
Christian religion and church and expect to reap a crop of sustaining
religious experience. When they cannot gather figs from thistles,
they cry out often that there is nothing in religion.

People sow the seeds of ease and idleness, and expect to reap the
harvests of real dedicated effort. This is true in the fields of education, of business, and of the building of a character and spiritual

life. For centuries men have expected the destructiveness of war to bring the fruits of human well-being and an orderly world. The opposite has been frightfully demonstrated for five thousand years, but hosts of men still look for the strange harvest.

This law of identical harvest has its terrible and its blessed side. It is terrible to think that whatever a man sows that shall he reap. When a man sows to the flesh, he reaps corruption, Nothing can change a tittle of that law.

But if a man sows to the spirit of God in committed allegiance, he will reap "the fruit of the Spirit," a very garden of God in a human life, "love, joy, peace, patience, kindness, goodness, faithfulness, gentleness, self-control" (Gal. 5:22). That, too, is a law of God. Nothing can change that bountiful harvest.

93. GLORY IN THE CROSS

But far be it from me to glory except in the cross of our Lord Jesus Christ. GAL. 6:14

These words are the culmination of Paul's epistle to the Galatians, the climax. They are also the culmination of Paul's mind and heart and life. He writes, "God forbid that I should boast about anything or anybody except the cross" (Phillips). His true glorying is in the outgoing love of God revealed in the cross of Jesus Christ.

We sing these very words in a great hymn, "In the Cross of Christ I Glory." But we must bow our heads in sorrow and shame to think that the cross of Christ has not always been a thing of glory to multitudes of people in many parts of the earth. The sign of the cross has been a curse in persecutions and pogroms of Jews in eastern Europe and elsewhere. Mary Antin has given a terrifying picture, in her autobiography, of the cross as a hated and feared symbol in the hands of professed Christians in a bloody pogrom in Russia. She writes,

I was afraid of the cross. Everybody was in Polotsk, all the Jews, I mean. For it was the cross that made the priests and the priests made our troubles, even as some Christians admitted. The gentiles said that we had killed their God, which was absurd, for they never had a God, nothing but images. Besides, what they accused us of happened so long ago. The gentiles themselves said it was long ago. Yet, they put up crosses everywhere and wore them about their necks, on purpose, to remind themselves of these false things. To worship a cross, and to torment a Jew was the same thing to them.

That was the betrayal and blasphemy of the truth of which the cross was the symbol, and should bring a deep contrition to the whole Christian world.

The cross must be seen in its true glory. There is a mountain in Montana, the Silver Bow, from which more wealth has been taken than from any other hill. It has been called "the richest hill on earth." But in a deeper and higher sense the richest hill on earth is Calvary. It is

> *a green hill far away,*
> *Without a city wall,*
> *Where our dear Lord was crucified,*
> *Who died to save us all.*

The cross is a window through which we see the realities of God beyond.

First of all, the cross of Calvary is a reality through which we see the nature of God. Those who have looked longest and deepest at Calvary have seen more than a tragedy, or a martyrdom, or what is called, loosely, "inspiration." They have been persuaded that they have looked through a window and seen the ultimate truth of the universe, a God of love. That is what makes Calvary the richest hill on earth. That God Himself has stepped into our human life, with all its pains, weariness, grief, and sin, making our struggle His own—this makes our gospel a breath-taking thing.

Arnold Bennett has put into words a memorable picture of the cross in its pull on the deep places of the heart. In his novel *Clayhanger* he tells how

Edwin Clayhanger, who said, "There is no virtue in believing," and his girl, Hilda Lessways, stared cynically at a Sunday School pageant in the streets of a midland town. They watched it with a good deal of derision, for it was not a very glamorous spectacle, until the children began to sing,
> "When I survey the wondrous cross
> On which the Prince of Glory died."

Then Hilda, hitherto unaffected by religion, was deeply moved, and when she turned her face away to hide her emotion, Edwin asked, sharply, "What is the matter?" Whereupon the girl flashes out, "It would be worth anything in the world to say those words and mean them."

We can say, not "It *would be* worth anything to mean those words," but "It *is* worth anything."

Second, we never really see Calvary in its full meaning until we see ourselves in it. There is a fierce light that beats about the cross. In that light we see ourselves; we see the play of motives that are active in our own lives. The motives that pushed Jesus to the cross are in our lives: greed, the desire for security, the grasp of advantage, the fear of the crowd, indifference to the suffering of others. Calvary was an event in history; but it is also an event in our lives if, with clear eyes and a heart that is not afraid to look at ourselves, we see our likeness to those who drove Jesus to the cross. Edwyn Bevan writes about the cross, "As a matter of mere psychological fact the thought of the cross has counted far more, as the mainspring throughout nineteen centuries, of Christian devotion, of Christian service and sacrifice, than the Sermon on the Mount. . . . What Jesus was and did was greater and more wonderful than what he said." The last sentence of that quotation implies more of *an opposition* than exists. It is really a matter of *extension*. The cross extends and dramatizes and personalizes the Sermon on the Mount.

Third, we do not really see the cross until we see it as a way of life for ourselves. Lent, if we use it thoughtfully in daily devotion, will show us that the cross is not only something to receive, but something to do. It is not merely something to sing about, "In the Cross of Christ I Glory," though we should thank God for that. It is a quality to put into action; "the love of Christ constraineth us" (2 Cor. 5:14, AV). That has been the most powerful source of social action the world has ever known.

There is a striking poem by Genevieve Taggard on the old superstition that was strong in Europe and in particular in Ireland, that it was not safe to die until one had taken a stick in his last hours and marked on the earth the Sign of the Cross. These are her words:

> *Mark the earth with a Cross before you die.*
> *Take a small stick and bend down*
> *And make two marks—two*
> *Only, on the ground. Ask no one why.*
> *Mark, before you die, the earth for a sign. You*
> *Are not a soul, you cannot die*
> *Rightly until you scratch a small mark on the ground.*
> *Lean and write and be done and gone,*
> *And the wind be with you.*

Lift that up to its larger meaning—not superstition, but reality. Leave somewhere on earth the sign of a cross written on your life. Some sign of unselfishness, sacrifice, love, that reminds men of Him who marked the earth with a cross.

The Epistle of Paul
to the Philippians

94. A TALE OF TWO EMPIRES

To all the saints in Christ Jesus who are at Philippi. PHIL. 1:1

Charles Dickens wrote that stirring novel of the French Revolution, *A Tale of Two Cities*. This greeting of Paul to the saints in Philippi suggests a parallel theme, "a tale of two empires." For in a real sense Philippi was the birthplace of two empires.

After the assassination of Julius Caesar, Brutus and Cassius, and their army of adherents, were defeated by Octavian and Anthony at Philippi in 42 B.C. That was a victory which led to the Roman Empire under its first emperor, Octavian, who took the name of Augustus. Octavian later defeated Mark Antony and Cleopatra at Actium and in 27 B.C. became the supreme ruler of the Roman Empire. Philippi was made a military settlement with many civil privileges.

Ninety-one years later another empire was founded at Philippi: the Christian Kingdom brought into Europe at Philippi when Paul crossed the narrow sea from Asia Minor to Macedonia. It was the first time in history when the gospel was carried from one continent to another. The Empire of Christ was brought to Europe and the West. It is stirring to the imagination to think of the cargo that was carried in the little ship in which Paul crossed. It was a far richer cargo than any ever carried by the treasure ships of Spain, which were loaded with the gold and silver of the New World. For this little ship brought the Gospel of Christ to Europe, and all the light and power brought into the Western world by that gospel.

It was the inauspicious beginning of a spiritual empire, a few women gathered for prayer at the seaside. It was a great anticlimax to Paul's vision of a man crying, "Come over to Macedonia and help us" (Acts 16:9).

But he began there. The gospel acted like yeast in the new continent. It was God's yeast and the Kingdom of grace, mercy, and peace was established. What a contrast there between the Roman Empire and that of Christ. And what a contrast now. The Roman Empire has dissolved into ruins and history books. The heralds of Christ still go forth conquering and to conquer. It shows the transience of physical empire and the permanence of Christ.

According to Shakespeare, Brutus replied to Caesar's ghost, "Why, I will see thee at Philippi then." According to the Book of Acts, God said to Paul, "I will meet you at Philippi."

95. DEFENSE AND DEMONSTRATION

I hold you in my heart . . . both . . . in the defense and confirmation of the gospel. PHIL. 1:7
Defending and demonstrating the power of the gospel. (Phillips)

Defending and demonstrating—those are two services to render the gospel. The effective defense of the gospel must include its demonstration in life. It is the demonstration on the proving grounds which vindicates the truth of the gospel. The two stages of this vindication are pictured in Sir Henry Newbolt's poem "Clifton Chapel," which depicts a father taking his son over to the old school where he himself was educated. In the school chapel he says,

> *This is the chapel: here, my son,*
> *Your father thought the thoughts of youth,*
> *And heard the words that one by one*
> *The touch of life has turned to truth.*

First the defense, "heard the words." Then the demonstration, "the touch of life."

It is much easier to defend the gospel by words than it is to demonstrate it by deeds. Defense may be an intellectual and debating operation. But demonstration gives a working proof. Joseph Butler, the Bishop of Bristol in England, wrote a defense of Christianity in 1736 entitled *The Analogy of Religion*, a book that had wide use. But a few years later the evangelical revival broke out in England under Wesley and Whitefield. This springtime of the gospel brought new life to multitudes of people. It demonstrated the power of the gospel to make new creatures in Christ Jesus. It was not a printed *analogy of religion* but the revival which swept over England and was a proof of the gospel in life.

Kierkegaard describes powerfully the true demonstration of the gospel in life without which all words of defense are weak. He writes,

What good would it do me to expound the significance of Christianity, to explain the many individual phenomena, if for me and my life it did not have any profound importance? What good would it do for me if truth stood before me naked and cold, indifferent whether I recognized it or not, producing rather a fearful shudder than a trustful devotion? To be sure, I am willing to recognize an imperative of the understanding, and to admit that persons may be influenced by this. But then it must be livingly embodied by me. And it is this that I now recognize as the principal thing.

"The words Incarnation, Atonement, Eternal Life, as also the words Segregation, Democracy, Liberty, are mere sounds or imprints on paper, without a picture of persons thinking or acting in concrete terms."

Demonstration is living. That is why it lives. Demonstration is the true defense. In the beginning when the gospel went out to the hard Roman world, there was a profound defense of the gospel in such works as the Epistle to the Romans, Corinthians, and Hebrews. But the victory that overcame the world was in the gospel as demonstrated in people, God's *dramatis personae.*

Religion is not something we defend. It is a power that defends us.

96. PROVE IT

That you may approve what is excellent.   PHIL. 1:10
That you may prove in practice the things that are excellent.   (Beare)

This does not mean a distant or languid approval. In fact, the word "approval" is an inadequate word to describe the intense striving for the excellent which is meant here. Christian achievement calls for vigorous athletic words, even agonizing words. "Strive to enter in at the straight gate" (Luke 13:24 AV). Strive means "agonize" to enter.

We all approve love. Indeed, it makes quite a pleasant mood to approve the whole gospel of God's love in Christ. But to prove it in practice comes harder. John Milton wrote, "A writer ought himself to be a true poem if he wishes to write well . . . in laudable things." The Christian must be a true poem of the gospel if he wishes to prove in practice the things that are excellent.

One real meaning of approving the excellent is to be able always to recognize what is highest and best. That is a giant step—to recognize the best when we see it. For one of life's great dangers is to be gullible over shoddy goods. Someone said of a woman that she was "destined to shop for cheap values."

Horace Walpole's biographer passed this judgment on him: "All his tastes were minor; they were for decoration and bibelots and curiosities, for historical paradoxes and antiquarian anecdotes and contemporary gossip." It is a great affliction, "all minor tastes." It means a person goes stumbling along and never even in dreams sees the things that are excellent.

Literally, "approve" means "that you may test the things that differ." Lay down a slide rule along with what you see. Test it by a Christian measurement. Test the difference between a genuine integrity of character and a showy pretense, between genuine self-giving and an easy imitation. With eyes set on the highest, you will not be misled or confused. If you really approve what is excellent—the Sermon on the Mount, for instance—that will bring a thoroughgoing revolution in life.

This proving in practice calls for a Christian exhibitionist. Exhibitionism is a vicious thing, corrupting a whole character, a "showing off." But there is a Christian exhibitionism which is a very different thing. It is proving to the sight of others the things that are excellent. It follows an excellent commission, "Let your light so shine before men, that they may see your good works and give glory to your Father who is in heaven" (Matt. 5:16).

97. THE BIG SURPRISE

What has happened to me has really served to advance the gospel.
PHIL. 1:12

Life under God is a surprise party. Here is Paul confronted with a big surprise. What looked like the end of his work, his imprisonment, has turned into one of God's surprise parties; an apparent calamity has served to advance the gospel. In life with God, the years turn into a series of boxes each with something unexpected hidden within it. We can detect Paul's amazement in his language, "What has happened to me has really served to advance the gospel." Really! We can almost see the exclamation points after that sentence.

We have a surprising God who has done amazing, unexpected things: a Baby in a barn and an opened tomb. It has been the way with God's dealing with His children. How many surprising things have turned out differently from the common expectation! People have gone into a valley of troubling and found surprisingly that

with trust in God it became a place of springs. People have demonstrated in their experience the amazing truth of Jesus' words, "He
that loseth his life for my sake shall find it" (Matt. 10:39, AV).

We can all remember the joy and excitement of a surprise
party during our childhood. Every year with God is an unknown
venture, the possibility of a divine surprise party.

98.   OVERFLOW OF A LIFE

Most of the brethren have been made confident in the Lord because of
my imprisonment, and are much more bold to speak the word of God
without fear.   PHIL. 1:14
Taking fresh heart in the Lord from the very fact that I am a prisoner
for Christ's sake.   (Phillips)

This is an example of what someone has called "the pretty ways
of providence." It is one of God's mysteries, the overflow of a life,
the plus of a life that empowers and fortifies and energizes the
life of another person. There is this strange overflow of Paul's life.
He was imprisoned, many scholars believe, at Rome, strangled as it
were in his witness at the very end of his work. But with this
strange overflow of his life to other people, his work and witness are
at a new beginning.

All through the years of Christian history, this mysterious overflow of life has gone on with amazing results. People have been
imprisoned with the shackling of their powers by the bonds of ill
health, by the barriers of financial limitations. It had looked as
though their work was all over. But it has entered a new chapter.

Operations have been performed by which one man's nerve has
been implanted into another man's body. Spiritually that has been
done, by God's grace, right along. The Apostle Paul's nerve has
given nerve to other men to speak more boldly. Again and again
people have been "nerved" for service by the nerve of another
person.

Two things are to be sharply noticed about this overflow of a
life. It has played a tremendous part in the history of Christianity.
In many ways and situations it has been Christianity's secret weapon.
It has been often the role of a mother, the contagion of courage and
power. It was so with Monica, the mother of St. Augustine. It was so
with Susanna Wesley, the mother of the evangelical revival. John
Wesley's practice, "Always look a mob in the face," was partly

the overflow of a slight little woman, his mother. In any great Christian achievement, we may usually say in seeking the secret, *"Cherchez la femme."*

The overflow of courage and fortitude often comes from a wife. Of course, there have been wives whose chief contribution to their husbands has been a timorous "Do take care of yourself dear. Don't take any risks." In that way "the native hue of resolution is sicklied o'er with the pale cast of thought," and the potential of a life is snugly bottled up. But very often the role of a wife has been that of a heartener, a quickener of nerve. A lovely picture of this is the wife of Wendell Phillips, who is said to have stated earnestly when he went out on a peace crusade where real danger would be met, not "Be careful, Wendell; don't get into any trouble," but a ringing "Don't shilly shally, Wendell." That is the high office of friendship. A true friend is not one in whose presence we may let down and relax, but one who holds us up to our best, whatever the best may be.

Again, this is a high vocation for anyone in bonds of any sort. He can be, as Paul was, "an ambassador in bonds" (Eph. 6:20 AV). He may be tempted to ask, "What difference does it make if I should be courageous or not? I am held down by afflictions." The answer is that it makes an enormous difference. It makes a difference of light, heat, and power in many centers if a dynamo is active and is generating power. It makes the same difference in life.

99. THE CHRIST OF RIVALRY

Some indeed preach Christ from envy and rivalry. PHIL. 1:15
Some are preaching Christ out of jealousy. (Phillips)

How could Christ be preached by rivalry and envy? Part of his mission was to end envy and jealousy and the spirit of rivalry in religion. It is a strange thing—on the face of it, a fantastic thing—but it can be done, it has been done, it is being done.

When the motives of envy and rivalry enter into the preaching of Christ or work for Christ, the center is all wrong. It is literally "eccentric," no center, in that it is not "Christ is the center" but "I am the center." It becomes not "I am committed to Christ," but "Christ is committed to me." That sounds impossible, but there are subtle ways of doing it so that it is not impossible. If envy and jealousy come into our preaching or serving Christ, we get a distorted view of

Christ, we lose our grasp of what manner of man he was. The process is like that of a man looking down a well and seeing his own face. So a man may look at Christ and see his own reflection and confuse that with Christ. So Christ is led captive in his train. Men suffer the illusion that Christ is more attached to them, is more like them, than he is to some other Christian group.

That has entered into the sorry part of the history of Protestant denominations. Christ has been preached with jealousy, with the feeling that we are more orthodox or more spiritual than the other group. Often there has seemed to be a more intense devotion to a denominational system than to the cause of Christ in the world. Some have even fallen victim to the childish view that Christ is a member of their denomination. Sometimes there has become a rather bitter rivalry. Heywood Broun once declared that some Protestant shepherds do not use their shepherd's crooks to guide the sheep, but to bean one another on the head. That is extreme, of course, but it is easy to see conditions that have led to such a statement.

The secret of the cure for this disastrous rivalry is given by Paul a few verses on in this same chapter. He writes, "For me to live is Christ." Our emotions must be attached to Christ and not to something possessed by ourselves. He must increase and we must decrease.

100.   WHAT DOES IT MATTER?

They preach in a partisan spirit, hoping to make my chains even more galling. . . . But what does it matter?   PHIL. 1:18 (Phillips)
But what difference does it make?   (Goodspeed)

These are four blessed words, "What does it matter?" They are liberating words. They liberate from a crushing anxiety over things that do not really matter.

Some people have never learned to say those words over the right things. They say, "What's the difference?" There the difference is tremendous. They say those words over the ethical quality of their lives, over a faith in a righteous and loving God, and over sympathy and sharing with others. These things make an immense difference. But in many other things, the words strike the manacles from a slave.

When it was a matter of his own credit or prestige, Paul cried impatiently, "What difference does it make?" The motives of his detractors who sought to do him harm were all wrong. But what of it? Christ was being preached and that was all that Paul really cared about. The words express a glorious freedom from self-concern. That is the most galling burden a man can be shackeld with. Unless a man is freed from a constant concern for his own prestige and importance, he can spend his whole life calling for his daily shot of prestige as a baby calls for his rattle till he is blue in the face. It is a great achievement in life to live without drugs, without the habit-forming drug of flattery administered daily like a drug by a hypodermic needle.

These words, "What's the difference?" act like the magic words "open sesame" in the story of Ali Baba in the *Arabian Nights*. For these words open the treasure house of freedom. They allow us to go on with our work, freed from the galling burden of the necessity of being a "big shot." For the grim necessity of being a "big shot" results in a crippling form of solitary confinement. It is a self-imposed bondage but none the less confining on that account. The victim is put on a slim diet of reputation and prestige, which has a vitamin content less than that of bread and water. At the door of the cell there is always the leering question "How am I doing?" If one has always to be a "big shot," that eliminates one of the finest luxuries of life, that of being himself.

The way to overcome the tyranny of little things that do not really matter is to put some big things in their place.

101. "YES, AND I SHALL REJOICE"

Christ is proclaimed; and in that I rejoice. Yes, and I shall rejoice. PHIL. 1:18-19
Yes, and I shall go on being very happy. (Phillips)

Paul here makes a strong affirmation of the durability of religious experience. He rejoices in the preaching of Christ. That joy is not going to change no matter what happens. His tremendous attachment to Christ and rejoicing in him is not at the mercy of tomorrow's happenings. Come what may, he will "go on being very happy."

This is a wonderful statement of faith in a permanent God and a permanent mood in Him. By such faith life is lifted out of the jeopardy of change. The joy Paul feels now, he knows he will feel always.

We sing in a hymn, "Peace, perfect peace, our future all unknown?" The future is all unknown as far as the details are concerned. We do not know the swift changes in detail of any tomorrow. But we can pray with assurance:

> Change and decay in all around I see;
> O thou who changest not,
> Abide with me.

The big thing is that we do know the unchanging God. "I know whom I have believed and I am sure that he is able to guard until that Day what has been entrusted to me" (2 Tim. 1:12).

The mood of life in Christ is not one of here today and gone tomorrow but here today and here tomorrow. As Goodspeed translates. "I expect to be glad." The earnest expectation will not be disappointed. So we may go into life with a great faith and joy that by the grace of God will be continuing and unchanging, whatever the outward changes, because it has been committed to an unchanging God.

102.   TO LIVE IS CHRIST

For me to live is Christ, and to die is gain. PHIL. 1:21

A minister was trying to write a sermon on this text and, strangely enough, found it hard going. It is one of the greatest texts in the Bible, the greatest human aspiration that can be conceived. Yet the preacher had trouble making the text fall into an orderly outline. Then a great idea came to him. "Suppose," his inner self said to him, "Suppose you give up trying to talk about this text, and just make it something to live." It occurred to him that after he had lived that aspiration he might be able to say something more effective and persuasive about it.

The text is an easy thing to say. It is a tremendous thing to *live*. We miss, so often, the glory of the all-consuming ambition because we want something else along with it. We like to make the best of both worlds. It was said of James Boswell that he wanted both the comforts of religion and the comforts of atheism. Not many of us crave the "comforts" of atheism, but the one goal of "to live is Christ" seems impossibly high.

When we can say "for me to live is Christ," it means that life is no longer a lonely trudge, but a life of fellowship with God. It becomes a life with a shining goal ahead of it: to achieve Christ-likeness in thought and act. It is a life that does not end in a blank wall. Life is a thoroughfare, living in the power of an endless life.

103. "NOT CARING TWO STRAWS"

Battling with a single mind for the faith of the Gospel and not caring two straws for your enemies. PHIL. 1:27-28 (Phillips)
Never be scared. (Moffatt)

Two straws makes a handy measure to carry around with one. It is a colloquial expression that reveals Paul's thought. It is the lowest amount of fear that could be designed, an apostolic measurement—"not caring two straws." Paul is writing to put courage into the Christians at Philippi. He does not envisage them crouching behind any kind of a barricade, but moving ahead with an erect forward stride.

"Two straws" are two great words to remember. Paul's words of encouragement to the Philippians were not a conventional slap on the back or an easy "cheer up." For there were real enemies facing them in Philippi. The little group which made the first fellowship in Europe was not yet facing the fierce persecutions that came later, but there was a real fight going on. Paul and Silas were thrown into prison in Philippi after being beaten with rods.

But Paul says, take my measuring tape for your enemies. Do not care two straws for them. It is as good advice and exhortation for today as it was on the far yesterday. Christians today face enemies of a vastly different kind. No more of being given to the lions in the arena. The lions today are not in an arena but in a zoo. That is part of our trouble. We have no enemies with whom to engage in deadly combat. Consequently, we degenerate and "take it easy." The valiant characteristics become subdued. The consequences can be expressed in a little equation—the gentler the enemies, the more dangerous they are to the spirit.

But there are enemies to a vigorous Christian witness.

1. As Christians, we face the "thumbs down" fraternity on social questions and we are very likely to care far more than two straws about them. We remember from reading of the gladiatorial contests in the arena at Rome that there were certain gestures from the Emperor's box, with the thumbs down meaning death. In our world we face the "thumbs down" of powerful groups when we attempt

to bring Christian teaching into concrete application. There are many groups, and they are the "enemies" who insist that the truths of the gospel are meant for mental performance only. We hear in different words the old command of the High Priests to Peter and John: "Let us warn them to speak no more to any one in this name" (Acts 4:17).

There are many warnings to those who undertake to bring about a more Christian industrial or political order. They say, "Speak no more in the name of Christ in the racial situation." Then it is a good time to remember Paul's word, "not caring two straws for your enemies." There is real danger that we care so much more than two straws that our witness is ruined by a shameful silence. Martin Luther King has pointed out this danger as it has been evident over and over again:

It may well be that the greatest tragdy of this period of social transgression is not the glaring noisiness of the so-called bad people, but the appalling silence of the so-called good people. It may be that our generation may have to report not only for diabolical actions and vitriolic words of the children of darkness, but also for the crippling fears and tragic apathy of the children of light.

2. There are also the dictators of private life for whom we should care less than two straws. There are many groups from which the word goes out to us, "Don't take your religion too seriously. It is all right to be a nominal Christian. In fact, that is quite fashionable." But to take it too seriously, to take religion into our private lives, is regarded as "fanaticism." "Fanaticism" has become a convenient blanket word for genuine thoroughgoing ordering of life on Christian principles.

The disapproving groups wield a tremendous power, flinging the same charge as that flung by the maid who charged Peter, "You also were with Jesus the Galilean" (Matt. 26:69). That was enough to win the strong social disapproval of the company in the courtyard. So it is with us. The charge is made, "You are an all-out disciple of Jesus." That does not go down too well with the country club set. On such occasions it is well to remember Paul's words, "not caring two straws." In fact one might see in a couple of straws a Christian symbol of great meaning.

104.   THE FINE ART OF MAKING ENEMIES

The fact that you have such men as enemies is plain proof that you yourselves are being saved by God.   PHIL. 1:28 (Phillips)

"They love him most for the enemies he has made." Those words formed a well-known tribute to an American statesman. That is something like the tribute which Paul here pays to the Philippians. He loves them for the enemies they have made. That means they are on God's side. That means they really count in God's holy war.

It is a tribute to be coveted today as in the far yesterday in Philippi. For having evil men as enemies means that one actually cuts deep. It means that one really counts. If a person has no enemies, he becomes, in the language of Dickens describing Mrs. Fezziwig, "one vast substantial smile."

There are two considerations to remember always about making enemies.

The first is that a spirit of pugnacity is the poorest, most miserable equipment for service. Paul had enemies aplenty. He was thrown in jail, beaten, and left for dead. Yet he never went out of his way to make enemies. He was never pugnacious. Under the most trying circumstances he was courteous. He made a gracious reference to the pint-sized official Agrippa before whom he was tried. He cared for the cause of Christ, not for his own satisfaction in thrashing around. He said he counted himself happy to defend himself before Agrippa.

Some people seem to take as the gospel for their personal conduct, Whistler's little book *The Gentle Art of Making Enemies.* They make enemies skillfully and successfully. They seem to think that by merely making enemies they turn in a great achievement for the Kingdom of God. They take this sentence of Paul's in tribute to having enemies in the wrong sense. Patience and conciliation count far, far more in God's warfare than a pugnacious spirit that picks fights. Humility is a powerful weapon. Lincoln, when he was criticized for taking without retaliation General McClellan's arrogance, said, "I would hold McClellan's horse if it would bring us a victory." Blustering animosity is a sure mark of adolescence.

So much is true. The other end of the paradox is also profoundly true. A forthright stand for the Christian faith and life is bound to make enemies, not always personal antagonistic enemies, but vigorous opponents of Christ's cause. This is, in a high sense, a "gentle art of making enemies." An out-and-out stand for the Christian way of life, in personal life and in the social order, is bound to make enemies. This is often forgotten in these days when such an idol is made of "adjustment." We are tempted to make adjustment to situations where a Christian has no right to get adjusted. We often hear it said, "He hadn't an enemy in the world!" That is given as a tribute. But if it were true, it is not a tribute but a terrible indictment. For that could mean that in many important ways he does not count. He cuts such a docile figure that he is not worth any frontal assault. Imagine anyone saying of that apostle of love, Paul, "He hadn't an enemy in the world!" He made enemies in every port and in all likelihood died with his head on the block. Imagine saying of Martin Luther or John Wesley, "He hadn't an enemy in the world!"

For a determined Christian who has put all of himself in the fight against evil makes a thorough nuisance of himself. There is a fine art of making enemies for Christ's cause. When the prophet Amos went to the seat of that court at Bethel, they did not say, "Come in and sit down." They said, "Get out." Early Christians were hailed in some quarters as those who "turned the world upside down." But often their successors would not upset a teacup. In fact, a teacup is their only weapon.

Robert Louis Stevenson wrote that as some people play the part of St. George meeting the dragon, they do not slay him, but tie a pink ribbon around his neck and say "nice pussy" and "give him a saucer of milk." We are called to a more deadly warfare against dragons. God grant that we may be rich in enemies.

105.   LIKE-MINDEDNESS

Complete my joy by being of the same mind.   PHIL. 2:2
Give me the utter joy of knowing you are living in harmony.   (Moffatt)

Like-mindedness can be a glorious thing as Paul pictures it here. Like-mindedness can be a vicious thing as it has been practiced from time out of mind and is practiced today.

Moffatt and Goodspeed give the meaning "of the same mind" as Paul was pleading for it: "living in harmony." It was harmony of life and spirit and purpose which Paul meant. It was not the parrotlike clatter of all saying the same thing, "Polly wants a cracker." The prize to be seized was that of harmonious minds having the same great goal, the same high allegiance. The verses following in this passage picture Paul's thought—humility of mind, extending high regard to others and having a great concern for them.

With that kind of like-mindedness established, variety of opinion and preference, of quality of mind, is a noble achievement, giving a variegated glory to God's Church. Gerard Manley Hopkins has given a memorable picture of this in his lovely poem "Pied Beauty":

> *Glory be to God for dappled things—*
> *For skies of couple-colour as a brinded cow;*
> *For rose-moles all in stipple upon trout*
> *that swim;*
>
> . . . .
> *All things counter, original, spare, strange.*

These differing wonders all praise God. What is true of nature is true of society and of the fellowship of minds in a church.

But a common type of like-mindedness can be a vast and dead mental desert. Minds can be cut with the same biscuit cutter, with the same form of words, and with endless repetition. Joseph Parker once said that the "church is a great brickmaker." That happens often when the church has sought to give the same form and shape to each mind. That is the like-mindedness of the cemetery, a dead uniformity.

What a tragic story it has been—church and state enforcing conformity of mind. It is the story of the torch and fagot, the prisoner's cell, the torture chamber, the executioner's ax.

In churches of a much more recent date there has been the stern demand, "Now say shibboleth." What has been desired has been uniformity of the larnyx, not of hearts. In these days of the search for unity in Christ's church, it is the unity of spirit we seek, the unity of great faith in Christ.

In our social world there is a terrible enforcement of mental conformity. The tyranny of a ruling code can be as bad in its effect on the mind as that of a dictator. That is important to remember in a day when there has been such high praise of togetherness as though it were the chief end of man. In city and in suburb (in some ways the compulsion to conformity is greater in suburban towns than in any other place), there is a stern demand for having the same mind, observing the same social code, and having the same political coloring as one's neighbors. If one is to have a separate mind, it will mean hard struggle. For multitudes of minds have been blinked out under the fierce pressure exerted by different agencies—the organization where a man works, the commuters' car he rides in, and, tragically enough, the socially correct church he attends.

In all these pressures there is one mind to strive for, described by Paul in this passage: "Have this mind among yourselves, which you have in Christ Jesus" (Phil. 2:5).

106.   HUMILITY AND THE INFERIORITY COMPLEX

Do nothing from selfishness or conceit, but in humility count others better than yourselves.   PHIL. 2:3
Modestly treat one another as your superiors.   (Goodspeed)

In the first chapter of Philippians Paul makes a prayer that the Christians in Philippi "may approve things that are excellent" (Phil. 1:10, AV). That involves the high art of distinguishing things that differ The ability to distinguish things that differ is a large part of one's equipment as a Christian disciple. The detection of differences is the beginning of all orderly mental power. It is the foundation of all science.

In our day one difference to be detected is that between Christian humility and an inferiority complex. For the grace of humility has been obscured by psychological and psychiatric jargon. In the last generation the term "inferiority complex" has been a new idea and phrase, and many people have ridden it to death. Paul was not recommending anything resembling an "inferiority complex" but something utterly different—a true humility. "Inferiority complex" is a term introduced by Alfred Adler and refers to a complex of emotionally toned ideas which are centered on real or imaginary handicaps. It is the distinct feeling that one is inferior to others. It often involves the individual's attempt to compensate for his feelings of inferiority by actions which would prove that those feelings are unjustified.

Humility, on the other hand, is defined as a modest sense of one's own significance. Its synonyms are lowliness and meekness. When the sense of true humility is destroyed by an inferiority complex the very beginnings of the spiritual life are destroyed. The first beatitude gives the quality of humility, "Blessed are the poor in spirit, for theirs is the kingdom of heaven."

A genuine humility can go along with an honest appraisal of one's abilities. In fact, Paul in Romans recommends that very thing: "I bid every one among you not to think of himself more highly than he ought to think, but to think with sober judgment" (Rom. 12:3). Sober judgment will induce a self-estimate not too high and, just as surely, not too low. John Keats wrote in a letter in 1919 to his brother that when at a certain place "nothing worth speaking of happened . . . I took down some thin paper and wrote on it a little poem called St. Agnesis Eve." A truly humble description of the creation of one of the world's great poems. Yet later Keats did write, "I think I will be among the English poets at my death." That was certainly an honest appraisal, yet it went along with a true humility.

Another common mistake about humility is to make it a flimsy and false excuse for laziness and irresponsibility. In that connection we find a different kind of Uriah Heep, not a scoundrel but a person with a ready excuse. Often a person says, "I can't do that. I am a very humble person." The real meaning of that false humility is that it is just serving as an excuse. The words really mean "I am too lazy or too fearful."

It is hard to develop humility in our time for two reasons among others. Here in America we are the wealthiest nation in the world. We are an island of abundance in a world-wide sea of poverty. We are the fortunate ones. That truth is easily distilled into the feeling that we are the competent ones, that we are leading the world's parade. That is not a good support for a true feeling of humility. A second reason for the difficulty of inducing a Christian humility, described in Phillips' translation of this verse—"in humility think more of one another than you do of yourselves"—is that we are in such a competitive world. Almost before the baby walks, his feet are planted on the bottom rung of the ladder of success. We are conditioned to getting on top in the race for advantage and prestige and wealth. That is not the ideal training for humility. The highly competitive spirit leaves little room for counting others better than ourselves.

We are led into a true and deep humility by the remembrance of all we have received, both from God and from men. The feeling of "selfishness or conceit" is driven out by a sharp remembrance of all that comes to us from the open hand of God. Paul traces it clearly: "What have you that you did not receive? If then you received it, why do you boast as if it were not a gift?" (1 Cor. 4:7). An honest view of ourselves, a keen remembrance of all that God has given us, brings about a true humility. Again and again Jesus urges the remembrances that make us humble. "When thou art bidden, go and sit down in the lowest room" (Luke 14:10, AV). "We are unprofitable servants: we have done that which was our duty to do." (Luke 17:10, AV).

107.   BEATING THE BOUNDS

Let each of you look not only to his own interests, but also to the interests of others.   PHIL. 2:4
Learn to see things from other people's point of view.   (Phillips)

This is a plea for the enlargement of a person. It is a plea to escape from the calamity of self-imprisonment. Roy Campbell, the South African poet, has written of some prisoners in Bloomsbury who were corked in a cask of self. He writes that of all the clever people he sees he most delights in himself. "Mine is the only voice I hear, and mine the only face I see."

In the first recorded words of Jesus' ministry, according to Luke, he proclaims his mission to bring "release to the captives . . . , to set at liberty those that are oppressed" (Luke 4:18). The gospel is a deliverance of liberation, of escape from calamity. It liberates from the prison of self, as well as from other jails. The solitary confinement of self is a dire imprisonment. The good news of the gospel is that in Christ there may be a jail break from self. There are people who have made prisoners of themselves, like the prisoner of Chillon. They are confined to a deep well of self and never climb to the top and look out on a human landscape.

Looking after the interests of others, for which Paul pleads here, is not merely a "nice" thing to do. It is absolutely essential if life is to be saved from catastrophe. Looking at the things of others is a life-saving enterprise.

There is an old Scottish custom of "beating the bounds," whereby the inhabitants of a town conducted a yearly inspection tour of its boundaries for defensive purposes. All of us ought to "beat the bounds" of our environment, to make the rounds of the people in our neighborhood or those to whom we are in any way related so that we really see them and know them.

We hear much of the dangers of "isms" of one sort or another. But the worst "ism" we can succumb to is *somnambulism*—sleepwalking. A person can go through life, in his exclusive attention to himself, walking in his sleep. A major sin of life is the sin of not noticing, the sin of lack of observation. That really was the sin of those condemned by Jesus in his parable of the Last Judgment. The sleepwalkers who never noticed any human need about them asked distractedly, as though they had been done a vast injustice, "Lord, when did we see thee hungry or thirsty or a stranger or naked or sick or in prison, and did not minister to thee?" (Matt. 25:44). They were guilty of going through life in their sleep, of not noticing those about them. The same is true of the man called Dives, in the Parable of the Rich Man and the Beggar. Dives was not an inhuman monster. He just didn't see. He was self-blinded. He had passed this beggar at the gate over and over and never really saw him. As he casually saw him, all he saw was a kind of impersonal bundle of rags. He was blind to the person involved. You can hear him in imagination, making a tap, tap, tap on the pavement in God's sight, a blind man.

Phillips' translation is very suggestive: "Learn to see things from other people's point of view." It is a difficult thing to do, so hard that many people never manage to do it at all. There is one point of view—their own. Consequently, they never learn anything and are never impelled to minister. Life's bitterest feuds and its great injustices come from failure to see things from the point of view of others. Lack of imagination is a major sin.

108. GET A NEW MIND

Have this mind among yourselves, which you have in Christ Jesus.
PHIL. 2:5
Let Christ himself be your example as to what your attitude should be.
(Phillips)

These words are the beginning of a great hymn found in Philippians 2:5-11. It is a great hymn of salvation recording the acts of Christ the Redeemer. Some scholars attribute the authorship to Paul. Others regard it as the work of various authors; some look on it as the work of a gifted writer of Paul's own circle.

In this hymn, recounting Christ's coming to earth, his life and death, the whole central core of the gospel brings the most powerful incentive to conduct which could be brought, the person and example of Christ. The high theme of the hymn gives the author's understanding of Christ, that he laid aside his heavenly prerogatives, regarding them as something not to be snatched at but relinquished. He took the form and work of a servant. So it should be with us. We should lay aside our privileges, whatever they may be, or we imagine them to be, and become a servant, and treat one another with the same spirit that we experience in Christ. These words operate in the realm of power, the power that transforms a life.

This is a plea for overhauling the mind, the demand that we get a new mind in Christ. That word "overhaul" is applied arrestingly to Lord Melbourne by his biographer:

His [Melbourne's] lack of system meant that he never overhauled his mind to set its contents in order in the light of a considered standard of value, so that the precious and worthless jostled each other in its confused recesses. Side by side, with fresh and vivid thoughts, lurked commonplaces, contradictions and relics of conventional prejudices of his rank and station.

So often the mind becomes a jumble, like an attic in which all sorts of things are put away in a hodgepodge of disorder. To have the mind that was in Christ Jesus, to have his attitude of a servant, is to give the mind the most drastic overhauling possible. We get a new mind for an old one.

Look steadily at the meaning marked up in the phrase "did not snatch at prerogatives." That comes close to us across the centuries. We are great "snatchers" at advantages. Notice the expressive words used in the effort to give a true translation; "grasp" is found in the RSV and Goodspeed; "set store upon" in Moffatt; "cling" is used by Phillips. May we ask ourselves, "Lord, is it I?" For special prerogatives are often the things by which we live. Laying them aside is like laying aside life itself. Prerogatives are often the last thing we let go. Rigor mortis will find some people clutching their prerogatives in the grip of death. We tend to love something which puts us above others, a decoration they cannot wear, an association they cannot join, a bauble of any sort they cannot use for strutting.

A good command for us all is to *lose your mind*. Lose it into the larger mind of Christ. It can be a terribly sad thing when we say of a person, "He has lost his mind." But it can be a glorious thing when we can say, "He has lost his mind and has the mind which was in Christ Jesus." It is a glorious thing to lose the insistent mind of self, the self-seeking mind which drives us to elbow other people out of our way, the mind which makes us feel, "Make way for me." David Livingstone once expressed what losing our mind and taking the mind of Christ means when he said that he held nothing in life which was not held in relation to the purposes of God.

A man once lost his mind while on the way to Damascus. He got a new mind, the mind that was in Christ Jesus.

109. ABOVE EVERY NAME

Therefore God has highly exalted him and bestowed on him the name which is above every name. PHIL. 2:9

This passage, as it appears in the hymn which is incorporated into this chapter, has a specific meaning. The words show the name of Jesus to be above every name in the threefold universe which is pictured here. The other names, specifically meant here, are the spirit-rulers of the three realms—of heaven, of earth, and of the underworld. Christ is hailed as the victorious Lord of all realms. He has a name that is above every name.

But as we look at those words today, "the name which is above every name," we see a larger meaning than the specific meaning as found in this hymn. We see these words placed in world history. History shows that the name of Christ has been above every name. No other name rivals it in the acclaim and veneration of men. This has not been universal, of course. There have been definite dismissals of Christ from the place of highest honor. But they look strange in the light of today. The gloomy poet of the nineteenth century, James Thomson, author of the poem *The City of Dreadful Night,* has put the name of Jesus down among the names of forgotten deities. He wrote these words and probably believed them:

More than 1800 years have passed since the death of the great god Pan was proclaimed; and now it is full time to proclaim the death of the great god Christ. Eighteen hundred years make a fairly long period even for a celestial dynasty; but this one in its perishing must differ from all that have perished before it, seeing that no other can succeed it; the throne shall remain void forever, the royalty of the Heavens be abolished. Fate, in the form of Science, has decreed the extinction of the gods. Mary and her babe must join Venus. . . . living with them only in the world of art.

How empty it all sounds. Mary's babe has not joined Venus. His name is above every name.

Consider one other affirmation. We read that Christ took the form of a servant. Henceforth the name "servant" is above every name. That has been true in history. The notable killers, the

Caesars, the Napoleons, have been awarded crowns and laurel wreaths. But in the long run the love and veneration has been accorded not to the killers but to the life bringers. Louis Pasteur has been given the palm of greatness over Napoleon, Jenner over Wellington, Socrates over Alexander the Great.

Test this by Wordsworth's line on Milton—"Milton, thou shouldst be living at this hour." To whom would we make such a plea today? Could we say, "Astor, thou shouldst be living at this hour"? John Jacob Astor was the richest man in the United States at his time. But we would not call him back for an encore. We would not plead, "Napoleon, thou shouldst be living at this hour." Hardly. The world has had enough Napoleons to last forever. We would call back not the ruler but the servant. Christ has a name above every name, the name of servant.

Jesus put that judgment in a powerful form, the final evaluation, "You know that the rulers of the Gentiles lord it over them, and their great men exercise authority over them. It shall not be so among you; but whoever would be great among you must be your servant, and whoever would be first among you must be your slave; even as the Son of man came not to be served but to serve, and to give his life as a ransom for many" (Matt. 20:25-28).

Above every name—servant.

110. YOURSELF AND GOD

Work out your own salvation with fear and trembling; for God is at work in you. PHIL. 2:12-13
Work out the salvation that God has given you with a proper sense of awe and responsibility. For it is God who is at work within you. (Phillips)

This text has been a great battlefield for centuries. An army has been on one side of the text and another on the other. Firing across the plain has been vigorous and determined. There have been many charges and assaults. One side, which might be called among other things the Calvinist side, has stressed mightily that salvation is God's affair, "for it is God who is at work." The other side, which might be given several names—free will, anti-Calvinist, liberal, Arminian—camp on the first end of the text, "Work out your own salvation."

By the grace of God, the order "cease firing" has been given in that battle, though some have not yet heard the order. Among most Christians, however, the old military conception of this text is merely an old unhappy, far-off thing and a battle long ago. A new order has been established, man at work *and* God at work. Man can work out his own salvation because God is at work in him. It is somewhat like attaching a piece of machinery to a powerful electric current. For here is the complete equipment for salvation, God's motive power and man's means.

Today we need stress on both man's part and God's. We need stress on the truth that "God is at work in you." For today there are many people who would read the verse in this manner: "Work out your own salvation, because science is at work." There has been quite a superstitious worship of science. Gilbert Highet has given a vivid picutre of this trust in science as the hope of man for anything needed.

There are naïve people all over the world—some of them scientists—who believe that all problems, sooner or later, will be solved by Science. The word Science itself has become a vague, reassuring noise, with a very ill-defined meaning and a powerful emotional charge; it is now applied to all sorts of unsuitable subjects and used as a cover for careless and incomplete thinking in dozens of fields. But even taking Science at the most sensible of its definitions, we must acknowledge that it is as imperfect as all other activities of the human mind.

Many times in the letters of Paul we find this God-plus-man relationship stressed. Paul stresses man's action: "I press on toward the goal for the prize of the upward call of God in Christ Jesus" (Phil. 3:14). He stresses also the action of God: "It is no longer I who live, but Christ who lives in me; and the life I now live in the flesh I live by faith in the son of God" (Gal. 2:20).

The truth "God in you" is an incentive to action, not an excuse for inaction. The position we take is not that of the burlesque of the hymn:

> *Sit down, O men of God!*
> *His Kingdom He will bring,*
> *Whenever it may please His grace*
> *You cannot do a thing.*

But the hymn as written:

> *Rise up, O men of God.*
> *His kingdom tarries long.*

For God works in us.

111. THEREFORE

Therefore, my beloved, as you have always obeyed, so now, . . . work
out your own salvation. PHIL. 2:12
So, then. . . . (Phillips)

"Therefore"—one of life's greatest words. It has motive power.
We can almost hear the hum of a great dynamo in it. Phillips expresses some of the divine propulsive power in this passage, "So,
then. . . ." The preceding verses have carried a great hymn on
the acts of Christ. That assurance is brought into life as a driving
power. The divine logic goes like this: "Christ has taken upon
himself the form of a servant and was obedient to death and has
been highly exalted above all, therefore our life is under a great
compulsion."

Of course, the word "therefore" can be used to enforce any premise.
It can have a downward push as well as an upward pull to the
high calling in Christ Jesus.

We can see this power of "therefore" in strong contrast. Some
people start out with the premise, "We are only physical creatures";
therefore, let us eat, drink, and be merry. Or the starting premise
might be, as it seems to be with some, "The great aim of life is to
rule, to be on top of the heap"; *therefore,* trample down everyone
you can.

Life can dwindle down to that, or it can follow this glorious sentence of Paul, with its divine logic. In view of all that God has done
in Christ, *therefore,* "work out your own salvation; . . . for God is
at work in you."

When life is stripped of its "therefore," it has no high compulsion,
no compelling direction, no shining goal ahead. Its potential is dimin-
ished. Instead of moving under power to a goal, it skids around in
varying directions. It has no saving "therefore." The lack of spiritual
power in a single life, when multiplied in a host of lives, results
in a depleted society. That has been happening. We often think of
the question of Jesus, "When the Son of man comes, will he find
faith on earth?" (Luke 18:8). We ask with deep concern, "How
much faith?"

Winthrop S. Hudson forswears any easy optimism about the
spiritual state of our society. He writes, "Spiritual capital available
to us in our lifetime has been largely depleted. For several decades
the American people have become increasingly illiterate religiously."

There is tremendous need for divine propulsive power—need for a strong "therefore" in our common life. Two convictions of this overwhelming need have come from Great Britain in recent years. The first is from Professor W. Macneile Dixon in his Gifford Lectures:

Our world has begun to doubt the power and sufficiency of unassisted reason to resolve its torturing problems, and of political and economic devices to meet and serve its needs. The search for material remedies to soothe or cure our spiritual distresses, can have only one end, failure. Only when we accept the truth that man does not live by bread alone, will there be laid a foundation stone of a civilization worthy of the name.

Another word comes from Canon F. R. Barry on democracy's need of spiritual power:

We are back on our ultimate ethical resources. What democracy needs for its survival is the leadership of spiritual conviction. Only so far as it is re-established on its true moral and religious basis is there any hope that it can endure and move to the next stage in its development. All that we value most in our tradition is the gift of our ancestral Christianity; all that we can hope to contribute to the future is inseparably bound up with it.

One of the most fascinating things in the history of nineteen centuries is to see the propelling power of the divine "therefore." "God so loved the world"; *therefore* men and women have gone out to the ends of the earth under its power. "The Son of man came . . . to give his life a ransom for many" (Matt. 20:28); *therefore*, there have been outgoing lives, lives of ransom.

112.   WITHOUT GRUMBLING

Do all things without grumbling.   PHIL. 2:14

This plea to avoid grumbling comes at the conclusion of the great hymn in the preceding verses describing the acts of Christ. Coming so close, the words indicate that grumbling is a major calamity, that the freedom of grumbling is one of the consequences of the ransomed and redeemed life.

Grumbling is more than a peccadillo, a somewhat unfortunate trait of personality. The habit of grumbling is a major sin, judged

by what it does to character. It can spoil the whole climate of a
life.

In Thomas B. Reed's poem on Sheridan's ride we read of

> *the rumble and roar*
> *telling the battle was on once more.*

In very unpoetic real life we hear the grumble, rumble, and roar
of a disturbed atmosphere whenever the grumbler gets within
"grumbling distance."

The habitat of the grumbler may be anywhere and take any
form. Ronald Knox of England has made a very reasonable point
in regard to Martha in the story in the gospel of Mary and Martha
in the home of Bethany when Jesus visited them. He writes that
our Lord's rebuke to Martha was not so much against those who
bustle as against those who *grumble*. That was what Martha was
doing when she asked Jesus to rebuke Mary for not helping to get
the dinner ready. She was grumbling! She thought Mary should
help, "plate breaker as she probably was." When we think it over,
we can still hear the note of grumbling in Martha's sharp words.

To allow oneself to become a pathological and habitual grumbler
is a major affliction, for such a one easily slides down the steep
descent to the state where nothing is right, something is the matter
with everything. Someone said, when he heard of the death of
Matthew Arnold, "Poor Matthew, he won't like God." That was
certainly unfair, but it does describe the critical, often scolding attitude
of Matthew Arnold.

Living with a grumbler is like living in a room with all the
window shutters banging in the wind. The tragedy, too, is that the
grumbler hears the banging all the time.

Grumbling does two big things, each of them fatal to the spiritual
life. It shuts thanksgiving out of a life. Gratitude to God is the
great antiseptic of life. It takes the poison out of what would
be without it a self-centered life. All through the Epistles of the
New Testament there is a running plea for the saving power of
thankfulness. It is the obligato which is the background of the whole
marvelous story of God in a human life. "And whatever you do, in
word or deed, do everything in the name of the Lord Jesus, giving
thanks to God the Father through him" (Col. 3:17). "Thanks be to
God for his inexpressible gift!" (2 Cor. 9:15). With thankfulness life
becomes a song instead of a snarl.

Grumbling also drives the spirit of service out of a life. How can
a person think of others with any ongoing love if he is always con-

cerned with his sore toe? How can his world open out to human need if it is full of his own complaints and bewailing? The constant clang of the riveting machine of his own dissatisfaction shuts out the still small voice of God and the still gay music of humanity.

But the grumbler can be saved by the Saviour. Christ proclaimed that he came to bring deliverance to the captive. The captive to the habit of grumbling can be delivered. When the mind is focused on what God has done, when one really sees as the great landscape of life the grace wherein we stand, the bars of a one-celled imprisonment are broken and a soul is freed.

113. CROOKED AND PERVERSE GENERATION

That you may be blameless and innocent, children of God without blemish in the midst of a crooked and perverse generation. PHIL. 2:15
Living in a warped and diseased world. (Phillips)

Watchfulness is needed in considering this description by Paul of his generation as crooked and perverse. It may lead into a great blunder. It may lead into an easy "times-are-out-of-joint" complex. It is easy, and often gives a more or less comfortable, self-righteous feeling to condemn our time as an evil time. That often results in missing the potentialities of a time. We may get to thinking that earlier generations were far better than this one. We read in Proverbs that the eyes of a fool are in the ends of the earth. They are also in the ends of the calendar. That leads to mooning sentimentally about yesterday, thus serving as an excuse for doing little or nothing about today. Frederick Denison Maurice wrote, "There is nothing more foolish than to have a complete disdain for the generation in which one lives."

Of course, there was plenty of the crooked and perverse in Paul's generation. We can hear the echo of it in the tramp of the Roman legions on their way to conquer the earth. We can hear the echo of crookedness in the shouts at the cruel carnivals of murder in the coliseums.

But a fine art needed in life is that of avoiding the easy wholesale condemnation of one's time, and yet clearly recognizing the perversion of our day. Just take a glance at some of the major perversities of our time. There has been far too little anguish of soul and action by mankind in our generation over the nuclear threat of our day. Here is the language of a scientist on the threat of destruction:

Moving out of the Neolithic age may be the world's most difficult problem. . . . It is the retention by atom age men, of the neolithic point of view that says, "You stay in your village and I will stay in mine. If your sheep eat our grass we will kill you, or we may kill you anyhow to get all the grass for our sheep. Anyone who tries to make us change our ways is a witch and we will kill him!"

Another mark of perversity in our time has been and is the all-consuming pursuit of profit. There has been and is a frantic frenzy for profit-making that has blocked some of the best possibilities of our communal life. One cause of our million juvenile delinquents has been that our values have been catching up with us. There has been and is the crookedness and perversity of racial conflict, the injustice and disdain of white superiority. Back of it all has been the banishment of God from large sections of our society. As Babette Deutsch writes, "There has been the dominance of an attitude that ignores whatever escapes the scientist's neat categories."

We are not to be part of this darkness but shining there like lights in a dark place.

114.   MAN OF THE WORLD

I have no one like him.   PHIL. 2:20
All the others seem to be wrapped up in their own affairs.   PHIL. 2:21
(Phillips)

Paul made many heartfelt tributes to Timothy in his letters. There was none greater than here in this paragraph. He gives Timothy a high role, the highest role anyone can aspire to, that of dependable helper in the work of Jesus Christ. The number of passages in which Paul mentions Timothy seem almost to picture a firm—Paul and Timothy, Incorporated.

There is along the railroad tracks in Milford, Connecticut, a building on which appears the sign *Ecclesiastical Brass*. Neither Paul nor Timothy was engaged in what is now called Ecclesiastical Brass. They did not care for rank or title, except for that towering title "Servant of Jesus Christ." Dependable helper—that is a far higher title than "Your Holiness," or "Your Beatitude," or "Your Grace."

There is a title often used of some glittering personality: "Man of the world." It is used to describe a person sophisticated, jaunty, concerned with the affairs of a coterie, the little world of fashion and indulgence. In a different and far more wide-reaching sense,

Timothy was a "man of the world," the world beyond self, beyond a fashionable crowd, the whole of God's world, the world of the things of Christ. In that sense today, many "men of the world" look quite unspectacular to outward view, but there is a global dimension in their mind and heart and life. They are dependable helpers concerned with the affairs of Christ in a globe.

Paul had no one like Timothy. For Timothy's chief concern was not for keeping his hands from activity, but to lay them on a task for Christ. The laying on of hands in the ordination of men to the Christian ministry is impressive, whether hands are laid on by bishop, ministers, or laymen. But even more impressive are the movements of hands being laid on a task of service to others. Barbara Hepworth's representation entitled "Hands Operating" portrays two pairs of hands wielding with blessed skill operating knives on a person. We cannot look at it without feeling, "Thank God for hands!" There are other blessed hands laid on tasks for Christ and for his brothers and sisters. Recall only a few among many of the tasks on which Timothy laid his hands. Paul enumerates them: "I hope, therefore, to send him just as soon as I see how it will go with me" (Phil. 2:23); "Therefore, I sent to you Timothy, my beloved" (Cor. 4:17); "Silas and Timothy remained there" (Acts 17:14); "Having sent into Macedonia two of his helpers, Timothy and Erastus" (Acts 19:22); "Timothy, my fellow worker" (Rom. 16:21)—and many more. There was none like him to Paul. There is none higher than such a role in the world.

Paul says that others "seemed to be wrapped up in their own affairs." All wrapped up. When a person gets too tightly wrapped, his spirit dies of slow suffocation. The best wrapped-up object in the world is an Egyptian mummy. A person wrapped up in himself becomes a mummy.

To be a dependable helper is not as glamorous a role as that of one in high adventure. Timothy's role was not as spectacular as that of Paul, the intrepid leader and pioneer. But it is an indispensable role in the work of Christ, none higher.

115. LIVING UP TO OUR NAMES

Epaphroditus my brother and fellow worker and fellow soldier, and your messenger and minister. PHIL. 2:25

Five names for a Christian disciple! Tremendous names! Epaphroditus has never been admitted to the New Testament Hall of Fame. He does not stand in wide remembrance along with Paul and John and Peter. He is not remembered with Barnabas and Silas and Timothy; not even as well known as Dorcas and Lydia. Fame has passed him by.

Yet, what a tremendous tribute Paul pays to him. What decorations of names he gives him! As we look them over, the thought comes strongly that these names are all ones that ought to fit every Christian, now as well as in far yesterday—"Brother . . . fellow worker . . . fellow soldier . . . messenger . . . minister." Notice what vigorous roles they describe! These are no gentle, namby-pamby compliments. They carry the echo of the clash of fighting, of blood, sweat, and tears.

It is a loss hard or impossible to measure when these names drop out as a common description. The familar names of those who belong to the church, "member," "communicant," and "layman," are noble ones. There can be a battlecry in them. But often they do not mean more than a statistic. Often the fighting and working quality is gone from them. The name "brother" has become obsolete, no longer conveying the meaning of a costly, dedicated relation. And as for the "fellow soldier" title, so often it is only a figure of speech. We sing "Onward, Christian Soldiers," but the nearest many such soldiers ever get to a battlefield is a parade ground or a rest camp behind the lines.

But every name Paul gives to this comrade-at-arms is a robust one. It conveys the feeling of action. Not one of the names suggests a spectator in a grandstand. The early church was to so large an extent a company of participants, not lookers-on. Arthur Hugh Clough wrote, "Life loves no lookers-on at his great game." The Christian church loves no lookers-on at God's Holy War. In the apostolic days it had no name for onlookers.

Also, the genius of the earliest day was expressed in the word "fellow." Most of these people did not engage in a one-man show. They marched, fought, and lived together.

Notice also the final tribute to Epaphroditus, "Risking his life to complete your service to me" (Phil. 2:30). This is an instance of the rating which Paul puts on "risk." He disdains an exercise in security other than the security of faith in God. This is a good thing to remember in an age so deeply marked by the search for security. It ought to be the mark of a Christian now, as it was then: he takes risks. It goes back to the very beginning. Jesus called some fishermen. They took the risk and followed him. He called a man, known to us only as a rich young ruler, and he chose security at home, without any risk. Epaphroditus risked his neck for Paul and the cause of Christ:

we take such good care of our necks, as though they were the most important part of our being.

May we recapture these great names and live up to them.

116. ESCAPE FROM BOREDOM

It doesn't bore me to repeat a piece of advice like this. PHIL. 3:1
(Phillips)
[It] is not irksome to me.
That never tires me. (Moffatt)

The advice which did not bore Paul was this: "Delight yourselves in the Lord." That can be endlessly repeated without a trace of boredom.

How easily we get bored by repetition! Some things, when we do them over and over, make our spirits sink. It can be called "our modern disease." Here is a description by a London physician:

After all, the greatest of human miseries, the most deadly of diseases, is one we cannot touch with the knife or save men from with drugs. I mean boredom. There is more real wretchedness, more torment driving men to folly or what you parsons call sin, due to boredom than there is to anything else. Men and women will do almost anything to escape from it; they will drink, drug themselves, prostitute their bodies, and sell their souls; they will take up mad causes, organize absurd crusades, fling themselves into lost hopes and crazy ventures; they will torment themselves and torture other people to escape the misery of being bored. And one who will discover a cure for that would put an end to more tragedy and misery than all the doctors and physicians put together.

That is a terrible indictment, no doubt exaggerated, yet freighted with a large burden of truth.

But Paul, here, discloses a cure for boredom. There is something "that never tires me." It is directing people to delight. That does not lead to the crushing boredom that lies in wait for us.

> *To-morrow, and to-morrow, and to-morrow,*
> *Creeps in this petty pace from day to day.*

In his words in the synagogue at Nazareth Jesus announced that he was sent to proclaim release to the captives. He does bring release to the prisoners in captivity to boredom. The secret of escape is in delight, our own delight in the Lord, and directing people to the unfailing source of delight in Him.

Look at Paul's demonstration of the delighted life. He had a steady routine of beatings and prisons, mobs and assaults, over and over. Enough to bore a person stiff and utterly tire him. Yet he is never worn down. He even sings at midnight in jail. He can always direct people to delight. "Again I will say, Rejoice" (Phil. 4:4). That is the escape from boredom—delight. Life is never an intolerable burden to one who is caught up in a great surge of joy, like the Gulf Stream. Boredom comes from never feeling God's favorable trade winds.

Because he has delight in the Lord, David Livingstone can say, deep in the heart of Africa, "I wouldn't be anywhere else for worlds." In any place or condition we can say,

> *What terror can confound me*
> *With God at my right hand?*

This very verse pictures it—"You will find it [delight] a great safeguard to your souls."

117. LIFE'S BARGAIN COUNTER

I count everything as loss because of the surpassing worth of knowing Christ Jesus my Lord.   PHIL. 3:8
I considered it useless rubbish.   (Phillips)

We spend a large part of our lives in measuring gain and loss. We love a bargain where the gain exceeds the loss in our figuring. Indeed, we make our way through the world's bazaar, like a comparison shopper, estimating costs and weighing comparative values. What is the greatest value? That is our question again and again. In this shopping expedition, there are some who have no value except price. They live up to the aphorism of Oscar Wilde, "A man who knows the price of everything and the value of nothing."

Here comes a man, Paul, who decides on life's greatest value at any price. The value is so great that price is an impertinent item. Compared to Christ, his greatest gain is loss, "rubbish" as Phillips translates it. A drama not long ago received this overwhelming appreciation: "The only essential missing is a story of any consequence." Paul so regards life's greatest possible gain without Christ. There may be much decoration, but the missing essential is a story of any consequence. For him, there is no story of any consequence compared to the eternal story of God's love in Christ.

What is included in life's greatest bargain is set forth in an old gospel hymn, no longer used to any extent. There were some so-called gospel hymns which were made out of pure syrup of sentimentalism. But not this one. It is the real thing, showing what gain there is in the knowledge of Christ:

> Out of my darkness, sorrow and night,
> Jesus, I come, Jesus, I come;
> Into Thy freedom, gladness and light,
> Jesus, I come to Thee.
> Out of my sickness into Thy health,
> Out of my want and into Thy wealth,
> Out of my sin and into Thy self,
> Jesus, I come to Thee.

What crowding of bargain counters there is in life's bazaar! Shoppers intent on gain by the fistful. The largest crowd, perhaps, at the money counters, eager to pay any price for money. Somewhat fewer, but no less frantic, are those bargaining for fame. Then there is the surging crowd, so eloquently described by Paul a few sentences later in this chapter of Philippians: "Their god is the belly."

But Paul counts all gain, the whole of it, as loss compared to Christ. Christ adds a dimension to life, height—reaching up to God —and another dimension, eternity—which is a quality of length. All is loss compared to the new dimensions of life.

Rudyard Kipling and William Booth, the founder of the Salvation Army, had honorary degrees conferred on them the same day by Oxford University. William Booth was not embarrassed by the famous Kipling. He strode across the quadrangle and asked him, "Young feller, how's your soul?" Booth asked the number one question. Beside that question all distinctions of fame and wealth are as nothing.

"Everything as loss."

118.   THAT I MAY KNOW

That I may know him and the power of his resurrection.   PHIL. 3:10
How changed are my ambitions!   PHIL. 3:9 (Phillips)

"I want to know" has been one of man's unending cries. The desire to know has been one of the greatest drives in human history. It has turned the eyes of men to the highest heavens that they may know the truth about the wheeling stars and galaxies. The passion to know has sent men across uncharted seas and around the globe. They have paid the price of life itself. The desire to know has sent men deep into the earth to learn its secrets. But the endless yearning "I want to know" is in the words of Paul directed with the deepest passion to the highest knowledge, "That I may know him and the power of his resurrection." It is not an easygoing wish that Paul utters, but wishing that is an active straining of every power in the changed ambition to know Christ.

The best way to feel the effects of the power of Christ's resurrection is to see its effect on life. Indeed, very often the best way to describe a thing is to describe effects. Chekhov gives a well-known example of this in one of his letters. He had been reading a story by a friend in which the moonlight was described at length in a highly poetic passage. He wrote, "No! No! Not that way. If you want to describe the moon, just mention that the old broken bottle on the side of the mill dam was glistening in the moonlight." So the best description of the power of God in Christ is that of lives from which light gleams.

The power of the resurrection is in our empowered life. Briefly, its power is that of God taken into a life and life poured out in service. Both intake and output. As Paul described that incoming of the Divine, "It is no longer I who live, but Christ who lives in me" (Gal. 2:20). "Christ in you, the hope of glory" (Col. 1:27). The outgoing life shares in his sufferings. There is no elimination of Calvary in order to have a resurrection. L. P. Jacks has written pointedly that too many people want the resurrection without Calvary.

Also the power of Christ's resurrection is in the power of an endless life. The words "He that doeth the will of God abideth for ever" (I John 2:17, AV) meet the deep need of life, of some hope of fulfillment which cannot be realized here. We feel the need of something that transcends human experience with all its insufficiencies. One of the most profoundly religious passages in modern English poetry is in John Masefield's long narrative poem "The Widow in the Bye Street," where a brokenhearted mother is making her last prayer for her son who is to be executed for murder:

And God who gives beginnings gives the end,
A rest for broken things too broke to mend.

There are so many of them in this world, "Broken things too broke to mend." Every day, in a home or a hospital, somewhere, things too broke to mend! An eye, a limb, a heart, too broke to mend.

Diseases from which one can never recover. Losses which one can never forget. Disappointments too great to be passed over. Failures too complete ever to be made over. Then Christ comes in the power of his resurrection and persuades that all broken things are still in the hands of the great Mender of Broken Earthenware with eternal life, with mendings beyond our resources.

119. STRAINING FORWARD

I press on toward the goal for the prize of the upward call of God in Christ Jesus. PHIL. 3:14
With hands outstretched. (Phillips)

What robust, intense, and athletic words are used for the Christian life all through the New Testament. Here are a few mighty ones from these verses in various translations: "straining forward," "press on," "grasping ever more firmly," "with hands outstretched," "to see if I can capture it." Are they not the echo of the earlier word of Jesus, "strive to enter by the narrow door"? (Luke 13:24).

Such words are far too vigorous to describe the casual, relaxed, easygoing type of Christian life that is so often found. Using any of these words for such a purpose would be like calling a quiet stroll in a garden an "agonizing race." The Christian has an agonizing role. It is well described in Philip Doddridge's rousing hymn, reflecting these very verses:

> Awake, my soul, stretch every nerve,
> And press with vigor on;
> A heavenly race demands thy zeal,
> And an immortal crown.

The intensity and strain is caught in Goodspeed's translation, "Pressing on to see if I can capture it" (Phil. 3:12). Some people never really capture anything in their Christian life, for "capture" is another strong word. They never lay strong hands on any prize. They just sit and listen and look. They have a perverse meaning to Christ's words, "My yoke is easy, and my burden is light" (Matt. 11:30). Their burden is easy because they have never lifted it; their yoke is easy because they have never really put their necks into Christ's yoke. The heavenly prize demands a strain, a grasp, calling on one's whole being. It demands a stern choice that sonship to God and His service are the best things of life. But other things have a way of slipping into first place. The massive merchandise mart in

Chicago has these words displayed in illuminated letters two stories high on its top façade: "The best things in life are here." The description of this claim is given in these words which warm a salesman's glowing heart:

More families are making more money; more new homes are being built; more new waves of working, living and having fun are coming into being. It's a new era in our nation.

All will admit that the mart is a gigantic showcase of national brands, but the claim "The best things in life are here" will cause two questions: "Are they?" "Can the best things in life be found in any merchandise mart?" Paul has another valuation. All marts are lost, even rubbish, compared to the prize of the upward call of God. The best things in life, a mature sonship to God, and a maturity in carrying burdens are the possession of those who are here called "mature." This high prize of Christian maturity differs from the childish traits of character in that it can view life in the long run, instead of the immediate now, and has escaped from the childish demand of "me," "me," "me."

The spiritually athletic life of pressing on brings life's deepest satisfaction and sense of achievement. It is life's high prize. A novelist said this of her demanding job of writing. She makes it a rule never to count the cost of work, time, effort, even health, providing she is building the book. In a higher sense those words apply to Christian discipleship. Nothing, not even a whole world's merchandise mart, can be compared to the surpassing worth of knowing Christ Jesus.

But such a prize comes only with striving, straining, grasping to "see if we can capture it." It is never found in a rest camp but on some kind of a battlefield. It calls for spiritual adventure. Alfred North Whitehead describes a civilization's need of adventure. He writes,

The Chinese and the Greeks both achieved certain perfections of civilization, each worthy of admiration. But even perfection will not bear the tedium of indefinite repetition. To sustain a civilization with the intensity of its first ardour requires more than learning. Adventure is essential, namely the search for new perfections.

That is profoundly true of the Christian life. New adventures are continually called for, new adventures in prayer, in understanding of God, in the service of God.

Keep the word "strain" in your working vocabulary. The great danger of the Christian life is not atheism or agnosticism. It is somnambulism.

120. THE GOD OF THE BELLY

Their god is the belly, and they glory in their shame, with minds set on earthly things. PHIL. 3:19
Their god is their own appetite; . . . and this world is the limit of their horizon. (Phillips)

The word "belly" is one we do not use much any more. It does not rank as a "nice" word. But what it stands for here, the domination of appetite, is not a nice thing. The word is a strong word of Tudor England, and the meaning is powerful and clear even if not now "genteel."

This verse suggests a study in comparative religion. The great competing gods in our world are not Allah or other gods worshiped in other religions. It is the god of appetite, with lavish temples for worship on almost every street. Food has become a paradoxical symbol. On the one hand, it is the symbol of high religion, the highest religion, as with the bread and wine of the communion service. "And he took bread, and when he had given thanks he broke it and gave it to them" (Luke 22:19). On the other hand, it can be the symbol of preoccupation with self and with the world. It can stand for degradation. For literally, when one's god is the belly, it means a degradation of values—life's top values graded down. Paul wrote, "I keep under my body" (I Cor. 9:27, AV). In other words, the soul was on top. But when one's worship goes out to appetite, the soul is graded down.

A man in a restaurant called the attention of a friend to a corpulent man busily writing an order check from a menu. "Look," he said, "that man is writing his autobiography from a menu card." That was no doubt cruel. But there are many people who could write the most essential parts of their autobiography on a large menu card. The god they worship and serve is appetite. In like manner, a widow was once asked by friends of her husband what ought to be carved on his gravestone. She said with real sadness, "I think a carving of a quarter-inch porterhouse steak would do very well. That seemed to be the thing he got most excited about." He was a devout worshiper of the belly god.

That cult finds hosts of followers in America. We are an island of plenty in a sea of hunger. "How can I reduce?" is one of our chief questions. As it has been said, in a hungry world our problem is fifty million "fatties."

The latter part of the verse gives the payment—and a tragically heavy payment it is: "with minds set on earthly things"; or as more vividly translated by Phillips, "this world is the limit of their horizon." The word "horizon" has been called by some students of phonetics as "the most beautiful word in the language." As defined here, our outlook goes beyond this world; the horizen of eternity is the most beautiful thing in life. We are familiar with the title of a novel: *Lost Horizon*. Here Paul writes of a lost horizon as the price of the worship and service of appetite and preoccupation with this world. For a man is truly measured by his horizon. The most beautiful sight in life is "a haze on the far horizon where the known shades into the unknown and the seen shades into the unseen." That is the glorious horizon of faith.

There has been an instrument on the panel board of an airplane called a "false horizon." Worship of the god of appetite gives life a very limited horizon, a very false horizon. For here we find man's true horizon: "But we are citizens of Heaven; our outlook goes beyond this world to the hopeful expectation of the Savior" (Phil. 3:20, Phillips).

121. CITIZENS OF HEAVEN

We are citizens of Heaven. PHIL. 3:20 (Phillips)
Our commonwealth is in heaven.

The newer translations of the New Testament add enormously to the meaning of the words in this text. The King James translation, "our conversation is in heaven," uses the word "conversation" with an obsolete meaning. As has been pointed out, "conversation in the King James translation always refers to conduct, behavior, or manner of life, and is never used in the sense it has today as a term for the give and take of talk." So it means conduct and behavior and allegiance. Moffatt has a still more vivid translation, the rendering "We are a colony of heaven."

All these translations take us away from the idea of "conversation" as talk, to the real meaning of allegiance to the rule of heaven. That is a Christian's highest loyalty. We are all familiar with the invitation "Make yourself at home." They are welcome words from friends in a strange place. But there is a sense in which the words are dangerous. When we make ourselves completely at home, if the world, in the words of Paul, "is the limit of our horizon," so that we are perfectly satisfied to conform to the ways of the world with no allegiance beyond, the words are an invitation to spiritual disaster. There is a true sense in which we must subscribe to the words of the old gospel song:

> *I am but a stranger here,*
> *Heaven is my home.*

If we acknowledge another kingdom and commonwealth, our behavior follows another pattern. The Moffatt translation carries this allegiance into more detail. Paul grew up in a Roman colony. He knew what the acknowledgment of allegiance to a distant authority meant, with its high gift of citizenship. The words "we are a colony of heaven" suggest high adventure in the Christian enterprise. It is the adventure of bringing new territories of life under Christ's rule. A colony is not a crowd on a picnic or a joy ride. It is not an expedition passing through the world, like a Pilgrim's Progress to some celestial city. It is a settlement. Our business on earth is to be colonizers of heaven, to set up an order of life which will incarnate the spiritual rule of Christ.

We get the high meaning of a colony in a close look at many of the things brought over to Massachusetts by the Pilgrims. As we look at those pieces of furniture and household equipment now preserved in Pilgrim Hall, Plymouth, we realize that every bit of it speaks of the homeland, the loved and noble heritage of England. These men and women did not come to the wilderness to live like savages, to drop their ways and go native. They carried England with them. In like manner, we are a colony of heaven.

The word "colony" suggests one ever-present danger to a church as a colony of heaven. Think of that tragedy of early American history known as the "lost colony" of Roanoke Island. In 1587, Sir Walter Raleigh planted an ill-fated colony from England on Roanoke Island off the North Carolina coast. A relief expedition did not get back to the colony until 1591; no trace of the colony was ever found. It was a lost colony. So a company of Christians may become a lost colony if they forget their high allegiance. If the salt of their witness has lost its savor, it is lost from its great purpose.

122.   A NAME IN A BOOK

Whose names are in the book of life.   PHIL. 4:3

How much of the busy, bustling, racing life which men live today consists of efforts to get one's name in a book! How many books there are to which we eagerly demand an entrance!

To begin at the lowest level—the telephone book. It is a large book, constantly adding to its list of names, so that it is not exactly a book of the elite. However, it is an elite of those who can afford to pay for a telephone, or at least those who do pay for one. So it is a minor prize to get our name in that book.

Then there is the tax collector's book. Men do not enjoy being given a high place in that book. They wail about it, but they would not be missing from it at any price. For it is a list of the taxable, and of those, presumably, who count financially. We do not love paying the tax, but we surely do love what is left!

We strain to get into the bankbook list of depositors. Now we are getting into a select company. Our name in that book is a high distinction. Some people even think of the bankbook as the Infallible Book.

Coming up in the scale, there is another book, the social register. That is the book with a real snob appeal. What terribly high prices have been paid and are being paid to get a name in that book. This abode of the blessed, the Elysian fields of Society, with a big "S," has been well compared to the ladderlike arrangement of the Hindu caste system, where one must kiss the feet of the one above and kick the face of the one beneath. So the gentle art of snobbery goes on to new refinements among those whose only measure of personal position is the wholly negative one of exclusiveness. To many people the top achievement is to be listed in the social register.

There is another book, larger than the social register, a book that is the goal of the frantic game of name in a book—*Who's Who in America.* It is, of course, a great convenience. But to some eager beavers, it is the goal of all existence. They must be rated among the "who's who." Some people aim at a much smaller volume, not yet compiled or printed but very real in the minds of people—"Who's Who in Jonesville."

Beside all these is another book—the Book of Life. It is the great volume of earth and heaven—to get one's name in that book is life's highest distinction. It is the book of those who have entered into the life of God. It is the book of those who have received life from God and who have given life to God. Those who serve have joined the top society of earth. What would happen if the men who joined the hundreds of lodges and societies would only join the human race, to feel the pulse of its brotherhood, its twinge of pain as their own, and lay its burden on their shoulders.

Someday God's Book will be opened, and what surprises! How the mighty will be put down from their thrones and those of low degree exalted. Take those who regarded themselves as the great in

Jesus' time in Jerusalem—Annas and Caiaphas and Pilate. What a surprise there will be when on the top of the list in the Book of Life will be a poor widow who dropped two small coins in the alms box.

A question for everyone: "Is my name written there?"

123. THE ART OF FORBEARANCE

Let all men know your forbearance. PHIL. 4:5
Have a reputation for gentleness. (Phillips)

Among the things that must gladden the heart of Satan is a mistranslation of a Bible passage. For often a mistranslation of the original Greek or Hebrew makes the reader see through a glass darkly. The dark glass has resulted in much harm. Here in this verse what was an exhortation to gentleness has been often taken by many people for an approval of halfhearted and slipshod work. The mistake is in the translation of the word rendered "moderation." To us that word brings a suggestion of laziness and mediocrity. It is a mistranslation of the Greek adjective which is here used as a noun. The word, as correctly translated for our time, means forbearing, gentle, gracious, kind. The plea is to let everyone with whom we have relations in daily life experience our forbearance. To us the word means patience, endurance, refraining from pressing our claims and rights. That is a long distance from what has been read into the verse by many people: the refusal to take an outright positive and vigorous stand on any question. Some people have let their cowardice and insipid "moderation" be known immoderately! Their watchwords are "never get excited" and "never risk going out on a limb. Be moderate."

How Christianity and the church have grievously suffered from those devoted to moderation! It inevitably makes for compromise with evil. The company of Christians who went out to turn the world upside down did not bring the message to the world, "Now, everybody be moderate." The younger Pliny, writing to the Roman Emperor, described the Christians by saying that they were obstinate as pigs. That was a high tribute, for an obstinate pig is never moderate. The call to the Christians was never moderate. It was a battlecry, "Put on the whole armor of God, that you may be able to stand against the wiles of the devil. For we are not contending against flesh and blood, but against the principalities, against the powers, against the world rulers of this present darkness, against the spiritual hosts of wickedness in the heavenly places" (Eph. 6:11-12). Here is what the author of Revelation thought of a cautious moderation, "So, because you are lukewarm, and neither hot nor cold, I will spew you out of my mouth" (Rev. 3:16).

This word "forbearance," translated as "gentleness" by Phillips, reaches out to an earlier word, "Blessed are the meek, for they shall inherit the earth." That word "meek" does not mean weakness or fear. It denotes power under control. The one who has forbearance forbears to use strength in a pugilistic manner. He does not have a get-out-of-my-way manner in his contact with people. There is a better highway direction he follows: "Yield right of way." It is not the way of self-pushing or self-appreciation but the way of love. Forbearance is the embodiment of Paul's word which occurs in this same epistle, "Let each of you look not only to his own interests, but also to the interests of others" (Phil. 2:4).

124.   FOR AN AGE OF ANXIETY

Have no anxiety about anything.   PHIL. 4:6

This is a timely word for our "age of anxiety." But telling our generation to have no anxiety about anything seems offhand like telling a company of people sitting on the edge of the crater of an active volcano to be not anxious. To the many anxieties of private life we have added the anxieties over human survival, or an obliterating nuclear war. In these days of potential strife with hydrogen bombs and long-range missiles, we feel strongly that there is "no place to hide," not even in the most remote spot of earth. We can say to the atomic bomb, "Whither shall we flee from thy presence?" We can easily imagine our time to be like that described by the prophet Zephaniah. Our day "is a day of wrath, a day of trouble and distress, a day of wasteness and desolation, a day of darkness and gloominess, a day of clouds and thick darkness" (Zeph. 1:15 AV). We are living in Anno Zephaniah.

That danger is put vividly in a bit of history on the South Pacific. Here it is as recorded in *The New York Times* by A .B. C. Whipple:

There was in Australia during the 1930's a scholar of world events who foresaw that a great war was sure to break out. He realized that Japan would be one of the belligerents. . . . Accordingly this twentieth century wise man studied the atlas in search of the perfect hiding place, the best possible island of escape from the storm about to break across the civilized world. By the employment of careful logic and the process of deduction, he finally selected the spot, an obscure virtually uninhabited island, and in the summer of 1939 he went ashore there. The name of the island was Guadalcanal!

No place to hide but every place to be anxious. Some people try to find a refuge from anxiety in many inadequate ways.

One has been to try to make a kind of vacuum out of the mind so that all disturbing thoughts are expelled. It is never to allow any thought which gives us worry or an anxiety. Here is a word of counsel recorded in a book by an exponent of the "be relaxed" school of thought. He gives this counsel: "If an unhappiness thought should enter your mind, stop, eject it, and substitute a happiness thought." How lovely! But suppose Jesus had followed this wise advice in the garden of Gethsemane. The cross was definitely an unhappiness thought. But he did not stop it, or eject it. He prayed, "Not my will, but thine."

One other inadequate way of escape from anxiety is to crowd mind and life with activities. A steamship company proudly tells us, "You're a world away from worry on the world's fastest ship." We respond, "Is that so?" In the most luxurious places in the world both normal anxiety and neurotic anxiety may thrive. Anxiety is not to be crowded out by activity. It is crowded out of the mind by faith. A certain amount of normal anxiety is necessary for the effective life. In *Moby Dick* Captain Ahab would not have a seaman who was not afraid of a whale. That, of course, was fear rather than anxiety. But there should be a preserving anxiety as well as a saving fear. There should be a deep concern for the affairs of one's life and one's world. Compared to fear which is a response to a threat which is specific and objective, anxiety is vague and diffuse. Rollo May's definition of anxiety is a good one: "Anxiety is a reaction to a threat to the existence of one's self as a human being, or to values that one identifies with that existence." That does not mean the obliterated mind. It can mean the *active* mind—one that does everything possible to meet a threatened situation, but which underneath the activity is a confident trust in God. Have no anxiety is a counsel not to allow the unceasing worry which causes nothing but useless agitation of mind, heart, and nerves. Paul gives the key to escape from endless anxiety in the word "rejoice" (Phil. 4:4). That is the positive affirmation of faith. No matter what happens, a rejoicing faith overcomes anxiety. For with Paul's direction, "Have no anxiety," there is the basis of victory over it in these resources: "Thou wilt keep him in perfect peace, whose mind is stayed on thee" (Isa. 26:3, AV). If God be for us, who can be against us? "I can do all things through Christ which strengtheneth me" (Phil. 4:13, AV).

125. THE QUEST OF PEACE

The peace of God, which passes all understanding, will keep your hearts and your minds in Christ Jesus. PHIL. 4:7

This passage has a pertinent and powerful word to our generation. Peace is a consequence of certain conditions. It is not something we win by direct assault. That is the blunder of a great multitude in our day. A great host of people have been making a frontal attack on peace of mind, determined to take the kingdom of peace by violence.

Peace of mind is a by-product of certain conditions and actions. Happiness is also a by-product. Those who go after it as an end in itself, miss it. A character in a modern novel cries out, "I want to take life by the throat and choke happiness out of it." But happiness does not come by choking. Neither does peace. There has been, of course, much psychological and religious wisdom in the search for peace of mind. But the search for peace in itself as an end to be captured is all wrong. It is a by-product of a higher search after a model set forth by Jesus, Seek ye first the kingdom of God *and peace of mind will be added to you*. The peace of God passes understanding. It does not come from understanding of ways to snare people. It is a consequence of dedication to God and His will, and trust in the goodness of God.

Some people have made a direct attempt to capture peace of mind by trying to shut out from their mind every indication of evil. They seek

> *Peace, perfect peace,*
> *In this dark world of sin*

by refusing to look at the real world where evil and sin abound. The peace of God does not come from running away from the world, by being blind to the evil in it. It is not a blind man's peace. St. Paul found peace of mind in the midst of turmoil. He tells of the secret, "Christ liveth in me" (Gal. 2:20, AV). His life as an evangelist was a continual parade of jails, mobs, and beatings. But in it, not by running away, he had the peace of a dedicated will.

In this very paragraph there is a trail marked out by Paul, leading away from anxiety to peace. "In everything by prayer and supplication with thanksgiving let your requests be made known to God" (Phil. 4:6). It resembles an equation. Prayer plus supplication plus thanksgiving equals the peace of God.

126.   FIX YOUR MIND ON THESE THINGS

Whatever is true, whatever is honorable, whatever is just, whatever is
pure, whatever is lovely, whatever is gracious, if there is any excellence,
if there is anything worthy of praise, think about these things.   PHIL.
4:8
Fix your minds.   (Phillips)
Let your minds dwell.   (Goodspeed)

There are two things, among many others, to be noticed and
stressed in this great exhortation to feed the mind.

One is to keep thinking on these things that appear in this glorious
list. Do not use it as a now-and-then exercise. Make it the steady employment of the mind. Phillips translates "think about these things"
as "fix your minds on the things which are holy," etc. Fix is a strong
word—it means steadily holding to a thing. With many people there
is no fixity to the mind; it swings like a weathercock, responding to
every wind of doctrine and every new occurrence. Goodspeed translates as "let your minds dwell." These great areas of life are not a
place to visit but to live. There is a great difference between the old-
fashioned parlor and the modern living room. The old New England
parlor was a place to use only occasionally, on a wedding or a funeral
or a formal call. What a triumph of grace when the parlor gives
way to a living room—airy, sunny, inviting and cheerful and warm,
a center of everyday life! Paul asks people to make these great
themes the places where our minds and spirits live. Move in and live
there.

A second thing to note in this appeal is that it urges us to look for
the positive values of life and experience. This is important, for in
our day the very opposite is followed by many. They make up their
minds as a cheap sensational newspaper is made up. The plan seems
to be, "Whatsoever things are shameful, shocking, or perverse, think
on these things."

That pattern is followed in quite a large part of today's fiction. The
direction that is followed seems to be, "If there be any virtue, if there
is anything to praise" in the book, you will have a dull book. So let's
take this road to the best-seller list: "Whatsoever is ugly, sinful, coarse,
degrading, think on these things for 350 pages!"

Sometimes the mind is merely filled with the trivial instead of the
pure, just, true, and lovely. Some people go through life like children
who are being taken on an automobile trip through magnificent

scenery but who sit glued to comic books or travel games. So they miss the beauties of holiness or give them a swift hurried glance. Paul asks for a life employment. Keep thinking of these things. Fix the mind on them.

127. WHATEVER IS TRUE

Finally, brethren, whatever is true. PHIL. 4:8

Note that "whatever is true" stands at the very top of Paul's great list of things to think about steadily. It is ahead of all the rest, "whatever is honorable, whatever is just, whatever is pure, whatever is lovely, whatever is gracious."

We are likely to forget that, just as a great host of people have forgotten it in their devotion to the pleasant, the lovely, the gracious. As we bring our minds to bear on the world, we must first face the truth about the world and life, no matter how difficult the truth may be. Many people have followed only the latter part of this marvelous list for thinking. They seek the pleasant, whether true or not. Facts that do not make for happiness or complacency are eliminated from their view. Here is one man, the poet William Butler Yeats, making a rightabout-face in the direction of truth-seeing and truth-speaking. He wrote toward the end of his life, in a pamphlet *On the Boiler*, "I must lay aside the pleasant truths I have built up for years and seek the brutality, the ill breeding, the barbarism of truth." All truth, of course, is not brutal or barbaric. There is the truth of God's revelation in Christ. That was what Paul had chiefly in mind in this very passage. That is the truth which makes us free. But a devotion to truth must not shrink from facing every truth, wherever it leads.

The tragic weakness that many people in the churches show is that they do not give a welcome to the truth when it attacks one of their sacred cows, or when it comes as a criticism of their brand of religion or church. When the herdsman of Tekoa, Amos, brought unpleasant truth to the capital city of Bethel, the top religious authorities did not welcome it or even allow its utterance. They had no use for this kind of religious truth: "I hate, I despise your feast days, and I will not smell in your solemn assemblies. . . . Take thou away from me the noise of thy songs. . . . But let judgment run down as waters, and righteousness as a mighty stream" (Amos 5:21, 23-24). They wanted a soothing song—a religious lullaby.

Many people in churches today shrink from truth in any book dealing with the ugly realities of life among us. That keeps them from dealing with harsh truth or bringing the Christian religion as a saving force in evil situations. Many in the churches have had a vicious preoccupation with the wholesome. Many parishioners can enjoy a sweet sentimental tale on the intellectual and ethical level of *Pollyanna* or *The Bobsy Twins in Camp* but will run from a searching examination of truth in racial relations in *Strange Fruit* or *Native Son*.

The failure of organized religion to appreciate and profit from present-day realism has been a calamity of the first order. It has meant a heavy handicap to its efforts to bring spiritual resources to bear on the life of the time. The attitude of many religious people, including ministers, has been too much that of shock at what offended their taste or their morals; they have been too swift in pulling down the shutters of their minds at the new, at the depressing, at what they disdain as "unwholesome."

One great weakness of the Christian churches as an agency for spiritual and ethical transformation lies in a commonly accepted idea of so-called "spirituality." In this view, the further religion is removed from the truth in social life and concrete situations, the more "spiritual" it becomes. A vague, abstract idea of the spiritual life does find wide enough acceptance to make it blur seriously the ethical understanding and spiritual insight of the churches. "Spirituality" has been so predominantly associated with emotional states and personal habits, so tied up with pious devotional practices, so measured by participation in services of worship, that problems and issues of tremendous concern to millions of people have been shut out from inclusion as spiritual issues.

Jesus never shut himself from any human need. There it was spread out before him in every roadway in Palestine. He sought it out. A question lived on in his life—"What wilt thou have me to do?" (Acts 9:6 AV). It was the way the Master went. Shall not the servant do it still? If we rely on God's truth in Christ, we should never hide from any other truth in our world.

"Whatever is true, . . . think. . . ."

128. THE SHINING SECRET

In any and all circumstances I have learned the secret of facing plenty and hunger. PHIL. 4:12

A large part of the history of the race has been the search for a secret. The shout of discovery, "Eureka!" has been a prominent word in many languages.

The long history of discovery and invention has stretched out around the world and through the calendar. It has been a far reach from the discovery of the wheel and fire—man's early learning of secrets—down through the adventures of Archimedes in, as has been reported, his bathtub, followed by the shout of "I have found it," Jenner's discovery of the cure for smallpox, Pasteur's learning the secret of the germ, to the Salk vaccine and nuclear explosions.

Some of the ultimate secrets of the universe have been locked up in the mind and soul of man. In these words in Philippians Paul proudly and gratefully affirms that he has learned a top secret of life, a secret that a great host of people have never unlocked—facing both plenty and hunger, abundance and want. It is a high secret— the discovery of a soul that is not a creature of outward conditions. He lived not by outward calms and storms but by the inward weather of the mind and heart, in any and all circumstances. That covers all outward weather.

It is a tremendous secret—that of keeping life on an even keel by the power of a great stabilizer. People have gone to pieces when they have missed it. People have gone to pieces by reason of want. They have become bitter and plunged into despair, with their resources collapsed. In equal manner people have gone to pieces from plenty. Jesus had seen much of the spiritual and moral collapse from a frightening cause, abundance. He said that it is hard for a rich man to enter the kingdom of heaven.

This secret is not one that he who runs may reach. Most good things in life are missed by running past them. But the secret is an open one to the person who will stop, look, and listen to God's working in life—in want and in plenty. The secret is to have something greater at the center of a life than want or abundance. The secret is the domination of God's grace in a life. With that on the throne hunger and plenty are both incidentals. Life does not follow a manic-depressive cycle, high one day and low the next. It stays steady, above all fluctuations of condition or fortune. The secret— Christ liveth in me. Paul spells it out in large letters in the next sentence: "I can do all things in him who strengthens me."

The Epistle of Paul
to the Colossians

129. THE CHURCH OF CHRIST

To the saints and faithful brethren in Christ at Colossae.   COL. 1:2

Here is one of the earliest names of the Christian church,—"saints and faithful brethren." Difficult, but what a glorious name to live up to!

Imbedded in the letters of Paul is the conception of the church as part of the gospel. That can be taken in a very bad sense. It is bad when a church substitutes itself for the gospel, when the organization gives itself precedence over the message. It must be one of the devices of Satan to bring that about.

Yet, the church is a real part of the gospel. The gospel was given in a fellowship and to a fellowship. It has moved in a fellowship and brought Christian persuasion to men in and through a fellowship. As the young church went out into the Greek and Roman world, people were drawn to the fellowship before they clearly understood the message. Paul asks, "Do you despise the church of God?" (1 Cor. 11:22). If you do, make light of it; you have missed a real part of God's work of grace. Paul prays and works for the unity of the fellowship of the church. There are strong bonds that bind the fellowship together. The leader of a mountain-climbing group which ascended Mt. Everest writes, "Morale was evidently high. Most satisfactory of all was to observe how our friendship and confidence in each other had increased. We had been together on the rope, and had had reason to respect each other's prowess." In the fellowship of Christ, men and women had "been together on the rope." Their spirits were tied together.

The highest conception of this fellowship is glimpsed in the gleaming sentence of Paul, "You are the body of Christ" (1 Cor. 12:27). It is hard to compass all the meaning of that phrase, but it is a great idea for the imagination. It brings a high conception of human significance. To be part of the body of Christ sharpens the sense of responsibility. It is sobering to realize that our weakness may represent a Christ with paralyzed hands; our dullness of perception may represent a Christ with blind eyes and deaf ears. But the highest churchmanship comes from the sense of serving as Christ's body.

There are many dangers which may befall a church. Two very subtle ones are respectability and dignity. Both may prove fatal to a church as a working, serving fellowship of Christ. A church may become so enamored of a respectable place in a polite society, and in love with a solemn dignity, that it fails in the lowly role of seeking and serving that which is lost.

There are many varieties of churches through the years. Let two stand in extreme contrast. One is the church, met with here and there, which has been preoccupied with mechanics. One scurrying activity follows another and looms larger than the practice of love. It might be called "The Church of the Holy Fidgets." In its busiest busy season it looks something like the practices of Moslem pilgrims at Mecca. They reverently kiss the Black Stone, solemnly go around the Kaaba three times running and four times walking, run to a neighboring holy hill seven times, run to a second holy hill, and then stop to catch their breath while they listen to a sermon. Quite a field day! "The Church of the Holy Fidgets" has the same kind of ecclesiastical genius.

The other church might be known by the name of an actual church in Chicago—St. Stephen's Church. It is called "The Church at the End of the Road." That is a fitting location for a church of Christ. There are so many people who come to the end of their road. They have reached the end of their hope, of their strength, of their money. Go through the gospels and recall how many people met Jesus at the end of the road. It is a high role to be a church at the end of the road, "saints and faithful brethren."

130. GOD'S POINT OF VIEW

We are asking God that you may see things, as it were, from his point of view COL. 1:9 (Phillips)
That you may be filled with the knowledge of his will.

This plea to the Colossians runs all through Paul's letter to them. He implores the Christian converts to learn God's will and do it, rather than follow the false teaching which was pulling them away from God's revelation in Christ. Part of the false teaching against which Paul bore down with all his might was that Christ was only one among many powers, that the Colossians could continue to be slaves to observances which had no foundation in the gospel. All through the letter there runs the conflict between God's will and man's will as represented by the proselyters.

The phrase "God's point of view" touches the imagination and starts it jumping. Inevitably, we see things from our own point of view. In fact, without putting the question into spoken words, we ask, "What other point of view could be valid?" It is often difficult to see or to remember God's point of view. God's will, His point of view, is represented in Christ. In Christ we see sharp differences between God's will and man's will. So much of the spiritual and social progress of the world has come from the substitution, as far as it has gone, of God's point of view to the views that take no account of God.

That difference is striking. For centuries, many men saw a slave. God saw a man created in His own image. It has been a long, long struggle to get God's point of view about man into the hearts and minds of many people. Great hosts of people do not yet share God's point of view, "All one in Christ Jesus." They prefer the horrors of *apartheid,* or some similar view of Negroes as a lower order of creation to be herded like cattle.

God's will puts the value of one man infinitely high. A common point of view held by multitudes of men is that a man is expendable without great loss. Napoleon after a battle wrote to his wife, Marie Louise, that he had won a great victory and "lost no one of importance." He lost hundreds, even thousands, of men—but they were of no importance to him. They were important to God.

In the Roman world into which the gospel came, girl babies were often exposed to the weather; murdered, in fact. The point of view was that they were nuisances. The Christians brought to that cruel world God's point of view, that girl babies were not nuisances but priceless daughters of Almighty God. Often, man sees an opportunity to make gain. God sees a sin.

We see the difference between God's point of view and what is often man's in the relative size of things. Man has seen small beginnings and has despised them. God's point of view is different. He sees things as small as a mustard seed. God measures size differently from the way man so often does. Here is God's slide rule: "The kingdom of heaven is like to a grain of mustard seed, which a man took, and sowed in his field: which indeed is the least of all seeds: but when it is grown, it is the greatest among herbs, and becometh a tree" (Matt. 13:31-32).

In the years of the early church, the great majority of men and women saw the little Christian groups, a company of unimportant fanatical people. God had a different point of view. That is sharply pictured in the ruins of the Roman Coliseum. It is a bit of sober, authentic history that the most important things that ever happened in that gigantic Coliseum were not the gladiatorial games. With 100,000 spectators at the murders, they were not the triumphs of emperors. In the divine view, they were Christian martyrs thrown to the lions and lit as torches. Those comparatively few unimportant people opened up a new world.

Drop down the centuries. In man's point of view—William Carey, making shoes with a map in front of him was a commonplace object. But in the divine view, he was a swinging door for the gospel into a continent. In man's viewpoint, the Haystack Prayer Meeting was the rather ridiculous adventure of a few impecunious students at Williams College caught in a rainstorm. In God's point of view it was an advance company of an endless line of splendor. We have a God of the long run, who makes a great tomorrow out of a mustard seed.

131. POWER FOR ENDURANCE

May you be strengthened with all power, according to his glorious might, for all endurance and patience with joy. COL. 1:11

We usually think of power as a hammer blow. Our world is full of tremendous blows of power. But here is a very different purpose of the giving of power, "for all endurance and patience with joy." It is a different kind of power. We can see one kind of power in a nuclear explosion, or a lifting power, raising a great weight to a height. There is another kind of power represented by a bridge. There is power to endure in the girders and cables, power to endure heavy loads, to carry them safely. It is that kind of power which Paul has in mind.

Life needs power for endurance. We have to endure more often than we are called on to assault. It takes more power of a special kind to endure. It is like the difference, as has often been pointed out, between an ocean liner driving through a heavy sea and a light ship which has to stand still and take any blow that comes. It is far more exhilarating to crash with power than to endure. Consequently, endurance of a difficult situation is a spiritual achievement calling for empowered patience. This is reflected in some ways in an old song:

It is not the jumping fences that hurts the horses feet
It's the hammer, hammer, hammer on the hard highway.

It is the hammer, hammer, hammer on the hard highway of life that calls for power for endurance, the daily march, the burden strapped on our shouders. No doubt the best commentary on bringing power from God for life's ardors and endurances is found in some of the various translations of this verse. Phillips translates, "able to pass through an experience and endure it with courage." That, by the power and grace of God, has been done. It is one of life's greatest victories. When we see a life passing with courage and victorious endurance through *any* experience that would flatten an ordinary person, witness one of life's greatest sights. Such enhanced and endowed people are among the world's greatest wonders. Goodspeed's translation will describe this wonder: "He will nerve you perfectly with strength for the cheerful exercise of endurance and forbearance in every situation."

But some people, Christian in name and profession, do not allow themselves to be nerved. A few years ago this want-ad appeared in the London *Times:* "Wanted by an invalid lady, a housekeeper. Must be a good churchly woman to take entire charge of house and four servants. A cheerful Christian, if possible!" Turn that last item over in your imagination—"A cheerful Christian, if possible!" The writer of that advertisement had probably had some experience with Christians in whom cheerfulness was impossible. They give the impression of undertakers' assistants on duty. They have not received power for endurance that is available to anyone who will receive it. The most thrilling use of the word "endured" in the Bible or in any literature is this: "who for the joy that was set before him endured the cross" (Heb. 12:2).

132.   NATURALIZED

He has delivered us from the dominion of darkness and transferred us to the kingdom of his beloved Son.   COL. 1:13

One scene gives a sharp picture of some of the meanings of this sentence of Paul—a naturalization ceremony, in which people have renounced their former allegience and are made citizens of the United States. Usually this is done in a drab office or courtroom, with a rather routine, uninspiring ceremony. Fortunately, efforts are being made in some cities to surround the ceremony with the dignity and impressiveness it deserves.

This ceremony of naturalization is a shadow of Paul's description of the Christian's experience. He renounces the old dominion of darkness over his life and takes on a new allegiance and responsibility.

He is transferred, is made a citizen of Christ's kingdom. This does not happen automatically. It comes as the gift of God. Phillips' translation makes this clear: "He rescued us from the power of darkness, and reestablished us in the kingdom of his beloved Son." God has acted for us. We find this perfectly expressed in First Peter: "The wonderful deeds of him who called you out of darkness into his marvelous light" (2:9). When we are naturalized we are brought from a dark pit into a floodlighted room, or better still, from midnight to sunrise.

Yet some have never really been naturalized or transferred. They bear the name of Christ formally, but even after years, they are still aliens, not naturalized citizens of "the kingdom of his beloved Son."

In order to be "transferred" from the dominion of darkness, we must renounce allegiances opposed to the Kingdom of Christ. That is easy when it is confined to normal worship. We have no worshipful allegiance to Baal, to Mohammed, to Buddha. But many still have an allegiance to old Mosler, to Bacchus the God of Alcohol, to Venus the Goddess of Lust, to Mercury the God of Speed and sharp dealing, all of whom are much worshiped among us.

Then there are the servants of a master, not listed in any work of comparative religion. The allegiance to self must be renounced, a hard rule to be given up. There is something very suggestive in one of our commonest exclamations, "Dear Me!" It is not too fantastic to think of that exclamation as the strongest profanity, swearing by the strongest and most revered person we know, ourselves. "Dear Me!" Our "Me" is very dear to us. We must be translated, naturalized out of the dark anarchy of lifting up our souls to the vanity of "Dear Me!" into the Kingdom of Christ. Instead of "Dear Me!" there must be other affections. "Dear Lord and Father of Mankind" and "O Mother Dear, Jerusalem."

133.   IMAGE OF GOD

He is the image of the invisible God.   COL. 1:15

The world has been full of images of God of every sort, all the way from the Olympian Zeus by Phidias, one of the Seven Wonders of the World, down to the crudest moldings of primitive man.

Much of the animal kingdom and much of the world has been scoured to make images of God, many of them looking like the products of a diseased imagination. All history has seen strange images of God.

One of the chief points of Paul's letter to the Colossians is here made—as it is made in this epistle over and over—that Christ is not one among many powers, but the very image of God. As Phillips translates it, "Christ is the visible expression of the invisible God." We believe in a Christlike God. The word in the Gospel of John expresses that perfectly: "He who has seen me has seen the Father" (14:9). Jesus going about doing good and holding out hands of help and healing to the suffering—that is the image of God. The Jesus who said, "Thy sins be forgiven thee" (Matt. 9.2, AV), the Christ of forgiveness—that is the image of God. That strange man on a cross, on a green hill far away, outside a city wall, pouring out life in love—that is the image of God.

But that image of Christlike God has been terribly blurred. It has been tragically blurred by the cruelties practiced under the name of God, such as the Inquisition and the many burnings and slaughters. The loving, compassionate Christ was a long, long distance from the stern God of many New England Puritans. The seeking God has been blurred. Christopher Morley has written, "As tragic as comic can be, I who am so unimportant, still seem so important to me!" That is a small part of it. The larger part of it is that we are important to God, the seeking God whose image is Christ.

A press dispatch from Rochester, England, a few years ago told of the ancient custom of "Sealing the child Bishop." The Rectory said that the installation of a thirteen-year-old boy as Bishop in St. Peter's Church was a part of the program to bring a return of "some of the old glamor" in St. Peter's Church. The "old glamor" of God will never be brought back by any kind of a show or ceremony and the glamor of God can be restored only by brightening the image of God in Christ. God is restored when His image, Christ, is seen in the lives of Christ's disciples.

134. BEFORE ALL THINGS

He is before all things. COL. 1:17

In this paragraph, as all through this letter, Paul is refuting the chief heresy that was bewitching many of the Christians at Colossae. He affirms, with every power of mind and every gift of speech in him, that Christ is not one of many powers, of angels and of the creatures, not just one of a chorus, a member of a hierarchy or of a group. Christ is not one of many, but One. He is the Son of God, the visible expression of God.

Paul fought a battle royal for the supremacy of Christ then. He won his battle. To Christians who trust the Christian tradition at all, the idea of Christ as one among many towers is an old, dead philosophy. But the battle for the *supremacy* of Christ as one takes an entirely different form. It is not primarily intellectual but practical. The rivals of Christ are not principalities and powers of any supernatural kingdom or realm, but practical powers of this world. The heresy of our day is allowing other things to take precedence over Christ in man's life. We have our own polytheism. Of course, to us polytheism as a formal belief belongs back in a book or the age of fable or ancient history. But polytheism, standing for allegiances and devotions that come above Christ, is part of our very life.

A picture of things which outrank Christ in man's mind appeared recently in a news item. Here it is:

To publicize a new history book, the publishers, Grosset and Dunlap, asked a panel of 28 historians, educators, and journalists to rate the 100 most significant events in history. First place: Columbus' discovery of America. Second, Gutenberg's development of movable type. Eleven events tied for third place. Tied for fourth place: U.S. Constitution takes effect, ether makes surgery painless, X-ray discovered, Wright Brothers' plane flies, Jesus Christ is crucified.

So Jesus ties for fourth place! That was the best he could do on this rating of importance.

Christ belongs first on the throne. Life needs one of its highest joys, the joy of a *priority*. Some lives have no priority at all. Everything is alike. Others have a commanding priority, Christ's priority. "Seek ye first the kingdom of God." In W. H. Auden's poem "For the Time Being, A Christmas Oratorio," he pictures Herod, with a startling anachronism, as an outraged scientific liberal who regards the Incarnation as a deplorable lapse from scientific enlightenment back to superstitious barbarism. But Simeon, the elderly patriarch of the Temple, hails the Incarnation in his ecstatic "Now lettest Thy servant depart in peace, for mine eyes have seen Thy salvation." And Auden takes those words to convey the idea that the Incarnation is the interpretation of the philosophy of history and the redemption of man. That debate between Herod and Simeon is still going on.

135. THE GOSPEL FOR A SPLITTING WORLD

In him all things hold together. COL. 1:17

This is a saving word for a world that is splitting apart. That word "split" seems everywhere in our world. It is a key word today. We have split personalities, split families, split nations, split atoms, a split world. We also have splitting headaches. Our world is in desperate need of a uniting power. It is in need of him in whom all things hold together. In the life of the individual our common phrase has real and tragic meaning: "go to pieces." The Christ in whom all things hold together keeps people from moral dissolution, from "going to pieces." He brings a unifying power: "Unite my heart to fear thy name" (Ps. 86:11).

In the larger circle—the circle of the round globe—we need to be held together by the bond of brotherhood in Christ. This splitting world needs him who can hold all things together. One of the best-known anthropologists in the English-speaking world, Ashley Montagu, has written with the passion of an evangelist and crusader to prove the supreme importance of loving-kindness in the social life of animals and the evolution of man and his works.

The need of our world in the contemporary situation has been well pictured in the words of one of the characters, an ex-pastor, in George Bernard Shaw's *Too True To Be Good.* He cries out,

I stand midway between youth and age like a man who has missed his train: too late for the last one and too early for the next. . . . I have no Bible, no creed: the war has shot both out of my hands. . . . I am ignorant, I have lost my nerve and am intimidated; all I know I must find a way of life for myself and all of us or we shall surely perish.

We need him on whom all things cohere.

A few years ago Winston Churchill said some deeply moving words:

What ought we to do? Which way shall we turn to save our lives and the future of the world? It does not matter much to old people. They are going soon anyway. But I find it poignant to look at youth in all its activities and ardor, and most of all to watch the little children playing their merry games and wonder what would lie before them if God wearied of mankind.

taken place among Christian thinkers. Hope has become a bad word, a refuge for unsophisticated innocents, a superficial attitude. Hope has been so far sponged out that some theologians, branding themselves as realistic hard thinkers, have really become inverted romantics. In their eagerness to get away from what they call—and often rightly—rose-colored glasses, they have the cult of dark glasses, and look on a dark world made even darker by the glasses through which they look. It is no great gain to change from a fool's paradise into a pagan's hell. Neither is Christian hope. Bishop Gerald Kennedy gives this acid picture:

Many influential theologians of our day have moved from the ruins of a devastated Europe to the libraries of the theological schools and have carried defeatism into these sacred precincts—locking themselves up in their little cells with their egos, their textbooks, their jargon and their pessimism.

The greatest arousement of some of these evangelists of doom seems to be as found in *Richard the Second:*

> *For God's sake let us sit upon the ground*
> *And tell sad stories of the death of kings.*

We do not believe that this is the best of all possible worlds, but Christians do believe in a God of hope. When hope in God dies out of our mind, a living center of our religion is gone. The Epistle to the Romans was hailed by the neo-orthodox as a gospel of realism. It certainly is no box of tranquilizers. But it is a declaration of hope: "We are saved by hope" (Rom. 8:24, AV). "Now the God of hope fill you with all joy and peace in believing, that ye may abound in hope" (Rom. 15:13, AV). "Rejoicing in hope" (Rom. 12:12, AV).

Even in the darkest day, we may light the candles of faith and be "born anew to a living hope" (1. Pet. 1:3).

137. HOPE OF GLORY

The glory of this mystery, which is Christ in you, the hope of glory.   COL. 1:27
The secret is simply this: Christ in you.   (Phillips)

The open secret of the Christian is the presence of Christ in the heart. That is the meaning here and should never be forgotten, and the great purpose, "Christ in you, the hope of glory," lends itself to various and wonderful meanings of the glory of God in human

Think that over with all its terrible gloom. Jesus Christ is th
pledge that God has not wearied and will not weary of mankin(
"He is . . . the upholding principle of the whole scheme of cre
tion" (Phillips).

136. HANG ON TO THE GOSPEL!

Not shifting from the hope of the gospel which you heard. COL. 1:2

In the moving world of our time people readily change from on
set of ideas to another, from one outlook on the world to anothe
In these psychological days they change from one "inlook" on then
selves to another. The tragedy is that in the process many peop!
have been shifted from the hope of the gospel. They have move
away from the basic affirmations of the good news, or pronoun(
them with a very faint accent. They have left any Christian hop
either for the individual or for society, quite a distance behind. I
any thinking on this subject of Christian hope we need to kee
a firm grasp on the difference between optimism and hope. The;
has been a radical shift both in sociological thinking and Christia
thinking away from pre-World War I optimism and those supe
ficial optimisms which lingered on till World War II. Many pr
dictions envisaged the coming of a Utopia, almost automaticall
Thus, a notable American economist, Sumner H. Slichter, reporte
in *Saturday Review* what the country could look forward to in
generation:

Based on statistics and on the assumption that the American peop
will not have suffered radical change, and leaving out the unpredictab!
our productions of goods and services will be doubled by a labor for
of more than seventy-two millions working only thirty hours a wee
There will be two cars in almost every garage, a greater portion of t!
population in colleges and high schools, and the arts will flourish
never before in the history of the world.

Let us rise for the sevenfold Amen!
How many factors are left out of that sunrise picture? The sa;
issue of *Saturday Review* mentions many, including the decline
religion and discontentment with an increasingly mechanical civili;
tion.
But the danger is that people, in being stripped of an immo
optimism, have been cast into a godless pessimism. This has ev

life. But the primary meaning here is the mystical presence of Christ
in the heart. That is the "mystery" of God. The word "mystery"
is not to be confused with our frequent use of the word. The mystery
of God is not a detective story mystery which we know so well—
although there is a resemblance, even there, for the detection of
the evidence of God's presence in the world is the world's greatest
detective story. But as used here and elsewhere in Paul's epistle,
mystery means "initiation." The Greek and Roman world in the
days of Paul and the whole first centuries of Christianity was full
of mystery cults and religions. It was full of initiation ceremonies
into secrets. Paul is here using a figure of speech which people
could understand. This initiation into the wonder of God in Christ
was not a guarded secret as in the mystery religions. This was an
open secret to be carried to the world. The mystical indwelling of
Christ has to be more fully realized in the future life. Hence, Christ
is the hope of glory to be fully revealed in eternal life. But Christ
in our lives is also the present experience of the glory of God.

That word "glory" needs careful and prayerful scrutiny. What a
magnet that word "glory" has been! Men have identified the fulfillment of their own desires with the achievement of glory. Said Robert
Burns of Tam O'Shanter, kings may be blest, but Tam was glorious. "O'er a' the ills o' life victorious, Poor Tam! His glory was a
bottle!" His victory over life's ills was an alcoholic calamity. Earthly
glory has been identified with walking "through slaughter to a
throne." Men have been lured by the hope of glory as they conceived it—like a false fire into the swamps of death. On this vast
spread of history, Thomas Gray has made the epitaph:

> The boast of heraldry, the pomp of power,
>   And all that beauty, all that wealth e'er gave,
> Await alike th' inevitable hour:
>   The paths of glory lead but to the grave.

What strange conceptions of the glory of God there have been!
A great pile of masonry erected to the glory of God in the midst of
appalling misery, poverty, and suffering of God's children. Is that
the glory of God? Or here is a great church, in South Africa or else-
where, erected to the glory of God, but cherishing an expurgated
Bible, from which the most glorious words, such as "all one in Christ
Jesus" (Gal. 3:28), and "He made from one every nation of men"
(Acts 17:26), have been expunged.

In the Inquisition, advertised as one of God's glories, torture and
murders were "acts of faith." Mercy and loving-kindness were violently heretical.

This sentence from Paul puts the truth clearly: "Christ in you, the hope of glory." The glory of God is in Christ, and wherever Christ's spirit lives and rules in a life and in an act, there is the glory of God.

We live in two realms, the wonderful and the probable. But most of our lives are spent in the narrow confines of the probable. In Christ, however, the wonderful becomes the probable. If a man opens his mind and heart to Christ, he moves into the realm of the wonderful. In showing God's love in our lives, the cross is an event which becomes an experience.

138. MATURE

That we may present every man mature in Christ.   COL. 1:28

This is the shining goal of the church and its ministry. It is a universal goal. The heralds of the gospel were not trying to capture an esoteric elite or a company of learned scholars, of which there were many in the first centuries of Christianity. The goal was everyman— the democracy of God. There is in this word "everyman" a clear echo of the Parable of the Lost Sheep. Ninety-nine is not high enough for a Christian goal. Paul sought to bring every man to Christian maturity.

That was so great a goal that he gave it his whole intense energy. Goodspeed thus translates Paul's striving to reach the goal of this undertaking: "That is what I am working for, fighting with all the energy with which he so mightily endows me" (Col. 1:29). Paul was not on a casual stroll through the Mediterranean world. He had a fighting job.

When we ask "What does maturity in Christ mean?" part of it at least is in the negative: the putting away of childish things, childish traits and childish qualities of mind. Paul writes in the great hymn to love, the 13th chapter of First Corinthians, "When I became a man, I gave up childish ways" (13:11). To do that is a life program of becoming a mature Christian.

There are many traits of a child which have great charm. But when the childish ways of behavior are carried on into adult years, the result is calamitous. It becomes a sad case of retarded mentality. Recall some of the childish immaturities as found in personality or rather in lack of personality development, particularly as they affect the religious life.

One trait of a child, essential to his survival in the earliest days, is *self-centeredness*. It is a sort of mental blindness to the rest of the world. In fact, the rest of the world has not yet swung into his ken.

> *The baby new to earth and sky*
> *What time his little hand that pressed*
> *The tiny circle of his breast . . .*

He does not have any clear consciousness of other people in the world with any rights and claims. The "baby" of advanced years, from thirty to seventy, is affected with the same type of blindness. He sees people, but he sees them as "trees walking," as far as any concern for their needs is felt.

A childish trait is that of knowing only one time—*today*. There's no tomorrow, as far as the child is concerned. Thomas Gray has put this in classic form:

> *Alas, regardless of their doom,*
> *The little victims play;*
> *No sense have they of ills to come.*
> *Nor care beyond today.*

So people have lived in the same bland unconsciousness of the future, when they must face some kind of a payday, the same disregard of the future. There is a childish clutch at today as being the whole of the calendar. There are too many Peter Pans, grown-up children. In the field of religion Peter Pans are a total loss. They have no power of projecting into tomorrow by imagination and do not qualify as servants of a long-range God.

A childish trait which has brought gray hairs to parents is the insistence on *having one's own way*. A child has the spirit if not the vocabulary of Monte Cristo: "The world is mine." A sign often seen along the road is "Perpetual Nursery." It is a place where hardy perennials and perpetual plants are raised. People who are adult infants demand a perpetual nursery where their infant cries are instantly responded to. Alfred Adler says emphatically that when an individual has difficulty in adjusting himself to a group, he demonstrates his immaturity. He is not normal. People who insist on "having their own way," regardless of all others, are sick people. In religion, the "having my own way" hangover from childhood has been a disastrous block to the church. It has often turned what might be a fellowship of brothers, devoted to a common cause, into a sort of Mad Hatter's Tea Party. Such an attitude has slowed down the motion of churches almost to a standstill. A familiar bit of doggerel, once much used in Christian Student Movement circles in England, pictures this:

Like a mighty tortoise
Moves the Church of God
Brothers, we are treading,
Where we've always trod!
We are all divided,
Separate bodies we,
One in basic doctrine
Yet wanting charity.

Maturity in Christ involves, for one thing, a mature relationship to our Father, God. A mature son has passed from the "give me" stage of sonship into a relationship that responds to the father's love, one of trust and devotion. Maturity in Christ means that one takes a grown-up share in God's work in the world. Too many adult children insist that they can carry only a child's portion of color. They go through life on a half-fare ticket. The mature Christian says with his Master, "My Father worketh hitherto, and I work" (John 5:17, AV).

139.   COOLING OFF

I want you to know how greatly I strive . . . for those at Laodicea.
COL. 2:1

Laodicea—the very name has a clang across the valley of the centuries like a funeral toll. This verse comes from the time when the church at Laodicea was in the first fine careless rapture of its history. The sharp condemnation of the church which we find in Revelation comes from the time when the church had "cooled off."

Laodicea was a city of Asia Minor, located at the crossroads of the great trade route from the East to Ephesus. The church there was one of the Seven Churches of Asia Minor (Rev. 1:9). It had begun as the early churches in Asia Minor and Greece and Rome so often began, in a house, the house of a woman Nympha (Col. 4:15).

But in a few decades it had cooled off. It lost the lilt of the faith. Its zeal and joy and drive were gone. It came under the scorching denunciation in Revelation, in which it is pilloried for all time to see and take warning:

I know your works: you are neither cold nor hot. Would that you were cold or hot! So, because you are lukewarm, and neither cold nor hot, I will spew you out of my mouth. For you say, I am rich, I have prospered, and I need nothing; not knowing that you are wretched, pitiable, poor, blind, and naked.   Rev. 3:15-17

Zeal cooled off. The sense of self-sufficiency set in like a withering blight. Contrast the two pictures: The young church making a grand beginning, dear to the Apostle Paul, object of his love and concern. Then, not many years later, a burnt-out relic which had lost its glow and warmth. In that contrast lies the tragedy which every church faces as a danger, the tragedy of the Falling Thermometer—sometimes with an individual it is called "middle age letdown." It can happen to a church as well as to a person.

We cannot analyze what caused the cooling off at Laodicea. The city had a great commercial center. Perhaps the souls got buried. It happens today as well as in the far yesterday. Perhaps the faith crumpled under the fire of later persecution. The very name, Laodicea, cries to us "Watch and Pray."

Often the cooling off happens when faith is pushed to one side or even clear out of the mind. The picture of one of the characters in Sinclair Lewis' *Main Street* stands, alas, for many Christians of today. "He believed in the church but seldom attended its services. He believed in Christianity but seldom thought about it. He was worried about Carol's lack of faith but was not sure just what it was she lacked." In connection with his religion he never got what G. K. Chesterton calls "uproarious thinking." Chesterton wrote, "Any mind that has not got the habit of uproarious thinking is, from the human point of view, a defective mind." The imperishable gospel is such an unspeakable gift that it demands uproarious thinking. Often a cooling-off tragedy comes from a dying down of a disposition to work. It is recorded on a tablet in an English cathedral that an eighteenth-century woman "died of an indisposition." Churches as well as people can do that. They die of an indisposition to take any vital part in the life and work of the Kingdom of God. Sometimes when we see a noble church structure on the avenue and step up to read the name, we have to control our imagination to keep from thinking the name might be "The First Church of Laodicea." It might be too languid to lift a hand in God's Holy War.

With all these lurking dangers, we need daily the grace of renewal.

140.   THE DELUSIONS OF LIFE

That no one may delude you with beguiling speech.   COL. 2:4
I write like this to prevent you from being led astray by someone or other's attractive arguments.   (Phillips)

Paul had never known personally the Christians at Colossae. But he goes out to them in fervent love and yearning as brothers and sisters in Christ. He is deeply concerned for their true understanding of faith in Christ, and in this passage he earnestly strives that they be not deceived by delusions about the Gospel of Christ. Paul is so eager that they be not deceived by those who bring in alien ideas that he returns to the same theme several verses later. He writes again, "See to it that no one makes a prey of you by philosophy and empty deceit" (Col. 2:8). As Phillips translates this verse, "Be careful that nobody spoils your faith through intellectualism or high-sounding nonsense."

The very word "delusions" kindles the imagination. There are so many delusions which run through our world today. They creep up on us with all kinds of "high-sounding nonsense," threatening to trap us by their deceit.

Look very briefly at some of the delusions about the faith which were invading the church at Colossae. Then glance at some of the powerful and familiar delusions of our own time.

One of the common delusions of our life today is the idea that life finds fulfillment in consumers' goods. People, many of them, strive to amass goods, as though a clutter of goods would bring happiness. So the piles of goods grow bigger and bigger—and very often, the bigger the pile, the less the happiness.

Another delusion is the faith that many have had that progress is inevitable, as though things were bound to get better and better. People ought to be through with that delusion with all the calamities that have come in the past fifty years. But many people are still fooled by that fancy. Moral and spiritual development is the only real progress. No kind of gadget will avail. When the populace at large was rejoicing at the prospect of the telephone, one observer, watching unimpressed the erection of telephone lines from state to state, asked, "But what if you have nothing wise to say to the person at the other end of the line?"

Another delusion is that great gain and happiness result from the general restlessness and hurry of life. Jet planes can fly at the rate of hundreds of miles an hour, but they may carry passengers of less spiritual worth and of less happiness than many people who ride in oxcarts. People are deluded by the eternal pursuit of material gain into thinking that it is the great purpose of life. They forget Jesus' question, "What shall it profit a man, if he shall gain the whole world, and lose his own soul?" (Mark 8:36, AV).

One strong delusion by which many are deceived is that nothing ever changes and that they may meet the future by going on in the same way that they have always done. A vivid picture of this delusion as it obtains in many realms is given in Ellen Glasgow's novel *Virginia*. She pictures a blind lady in her Elizabethan chair, believing in her blindness that the confederacy went on, and that she still had three hundred servants.

A dangerous delusion, shared by millions in many nations, is the conviction that deadly weapons will end war. Alfred Nobel, many years ago, predicted that his high explosives would put an end to war sooner than peace meetings because as military weapons became more deadly, horrified nations would disband their troops.

What we desperately need is not to live in a world of delusions but in a world of sanity. We often hear the phrase "a world gone mad." H. G. Wells asks the pertinent question, "What would a world of human beings gone sane be like?"

The answer to that question is found in the New Testament.

141. ROOTED LIVES

Rooted and built up in him. COL. 2:7

Our generation ought to have a special interest in this word "rooted." For in so many ways we have been a rootless generation. There are two aspects of this calamity. Since World War II this has been so largely a world of uprooted wandering refugees. People have been made rootless and homeless by cruel and vindictive deportations, such as that of the Israelites carried off into alien Babylon. They have been pulled up by the roots and driven into new surroundings, usually into concentration camps. It has created one of the greatest social problems of the centuries. The United States may well be proud of the people who have sponsored refugees and made it possible for them to come to America. West Germany threw open her gates to great numbers, even when the nation was ill-equipped to receive them. Austria opened her frontiers to the harassed refugees from ravaged Hungary. There is still aching, hungry need among rootless peoples.

There is another kind of rootlessness in our own and other lands. This is found in people who have no real, deep, life-sustaining roots in a community. To them the words of the Parable of the Soil applies: "Rocky ground, where they had not much soil, and . . . since they had no root they withered away" (Matt. 13:5-6). That has been a sad feature of so many lives in a city. The life has been trying to sink roots into a concrete pavement. Willa Cather paints a vivid picture of much urban life:

But off there in the cities we are thousands of rolling stones like me. We are all alike, we have no ties, we know nobody, we own nothing. When one of us dies, we scarcely know where to bury him. Our land-lady and the delicatessen man are the chief mourners. And we leave nothing behind us but a frock coat, a fiddle, an easel or a typewriter, or whatever tool we get our living by. We live on the streets, in the park, in the theaters. We sit in the restaurants and concert halls and look about at the hundreds of our own kind and shudder.

Among the lacks of the rootless city dwellers is often the big one, that they have never put down roots in the fellowship of a church, a communion of faith. Having no such life-giving roots, they wither and die. J. B. Priestley has reported on a rootless generation in England, people leading a "thin, brittle, mechanical" life:

Now people like my parents lived in a real society, were members of a community, whereas a great many of these young flat-and-bungalow couples do not live in a society and are not members of a community. They are young people eating and sleeping and trying to enjoy them-selves in a certain place, with no interest in or feeling of responsibility for that place. They are nearly as far removed from the main stream of civic life as those melancholy souls who exist perpetually in hotels. There is something thin, brittle, mechanical about their life. It lacks richness, human variety, sap and juice, just because it has no real social background. Higher wages, shorter hours, more labour-saving devices, bigger garden suburbs, though excellent things in themselves, will not greatly improve this way of living. What they cannot restore to it is the social background, the civic feeling, the deep sense of being a member of a community. The people do not really belong to the place they are in, but are camping in it. They are nomads without a tribe.

Such rootless people are like trees growing on rocky soil. All their roots are horizontal.

The deep trouble in our world is that so often there is no *spiritual* rootage. There is no religious subsoil of belief from which people can draw nourishment for life. They are baked by the sun and dry up. This passage gives the cure for rootlessness. Phillips' rendering of the verse gives the deep secret, "Grow out of him as a plant grows out of the soil it is planted in." So many of our motives and goals and principles do not grow out of Christ. They grow out of our culture about us. Make the soil of our lives the mind of Christ, the spirit of Christ, and let the actions and words of our lives grow out of that. And do not make a visit to Christ just every once in a while, but in the glorious words of the epistle, "So live in him" (Col. 2:6). Dean Willard L. Sperry wrote a book entitled *Jesus, Then and Now.* A woman ordered it in a store, giving the title *Jesus, Now and Then.* That has been too often the trouble. It has been a case of "Jesus, Now and Then." Paul has something better than that. As Phillips translates it, "Go on living in him—in simple faith."

142. FULLNESS OF LIFE

You have come to fulness of life in him. COL. 2:10

In this passage we have one of the high spots of Paul's doctrine of Christ—his high Christology. Paul describes the delusion that had attacked many at Colossae, that Christ was but one of many powers, as "nonsense." He writes in an earnest plea, "Be careful that nobody spoils your faith through intellectualism or high-sounding nonsense. Such stuff . . . disregards Christ!" (Col. 2:8, Phillips).

This passage contains not only the Christian *doctrine* of Christ but also the Christian *experience* of Christ. It is the experience of a Christ-filled life. That, Paul declares, is the true fulfillment of life. "It is in him that you reach your full life" (Moffatt).

Many psychologists hold that the impulse toward completeness is the most compelling motive in life. That joins with the word of Paul, "Ye are complete in him" (Col. 2:10 AV).

The novelist Joyce Cary, in an essay entitled "The Revolution of Women," has written on this matter of fulfillment, "You don't find any woman who would change places with her grandmother. For the fact seems to be that people do not seek peace or happiness in life but fulfillment, and to get fulfillment they are ready for any kind of hardship."

Completion in Christ meets life's deepest need. The first great experience in life, its highest value, is not in doing but in receiving. It is in being, not acting. It is receiving the fullness of God in Christ which is open to us if we open our lives to God's gift in Christ. We have much to learn in receiving. Charles Morgan has written, "We know how to demand, acquire, capture; not how to receive. Social conscience has taught us how to perform an active service, even how to inspire others, but not how to receive inspiration." To receive the gift of God's fullness of life is the great step in Christian experience. The endless frontier in the world is not science but God. In a memorable picture the late Charles Cuthbert Hall, beloved president of Union Theological Seminary, likened the coming of God's fullness in life to the coming of the tide in the Bay of Fundy, up from the unfathomable deep:

> You could *hear* it coming, with a distant sound of motion and life. You could *see* it coming, with a pure, white girdle of foam, that looked like sunlight in a zone of fire. You could *smell* it coming, with a smell of freshness, a breath of coolness, the waft of far-off scents from breeze-blown ocean leagues. You could almost *feel* it coming, for the heart stirred at the sight of it, and the pulse quickened at the rush of it. . . .

Dr. Hall drew the parallel "So Christ comes into empty human lives and fills them with his fullness."

The question from the German, "How do you find yourself?" can be asked of each of us with complete seriousness. "How *do* you find yourself?" In other words, how does one find his *real* potential, the possible self? Paul in this passage has an answer to that. He writes, "Your own completeness is only realized in him" (Col. 2:10, Phillips). Man's real potential is realized in God. Our true end is realized when we say with our whole being, "Beloved, now are we the sons of God" (1 John 3:2, AV).

We have a common saying that a person is keeping "open house." It is a good phrase. Keep an open house to God. "Behold, I stand at the door and knock; if any one hears my voice and opens the door, I will come in to him and eat with him" (Rev. 3:20).

143.   SHADOW AND SUBSTANCE

These are only a shadow of what is to come; but the substance belongs to Christ.   COL. 2:17

This is a word from an early battle in a war that has gone on endlessly, the battle between the forms of religion and the inner reality. Paul warns the Colossians against making the trimmings of religion,

"food and drink, . . . a festival or a new moon or a sabbath," take
the place of the substance of Christ. How often in Christian history
the substance, the inner life of Christ, has been lost! The Battle at
Colossae is a continual war that must go on. The converts there
were being lured into barren asceticism. That is occasionally true
in our time, but more often the danger comes from an equally barren
opulence. The living center of Christ, the true substance, can be
and has been swamped by festivals and trimmings. Equipment is
one of the fetishes of our age. The shadow displaces the substance.
The substance of Christianity is "a mind at home in Thee." Just as
many a play of Shakespeare has been swamped with scenery, so, all
too often, the substance of Christ has been swamped with festivals,
new moons, and sabbaths. No outward paraphernalia will suffice
for the lack of substance of Christ in the heart and mind. To set
out on life with nothing but the shadow of observances is like setting
out on a trip across the country with a box of soda crackers and a
can of sardines. It won't last the journey!

144. DON'T BE CHEATED

Nor let any man cheat you of your joy in Christ. COL. 2:18 (Phillips)

Many people have been cheated. They have been cheated out of the
joy that is the mark of the Christian faith and discipleship. What
should and may be a joyful leap becomes a dull trudge.

How much that can cheat a person out of his joy in Christ! Legalism can do it, has done it, and still does it. Paul, in verses following
this one, protests vehemently against a joy-killing religion of prohibitions. When a person substitutes a religion of prohibitions for
freedom in Christ, he has been tragically cheated. Paul asks, "Why
do you submit to regulations, 'Do not handle, Do not taste, Do not
touch?' " It is a poor trade to accept the heavy gloom of a religion
of do not, do not, do not, in exchange for the light of the glory
of God in the face of Jesus Christ. Prohibitions are easier to see
than the love of Christ; they are more tangible. And they miss entirely
the deep joy of the Lord.

We are also badly cheated in our religious life when we allow
ourselves to be persuaded that the Christian life is something less
than what we meet in the New Testament and what we can
experience in following Christ. In Browning's *The Ring and the
Book*, the Pope asks a question about an inadequate religious ex-

perience. "Is this little, all there is?" We may well ask it of ourselves. There is more than "this little" that is infrequently realized. There is so much that it cannot be measured. "Eye hath not seen, nor ear heard, neither have entered into the heart of man, the things which God hath prepared for them that love him" (1 Cor. 2:9). That is the top prize of life. Do not allow yourself to be cheated out of it.

145.   THE SET OF THE MIND

Set your minds on things that are above, not on things that are on earth. COL. 3:2

Paul pictures here a vigorous, demanding operation. It calls for strong words. Goodspeed translates, "Fix your thoughts." Phillips brings in every power—"Give your heart."

The task of setting the mind is like setting the wheel of a ship against heavy winds. It is a terrific undertaking. So, the task of setting the steering wheel is a tremendous job. Often in the guidance of life, a person will give the wheel a light and easy spin, and then take his hand off the wheel and his mind off the guidance of life. The ship becomes a derelict.

In our day the tendency of many people is against "setting the mind." It is regarded as "dogmatic" and that, in the opinion of some, is the last calamity of a mind. They extol the "open mind." A mind open to the presentation of all truth is a good thing. But with the mind perpetually open nothing is ever really decided. The mind is open to anything, axiom or whim, it makes no difference. But turning the mind, setting it on things above, is like setting a great ship on the course, against all currents and tempests. This is man's part in God's transformation of the life.

"Let this mind be in you, which was also in Christ Jesus" (Phil. 2:5, AV). Set your mind on that as the steering star of life. To set the mind on things above the earth is man's highest use of mind. Wordsworth wrote,

> *Unless he can, above himself,*
> *Erect himself*
> *How poor a thing is man.*

To use a figure of speech, our heads should "bump the sky." That was the point of an expression James Russell Lowell once used of young people listening to Emerson. He wrote, "After hearing him, we went out, not entirely sure of what he said, but with our heads hitting the stars." If we are the true size of men and women, our heads must "hit the stars." We should seek those things that are above.

146. THE LATE JOHN DOE

For you have died. COL. 3:3

That is what the Christian ought to be and, by the grace of God, may be: the late John Doe. Paul writes, "You have died." There is a finality about the old life before Christ. These words make a plea for finality in the Christian life. There ought to be no shifting question about it. If any man is in Christ, he is a new creature. Something old, the old life, has ended with a finality compared to death; "You have died." In the victorious Christian life, you are no longer John Doe. He died. Remember? The great Christian enterprise is to go in for murder. The inducement to kill is found in verse 5 of this chapter, "Put to death therefore what is earthly in you: immorality, impurity, passion, evil desire, and covetousness." Have a first-class funeral for all those things. The church and the world need more funerals for the late John Doe. That means all of us, dead to the old life, and born anew to a life of hope. For you have died and you ought to treat as dead the person you once were. There is a glorious finality about the gift of a new life, and the death of the old one. As Phillips translates, "You have finished with the old man and all he did and have begun life as the new man" (Col. 3:9-10).

147. THE HIDDEN LIFE

Your true life is a hidden one in Christ COL. 3:3 (Phillips)

A life of power and joy has at its center a hidden life. Henry James made a vivid plea for this truth: "Let your soul live. Every other kind of life is, on the whole, a shell." Many biblical scholars have pointed out that this phrase, a hidden life in Christ, carries a double meaning; it cannot be wholly explained. It is the mystery of the indwelling God in a human life. It also denotes the life made secure, hidden from all the tempests that would overwhelm it. It is hidden with Christ in God. This gift in Christ fills a wide and deep need.

So many lives have nothing hidden. All the life is public, as public as the waiting room in a railroad station. There are throngs of many things; many comings and goings. This is what might be called a version of the story of Bluebeard. The inner soul of many people is not that it conceals some shameful secret. It is just that there is nothing there. There is no hidden life, no inner life in any deep sense. It is all outer. Old words that have been the foundation of life's security mean nothing to them, great words such as "He shall hide me in his pavilion: in the secret of his tabernacle shall he hide me" (Ps. 27:5).

A strong light is thrown on the power and influence of the hidden life. "There is nothing covered, that shall not be revealed; and hid, that shall not be known" (Matt. 10:26, AV). The life that is hid with Christ in God reaches out to the making of a more Christlike world.

148.   CHRIST IS ALL THAT MATTERS

Here there cannot be Greek and Jew, circumcised or uncircumcised, barbarian, Scythian, slave, free man, but Christ is all, and in all. COL. 3:11

This verse reads like a sunrise. It *is* a sunrise. With the revelation of this unifying power at work in humanity, "the sun of righteousness shall rise, with healing in its wings" (Mal. 4:2). This picture of Paul's of a unified human race in Christ is like the new view of the heavens of Copernicus and Galileo. The person who first truly realizes it can feel with the poet "like some watcher in the skies when a new planet swims into his ken." For a planet in which Christ is all that matters is a new planet.

We can say of Paul, bringing this revelation of the oneness of humanity to the infant church, that he was the first that ever burst on the world with the basic truth about it.

Today our world needs that sunrise of truth. As we look at our world, divided by picket fences of race and clan, and by barbed-wire fences of superiority and hostility, we see the greatest need of the world; that there cannot be Greek or Jew, and must not be, if the human family is to endure. The crowds of aliens must become a family. The Christian contention to the ongoing of the world is that "Christ is all that matters." In our segregated United States the imperative of faith is for Christians to believe their own gospel that "Christ is everything and in us all" (Goodspeed).

We sing heartily on Palm Sunday, "Ride on, Ride on in Majesty."

That salutes Christ at the head of the procession. But all too often, as we arrange our own ideas and prejudices, Christ is not "all in all" but comes well toward the end. Rearrange the procession.

149. THE FORBEARING MIND

Forbearing one another. COL. 3:12
Be most patient and tolerant with one another, always ready to forgive if you have a difference with anyone. (Phillips)

Forbearance seems at first glance an obvious duty. But it is one of the very hardest Christian virtues to practice. The dictionary makes the task clear: "An abstaining from the enforcement of a right. Patient endurance." He who calls that easy has never tried it!

It is hard to make allowances for people who irritate us, or at times for those who are stupid enough not to agree with us. It is hard to bring sympathetic understanding and response to conduct which we strongly disapprove. We have such a ready collection of verbal missiles to hurl at people, choice names which rush to our lips: "Simpleton" and "Dumbbell," and under great provocation, "nitwit," "moron," "addlepated," and "jackass." This is not the vocabulary or attitude which Paul pleads for in dealing with people, but "compassion, kindness, lowliness, meekness, and patience." In other words, "Put on love" (Col. 3:14).

Forbearance includes overcoming any attitude of disdain or contempt. Lack of forbearance is too much like the contempt described by Dean Swift in the lines:

> *We are God's chosen few*
> *All others will be damned.*
> *There is no place in Heaven for you,*
> *We can't have Heaven crammed.*

To be truly and fully forbearing we need the gift of God in Christ. It is the very essence of the spirit of Christ—" . . . forgiving one another, as God in Christ forgave you" (Eph. 4:32). This not only gives direction, it gives power. One man has reported asking Bertrand Russell two question, "Do you understand the Einstein theory of relativity? Do you go with him all the way?" Our attitude to Jesus, as it includes forbearance and making allowances, ought to be like that. Although we do not completely understand the central mystery of our faith, that God was in Christ, we can go all the way with

Christ's love. Indeed, if we are his we must go all the way in patient forbearance.

Moffatt brings into his translation of this passage the expressive word "clothed." We give so much attention, as a rule, to clothing. We like to be in style. We are urged by the advertisers to "get a new outfit," "get the new styles." Here is God's style for the clothing of the spirit: "Be clothed with compassion, kindliness, humility, gentleness, and good temper."

150.   CONCERT PITCH

Sing psalms and hymns and spiritual songs.   COL. 3:16

In these words Paul's thought breaks forth into music. The preceding words, "And be thankful. Let the word of Christ dwell in you richly," are like the tap of a conductor's baton. Then the whole of life, like an orchestra and chorus, bursts into marching music. Life in Christ rises to concert pitch. As Phillips describes the high and brisk stepping march of life, "Help one another along the right road with your psalms and hymns and Christian songs, singing God's praises with joyful hearts." That is truly life at concert pitch. The stress in this passage is on thanksgiving from first to last. At the beginning the note is heard—"And be thankful" (3:15). Again at the end the theme sounds—"giving thanks to God the Father through him" (3:17). It is thanksgiving which puts life into a marching mood and supplies the marching music. Life is stripped of its highest joy when it has no music of thanksgiving to march by. Without the lifting power of the music of thanks for God's gift, life becomes a treadmill. But with Christ at the head of our procession, there is divine music.

151.   DISCOURAGED CHILDREN

Fathers, do not provoke your children, lest they become discouraged.
COL. 3:21

This insight of Paul on the nurture of children brings spiritual and psychological truth which is in close harmony with much psychological understanding and teaching. The spirits of children have suffered great harm from parents who have "overcorrected" them. This appears sharply in the translation of Phillips, "Fathers, don't overcorrect your

children, or they will grow up feeling inferior and frustrated." The
lack of Christian love, of understanding sympathy, the lack of
restraint on the part of a parent from exercising his sheer power
in forcing the shape of a little replica of himself in his child, has resulted in countless hosts of children marked with a sense of inferiority
and mangled with frustration.

That there is a need for love in a young child's environment has
been one of the discoveries of recent generations. Love has found a
place, not only as a Christian ideal, but as a powerful medical
prescription. It has a name. Doctors prescribe it seriously T.L.C.:
"Tender, Loving Care." Without it, children often die. They get
discouraged. Babies need encouragement to live. Large numbers of
children are overcorrected and frustrated and made to feel inferior by
parents who have suffered from a Jehovan complex. Their slightest
word of constant correction becomes a peal of thunder from Mt. Sinai.
Paul's word to parents is found here, and a few verses earlier (Col.
3:14): "Put on love, which binds everything together in perfect
harmony." Love binds a young life together far, far better and more
strongly than the endless correction of nervous watchfulness.

152.   ZEST FOR PRAYER

Attend to your prayers, maintain your zest for prayer by thanksgiving.
COL.   4:2 (Moffatt)

This passage ties together closely two words that belong together,
but are frequently separated: "zest" and "prayer." In wide experience
prayer is more frequently thought of in connection with "duty"
rather than with "zest." Paul has a much livelier word both in his
plea to others and in his own experience. Prayer should have zest.
"Maintain your zest for prayer by thanksgiving."

The world has known only too well the blight of dull, sleepy
prayer. It is not surprising that prayer should be regarded as hard
work. But it seems incredible that it should ever be regarded as dull,
the living contact with God the Creator and Father. It has been
said by devoted scientists that science is "at the edge of mystery." True.
But prayer brings us to the edge of the greatest mystery in the
universe: the mystery of God. The Christian is a steward of that
mystery. We all disapprove of an Oriental prayer wheel as an empty
and futile exercise. But a sleepy prayer which takes hold of little of
a person's mind and heart, and does not hold even that little for

long, will give the same drugged result. One very practical observation is in order. Surely one reason for much sleepy praying is that so many put off prayer till the moments of falling off to sleep, and the Lord God Almighty is dimissed by a sleepy yawn. Prayer should also be made when one's senses are at the highest. For prayer is a great undertaking. As has been wisely said, "Prayer takes you out of life and puts you into life." It may be said with equal truth that when zest is brought to prayer, prayer brings zest to life.

When prayer in the life of an individual dwindles down till it is merely a "give me," "give me" demand, all true zest is gone. It is reduced to a beggar-with-a-cup routine. On this truth Emerson observes acutely, "Prayer that craves a particular commodity, anything less than all good, is villainous. Prayer is the contemplation of the facts of life from the highest point of view." H. G. Wells shamelessly recounts his top experience of prayer by telling us that in his schooldays he prayed during an examination for the right answer to a problem in accounting. No correct answer came to him. He adds solemnly, "From that day on I never prayed again." That is on an intellectual level with saying, "There is no God. I tried Him out with a daisy." No wonder Wells wanted a "one-way telephone." On the other hand, prayer may have the zest of a great companionship. To overtake that great possibility, however, it must get off the center of itself. In Jules Romains' poem "The Church," he gives samples of futile begging prayers. He puts these requests into the mouth of a French storekeeper: "Vouchsafe to fill my shop with customers"; "Let my son pass his examinations"; "O God, cure my sore eyes"; "Thou shalt have a great big candle"; "I will put nine pence in Saint Anthony's box." That sounds like a cash transaction over the counter in a bargain basement.

Paul writes that a sure way to bring zest to prayer is by a continual thanksgiving.

153. THE LETTER CARRIER

Tychicus will tell you all about my affairs; he is a beloved brother and faithful minister and fellow servant in the Lord.   COL. 4:7

Tychicus is another name that does not appear in the New Testament Hall of Fame. But he really deserves a place on the list. He had a remarkable career, crowning it as the man who carried this letter of Paul to the Christians at Colossae in Asia Minor. Evidently he also carried the letter to Philemon (Col. 4:9), and the letter to the

Ephesians, if the latter is a genuine letter of Paul (Eph. 6:21). Another man, Epaphroditus, carried the letter of Paul to the Philippians (Phil. 2:25-29).

Paul's letter carrier. God's letter carrier. What a role to play! Think of arriving with the mail at a little house on a side street in which a church was gathered. So in Colossae, Philippi, Ephesus. They would pass the thrilling word along in whispers, "We have a letter from Paul tonight. Tychicus has brought it." Carrying the Kohinoor diamond would be a comparatively trivial errand.

That was a long time ago. It also happened yesterday. It is happening today. We have been entrusted with the Gospels and with the letters of Paul. Are we truly filling the role and responsibility of being God's letter carrier? Do we deliver the letters to those to whom they are written—to the whole human race? Or are we negligent letter carriers—just reading them ourselves, as though these letters were written only to us?

People up and down the streets and country lanes in all the world are waiting for the letters written to them. May we grow up to this role, that of being God's letter carriers.

154. CHEERS FOR A SMALL CHURCH

Only these few are working with me for the kingdom, but what a help they have been! COL. 4:11 (Phillips)

Only a few—but what a help! How often has that been repeated in Christian history! Only a few but what a power! That makes the history of the church such fascinating reading. Paul lists in this passage a very few helpers: Aristarchus, Mark, and Jesus who is called Justus (Col. 4:10-11). Tychicus had been there but left on a trip through Asia Minor, in the course of which he carried this present letter to the church at Colossae. Onesimus had also been there (Col. 4:7, 8). What a pitiful line-up with which to face the Roman Empire. But four with God was a majority. This little group had an unseen ally. God Himself! It was one example of the powerful and triumphant mustard seed.

Only a handful of people working at a few spots—but from them there went out a stream of tremendous influence! It was like the Mississippi or the Amazon issuing from a tiny spring the size of a cup!

There were only a few in the little company of Christians at Blantyre, where David Livingstone received his first Christian nurture. Only a very few in the little group in Glasgow, where as a medical student he formed his desire to go as a foreign missionary! There were only a few in the small group in Elstow near Bedford, where John Bunyan received his impetus to a Christian life and witness. Only a few but how many they became! There were only a very few in the little village of Epworth where John Wesley grew up as a child. Not many more than his own family. We can stand at Epworth today and repeat this scripture, "Only these few are working with me for the kingdom, but what a help they have been!" We can say the same of a little parish church at Nottinghamshire in North Central England. From Scrooby the Pilgrim Church emigrated, first to go to Holland and then to America, sailing on the *Mayflower*. Only a few—but what a power under God in the history of the world!

These words could be a fitting motto for a large majority of churches in Christendom. In the providence of God, small churches have been the most powerful forces in history.

155.   THE CHURCH IN THE HOUSE

Give my greetings . . . to Nympha and the church in her house.   COL. 4:18

The name Nympha is totally unknown to most of us. We do not find her name among the small list of notable women in Apostolic times: Lydia, Priscilla, Dorcas. But what an example Nympha set in allowing her home to be used by the church. That is an example that has been fruitfully and gloriously followed for nineteen centuries. The Christian home has been the church's secret weapon in God's Holy War against evil.

The Book of Acts is particularly effective in showing clearly the place of the Christian home in the spread of the gospel and the work of the church. This was inevitable because the first Christian home appeared in the early years of the Christian Era, the time in which the history recorded in the Book of Acts took place. The first churches were in the homes long before there was any organized church at all.

Here are a few of the homes mentioned in the Book of Acts which the owners permitted to be used for the cause of Christ:

In the very beginning the Upper Room, in which the Spirit of God descended on the disciples, was in someone's house. Someone was willing to go to all the trouble of having such a meeting place in the house. Think of the high joy of having your home become the cradle of the Christian church!

Lydia, the first Christian convert in Europe, was also the first Christian hostess, for she invited the Apostle Paul to stay in her home, and he did so (Acts 16:14-15). From her home, so freely offered, the first evangelism in Europe went forth.

In Acts 17:6-7 we get a glimpse of the generous and courageous Jason, who at the risk of his life received the apostles Paul and Silas into his home. We read that a mob dragged Jason to the city authorities in Thessalonica and cried, "These men who have turned the world upside down have come here also, and Jason has received them." He made a tremendous contribution to Christian history by allowing his home to be used.

Then, think of Aquila and Priscilla, the wise and loving couple who opened their home to Paul for a long time (Acts 18:2). Who can say how great a gift they made? And turn to I Corinthians 16:19 and read: ". . . together with the church which meets in their house." This couple made their home a place for worship!

There are many other such references to those who let their homes be used for Christ. The home became in New Testament times, and remains today, a center and a power for the spread of the gospel.

So it was with Nympha. So may it ever be.

NOTES

Page *Line*

19 14   William Wordsworth, "Lines Composed a Few Miles above Tintern Abbey."

19 18-23 John M. Mecklin, *My Quest for Freedom* (New York: Charles Scribner's Sons, 1945).

20 26-27 Charles Wesley, "Love Divine, All Loves Excelling."

27 30-31 Elizabeth Spriggs, *Gertrude Stein: Her Life and Work* (New York: Harper & Brothers, 1957).

31 12-13 Phillips Brooks, "O Little Town of Bethlehem."

32 14-17 H. M. Tomlinson, *The Wind is Rising*, War Diary, Aug. 1939 to Aug. 1941 (London: Hodder & Stoughton, Ltd., 1941).

32 21-26 Gilbert Murray, *Five Stages of Greek Religion* (New York: Columbia University Press, 1930).

33 23-27 Denis de Rougemont, *The Devil's Share* (New York: Pantheon Press, 1944).

34 39   J.W. Dodds, *Age of Paradox* (New York: Rinehart & Co., 1952).

34 40-41 Sir Spencer Walpole, *History of England*, Vol. III (London and New York: Longmans, Green & Co., 1890).

37 22-24 Jerome Hamilton, *William Ernest Henley*, A Study in the "Counter Decadence" of the Nineties (Princeton, N.J.: Princeton University Press, 1945).

38 25-26 Frances R. Havergal, "Lord, Speak To Me."

39 10-12 William James Durant, *The Renaissance*, A History of Civilization in Italy from 1304-1576 A.D. (New York: Simon and Schuster, Inc., 1953).

40 20-30 Hesketh Pearson, *The Man Whistler* (New York: Harper & Brothers, 1952).

42 12-13 Frederick W. Faber, "Faith of Our Fathers."

43 3-12 William James, *Varieties of Religious Experience* (New York: Longmans, Green & Co., 1902).

44 13-19 Emmet Dedmon, *Fabulous Chicago* (New York: Random House, 1953).

45 12-14 Margaret Webster, *Shakespeare without Tears* (Cleveland: World Publishing Company, 1955).

45 19-26 Charles E. Raven, *A Wanderer's Way* (New York: Henry Holt & Company, 1929).

Page *Line*

45 39 Henry D. Thoreau, *A Week on the Concord and Merrimac Rivers* (Boston: Houghton, Mifflin Company, 1893).

47 5-8 John Cheever, *The Housebreaker of Shady Hill and Other Stories* (New York: Harper & Brothers, 1958).

47 21-27 Norman Cousins, editorial in *Saturday Review*, Aug. 18, 1945.

49 33 John Milton, "On His Being Arrived to the Age of Twenty-three."

50 4-10 Herbert Joseph Muller, *The Loom of History* (New York: Harper & Brothers, 1958).

50 19 Vachel Lindsay, *Collected Poems* (New York: The Macmillan Company, 1931).

54 17-20 L. P. Jacks, *The Confessions of an Octogenarian* (London: G. Allen and Unwin, Ltd., 1942).

55 13-17 News Exchange of Planned Parenthood, London, 1950. *Mind at the End of Its Tether* (London and Toronto: W. Heinemann, Ltd., 1945).

56 9-10 Reginald Heber, "The Son of God Goes Forth to War."

56 25-26 Ambrose Bierce, *The Devil's Dictionary* (New York: Dover Publications, 1957).

57 3-10 Bayard Tuckerman, ed., *Diary of Philip Hone, 1828-1851* (New York: Dodd, Mead & Co., 1889).

57 22-24 Geoffrey Chaucer, *The Canterbury Tales.*

57 26-27 John Masefield, *Collected Poems* (New York: The Macmillan Company, 1925).

60 4-5 John Milton, item in *New York Herald Tribune*, Feb. 23, 1958.

60 26-27 Lord Byron, "Childe Harold's Pilgrimage," Canto IV, Stanza 145.

61 15-22 Thomas Carlyle, *Miscellanies* (Boston: J. Munroe & Co., 1838-39).

61 26-31 William James, *Varieties of Religious Experience* (New York: Longmans, Green & Co., 1902).

64 2-5 Louis Kronenberger, "Unbrave New World," in *Harper's Bazaar*, Sept., 1957.

65 27-35 Barbara Ward, *The West at Bay* (New York: W. W. Norton & Co., Inc., 1948).

66 37 A. S. Tuberville, *English Men and Manners in the Eighteenth Century* (Oxford: Clarendon Press, 1926).

68 9-12 Bertrand Russell, *Portraits from Memory and Other Essays* (New York: Simon and Schuster, Inc., 1956).

69 8-9 *The Interpreter's Bible*, Vol. 10 (Nashville: Abingdon Press, 1953).

69 16-23 William James Durant, *The Renaissance*, A History of Civilization in Italy from 1304-1576 A.D. (New York: Simon and Schuster, Inc., 1953).

Page	Line	
Page	*Line*	

69 33-34 Samuel Shellabarger, *Lord Chesterfield* (London: Macmillan and Co., Ltd., 1935).

71 12-15 Randall Stewart, *American Literature and Christian Doctrine* (Baton Rouge: University of Louisiana Press, 1958).

72 17-18 A. E. Housman, *Last Poems* (New York: Henry Holt & Company, 1937).

73 21 John Masefield, *Collected Poems* (New York: The Macmillan Company, 1925).

73 33-39 Margaret Webster, *Shakespeare without Tears* (Cleveland: World Publishing Company, 1955).

74 15-17 Aubrey de Selincourt, *On Reading Poetry* (London: Phoenix House, 1952).

75 14-19 Agnes Repplier, *Eight Decades* (Boston: Houghton, Mifflin Company, 1937).

76 13-19 Thornton Wilder, *Our Town* (New York: Coward-McCann, Inc., 1938).

76 40-42 H. G. Wells, *The World Set Free* (New York: E. P. Dutton & Co., 1914).

78 35-36 Augustus M. Toplady.

80 23-24 Ola Elizabeth Winslow, *Master Roger Williams* (New York: The Macmillan Company, 1957).

81 13-16 "How Dreary To Be Somebody," from *The Complete Poems of Emily Dickinson* (Boston: Litttle, Brown and Co., 1930).

82 12-15 Winston Churchill, *The New World* (New York: Dodd, Mead & Co., 1956).

85 16-17 Odell Shepard, *Pedlar's Progress; the Life of Bronson Alcott* (Boston: Little, Brown and Co., 1937).

86 4-9 Quoted in *The American Treasury*, edited by Clifton Fadiman (New York: Harper & Brothers, 1955).

86 29-33 Charles E. Raven, *Science, Religion and the Future* (Cambridge, England: The University Press, 1943).

87 9-12 William Wordsworth, "The Excursion," Part 4, line 244.

88 18-20 John Mecklin, *My Quest for Freedom* (New York: Charles Scribner's Sons, 1945).

88 27-28 John Betjeman, *Collected Poems* (London: J. Murray, 1958).

90 16-17 Bayard Tuckerman, ed., *Diary of Philip Hone, 1828-1851* (New York: Dodd, Mead & Co., 1889).

90 32-33 Vachel Lindsay, "Foreign Missions in Battle Array."

92 11-16 Laurence Housman, ed., *What Can We Believe?* (London: Jonathan Cape, 1939).

94 38 *Giants in the Earth,* a tragedy by Thomas Job from the novel by O. E. Rölvaag (New York: Harper & Brothers, 1929).

Page Line
95   39   Michael St. John Packs, *Life of John Stuart Mill* (New York: The Macmillan Company, 1954).
97   20-22 *Emerson's Journals*, Dec. 22, 1834.
98   22-32 Walter Millis, in *The New York Times*, Feb. 2, 1958.
99   19-24 Quentin Reynolds, *Officially Dead, The Story of Commander C. D. Smith, U.S.N.* (New York: Random House, 1947).
101   3-8   Robert Chelsey Osborn, *On Leisure* (New York: Simon and Schuster, Inc., 1957).
104   1-4   Samuel Dill, *Roman Society in the Last Century of the Western Empire* (London and New York: The Macmillan Company, 1898).
105   5-14 Edward Rowland Sill, "The Fool's Prayer."
107   8-9   W. H. Auden, *For the Time Being, A Christmas Oratorio* (New York: Random House, 1944).
109   23-24 William Cowper, "The Task."
110   8   *The Decline of the American Male*, by the Editors of *Look* (New York: Randon House, 1959).
110   28-31 J. B. Priestley, *The Magicians* (New York: Harper & Brothers, 1954).
112   5-10 Paul Hutchinson and Winfred E. Garrison, *Twenty Centuries of Christianity* (New York: Harcourt, Brace & Co., Inc., 1959).
112   22-23 Attributed to Peter Williams, eighteenth-century Welsh poet.
112   27-28 Samuel Taylor Coleridge, "The Rime of the Ancient Mariner."
113   3-4   Washington Gladden.
117   14-17 Charles Hartshorne, *Reality as a Social Process* (Glencoe, Ill.: Free Press, 1953).
117   29-30 Robert Browning, "Rabbi Ben Ezra," Stanza 6.
118   8-10 Carl Sandburg, *Abraham Lincoln, The War Years*, Vol. 3 (New York: Harcourt, Brace and Co., Inc., 1939).
118   26-29 Elizabeth C. Clephane, "Beneath the Cross of Jesus."
119   28-33 Jacques Barzun, *Teacher in America* (Boston: Little, Brown and Co., 1945).
127   15-16 Isaac Watts, "When I Survey the Wondrous Cross."
128   32-36 Quoted in *The American Treasury*, edited by Clifton Fadiman (New York: Harper & Brothers, 1955).
129   1-4   Margaret Halsey, *The Folks at Home* (New York: Simon and Schuster, Inc., 1952).
129   9-21 Arnold Toynbee, *An Historian's Approach to Religion* (London and New York: Oxford University Press, 1956).
132   18-22 Denis de Rougemont, *The Devil's Share* (New York: Pantheon Press, 1944).

Page Line
161 35-39 Irwin Edman, *Philosopher's Holiday* (New York: Viking Press, 1938).

163 30-38 Mary Antin, *The Promised Land* (Boston: Houghton, Mifflin Company, 1912).

164 9-12 Cecil F. Alexander, "There Is a Green Hill Far Away."

164 27-36 Arnold Bennett, *Clayhanger* (New York: George H. Doran Co., 1910).

165 28-36 Genevieve Taggard, "Do As I Tell You," from *Not Mine to Finish* (New York: Harper & Brothers, 1934).

169 14-17 Sir Henry Newbolt, *Clifton Chapel and Other School Poems* (London: J. Murray, 1908).

169 34 Walter Lowrie, *A Short Life of Kierkegaard* (Princeton, N.J.: Princeton University Press, 1942).

170 7-10 W. L. Caswell, in *The Churchman*.

173 7-8 William Shakespeare, *Hamlet*, Act III, sc. 1.

176 5-7 Henry F. Lyte, "Abide with Me."

178 15-20 Martin Luther King, Jr., *Stride toward Freedom: The Montgomery Story* (New York: Harper & Brothers, 1958).

179 3 Edward S. Bragg, "Seconding Speech for Grover Cleveland," July 9, 1884.

179 12 Charles Dickens, *A Christmas Carol*.

185 5-9 F. W. Beare, *Epistle to the Philippians* (New York: Harper & Brothers, 1959).

186 9-14 David Cecil, *Melbourne* (Indianapolis: Bobbs-Merrill Co., Inc., 1954).

187 21-29 James Thomson, *Satires and Profanities* (London: Progressive Publishing Co., 1884).

189 16-23 Gilbert Highet, *Man's Unconquerable Mind* (New York: Columbia University Press, 1954).

190 36-38 Winthrop S. Hudson, *The Great Tradition of the American Churches* (New York: Harper & Brothers, 1953).

191 5-10 William Macneile Dixon, *The Human Situation;* the Gifford Lectures delivered in the University of Glasgow, 1935-1937 (New York: St. Martin's Press; London: E. Arnold and Co., 1937).

194 1 Charleton S. Coon, *The Story of Man* (New York: Alfred A. Knopf, 1954).

194 15-16 Babette Deutsch, *Poetry in Our Time* (New York: Henry Holt & Company, 1952).

197 13-23 Quoted by G. A. Studdert-Kennedy, London.

197 29-30 William Shakespeare, *Macbeth*, Act V, sc. 5.

198 13-14 James Montgomery, "God Is My Strong Salvation."

200 37-38 John Masefield, "The Widow in the Bye Street" (London: Sidgwick and Jackson, Ltd., 1912).

Page	Line	
202	31-35	Alfred North Whitehead, *Adventures of Ideas* (New York: The Macmillan Company, 1933).
204	6-9	Ronald Bridges and Luther A. Weigle, *The Bible Word Book* (New York: Thomas Nelson & Sons, 1960).
207	10	*Ibid.*
209	27-30	Rollo May, in *The Best of Pastoral Psychology*, edited by Simon Doniger (Great Neck: Pastoral Psychology Press, 1952).
210	24-25	Edward H. Bickersteth, "Peace, Perfect Peace."
222	18-19	Christopher Morley, *The Man Who Made Friends with Himself* (Garden City, N.Y.: Doubleday & Co., Inc., 1949).
224	18	Ashley Montagu, *Man: His First Million Years* (Cleveland: World Publishing Company, 1957).
224	22-26	*Too True To Be Good, Villiage Wooing,* and *On the Rocks,* 3 plays by George Bernard Shaw (London: Constable and Co., Ltd., 1934).
225	19-25	Sumner H. Slichter, in *Saturday Review*, Nov. 19, 1949.
226	11-15	Bishop Gerald Kennedy, in *Time Magazine*, April 11, 1960.
229	3-5	Tennyson, *In Memoriam.*
229	14-17	Thomas Gray, "On a Distant Prospect of Eton College."
231	19-22	Sinclair Lewis, *Main Street* (New York: Harcourt, Brace and Co., Inc., 1920).
233	11-13	Ellen Glasgow, *Virginia* (Garden City, N.Y.: Doubleday & Co., Inc., 1913).
233	15-18	Alfred Nobel, in *Saturday Review Gallery*, edited by Jerome Beatty, Jr., *et al.* (New York: Simon and Schuster, Inc., 1959).
233	21-22	H. G. Wells, *Star Begotten* (New York: Viking Press, 1937).
234	11-18	Willa Cather, *O, Pioneers!* (Boston: Houghton, Mifflin Company, 1913).
234	24-38	J. B. Priestley, *Rain upon Godshill.*
235	30-35	Joyce Cary, "The Revolution of Women."
236	12-17	Charles Cuthbert Hall, *The Christ-Filled Life* (New York: Thomas Y. Crowell, 1907).